CITIZENSHIP
IN A CONNECTED CANADA

CITIZENSHIP
IN A CONNECTED CANADA
A Research and Policy Agenda

EDITED BY

Elizabeth Dubois and Florian Martin-Bariteau

University of Ottawa Press

2020

University of Ottawa **Press**
Les **Presses** de l'Université d'Ottawa

The University of Ottawa Press (UOP) is proud to be the oldest of the francophone university presses in Canada as well as the oldest bilingual university publisher in North America. Since 1936, UOP has been enriching intellectual and cultural discourse by producing peer-reviewed and award-winning books in the humanities and social sciences, in French and in English.
www.press.uOttawa.ca

Library and Archives Canada Cataloguing in Publication

Title: Citizenship in a connected Canada : a research and policy agenda /
   edited by Elizabeth Dubois, Florian Martin-Bariteau.
Names: Dubois, Elizabeth, editor. | Martin-Bariteau, Florian, 1987- editor.
Series: Law, technology, and media.
Description: Series statement: Law, technology, and media | Includes bibliographical references
   and index
Identifiers: Canadiana (print) 20200281321 | Canadiana (ebook) 20200281429 |
   ISBN 9780776629254 (softcover) | ISBN 9780776629292 (hardcover) |
   ISBN 9780776629261 (PDF) | ISBN 9780776629278 (EPUB) | ISBN 9780776629285 (Kindle)
Subjects: LCSH: Information society—Canada. | LCSH: Citizenship—Canada.
Classification: LCC HM851 .C58 2020 | DDC 303.48/330971—dc23

Legal Deposit: Fourth Quarter 2020
Library and Archives Canada

Production Team

Copy editing   Alicia Perez
Proofreading   Robbie McCaw
Typesetting   Édiscript enr.
Cover design   Steve Cress.

Cover image

By Michelle Wronski

SSHRC CRSH

This book was published with funds provided by the Social Sciences and Humanities Research Council of Canada, the University of Ottawa Research Chair in Technology and Society, and the Fund for Law, Risks and the Internet at the University of Ottawa Centre for Law, Technology and Society.

The University of Ottawa Press gratefully acknowledges the support extended to its publishing list by the Government of Canada, the Canada Council for the Arts, the Ontario Arts Council, the Social Sciences and Humanities Research Council and the Canadian Federation for the Humanities and Social Sciences through the Awards to Scholarly Publications Program, and by the University of Ottawa.

ONTARIO ARTS COUNCIL
CONSEIL DES ARTS DE L'ONTARIO
an Ontario government agency
un organisme du gouvernement de l'Ontario

Canada Council   Conseil des arts
for the Arts   du Canada

Canadä

uOttawa

Table of Contents

Part III: Rethinking Legal Frameworks for the Digital Context

Preface

Elizabeth Dubois and Florian Martin-Bariteau

In 2017, we brought together academics, policy-makers, and technologists for the Connected Canada conference at the University of Ottawa. We wanted to generate discussion and build a network of people interested in mobilizing research about what it means to be a citizen in a connected Canada and how we, as researchers, policy-makers, and members of civil society, can overcome gaps in data that limit our understandings of the impacts of digital tools on civic life.

In 2018, we published *Canadians in a Digital Context: A Research Agenda for a Connected Canada*, a knowledge synthesis report presenting the perspectives of participants in order to facilitate discussion and collaboration, and to propose a collaborative research agenda. In the next days, we reached out to some of Canada's pre-eminent leading and emergent voices with the idea of an edited collection expanding on some of the noted issues through short policy papers, informed by evidence-based research.

In this collection you will find a range of policy-oriented pieces that tackle some of the most pressing research and policy gaps we identified over the past few years of work on the Connected Canada Initiative. This collection has been made possible thanks to the support of many—from academia, government, and civil society—as well as the University of Ottawa Press. This multi-year project will continue beyond this book, and we wish to thank several people and organizations without whom none of these efforts would have been possible.

*

The Connected Canada conversations, from the conference to the report and this edited collection, were possible thanks to a Canada 150 Connection grant from the Social Sciences and Humanities Research Council of Canada (SSHRC). We also received additional financial support for the conference from the University of Ottawa— namely the Office of the Vice-President, Research; and the Office of the Vice-Dean, Research, at the Faculty of Arts—as well as from Elections Canada, the Public Policy Forum, Fulbright Canada, and the National NewsMedia Council of Canada. The Black Arcs, Home of the Creative Minds, and iVote-jeVote were also key supporters of the event. The publication of the edited collection has been made possible in part thanks to the Fund for Law, Risks and the Internet at the University of Ottawa Centre for Law, Technology and Society.

This collection would not have been possible without the involvement of many collaborators, and we wish to express our sincere gratitude to them. First and foremost, our profound thanks go to Ellie Marshall. Ellie and Elizabeth first hatched the idea for Connected Canada over a conversation in a coffee shop. They were frustrated by a lack of publicly available data about how Canadians use the Internet. Ellie and Elizabeth observed and participated in conversations about how to develop policy related to the Internet that were based on limited data or data from studies in the United States or the United Kingdom. They knew the response to these challenges would require a range of stakeholders and decided a conference bringing a diverse array of people together was the ideal first step. For their help in that crucial first step, we wish to offer a special thanks to Megan Beretta, Céleste Côté, Sara Minaeian, and Caitlin Myles, who all joined the crazy adventure at its inception, as well as Jon Penney, Alfred Hermida, Amanda Clarke, and Kent Aitken who led some of the initial breakout sessions at the conference. We are also indebted to the Ottawa Civic Tech community. Many of our conference planning sessions happened at Tuesday night meet-ups which shaped how we thought about which problems were most crucial to tackle, and who we most needed in the room. We would like to thank the many other colleagues, collaborators, members of civil society, and policy-makers who got involved and supported the creation of this conversation. We would like to thank the participants, experts, and volunteers who took part in the Connected Canada conference. We are also grateful to Catherine Ouellette and Chris Casimiro for their research assistance in the preparation of this collection. Thanks also to Jasmine Law, Eryn Heidel, and Véronique Poulin who provided assistance for the copy editing of this collection. Crucially, we are extremely grateful to Guillermo Renna who was immensely supportive in the final stages of the collection, notably through research and copy editing. Thanks are due to the authors of the chapters included in this edited collection, as well as the numerous anonymous peer reviewers, each of whom spent part of their summer to assess, comment on, and improve these chapters. We also thank the two anonymous experts who reviewed the collection itself. Finally, we wish to thank the team at the University of Ottawa Press who agreed to consider this unusual book for publication in their collection under an open access licence, and for the work of their editorial team on the manuscript.

Citizenship in a Connected Canada

Elizabeth Dubois and Florian Martin-Bariteau

C itizenship has become digital.
   In 2020, all experiences and expressions of civic and political
life in Canada are impacted by digital technologies in some way.
Whether they use a mobile app to listen to a news podcast, log in to
their online banking profile, order food online, or connect through
social media with co-workers, friends, or family, most people's lives
are necessarily digital to some degree. Even for those who choose not
to use digital technologies in their daily lives and for those who do
not have the needed access, resources, or skills to employ these tools,
governments and other institutions make use of digital technologies
in ways that impact everyone. For example, even unconnected citizens are impacted by automated decision-making in government—
from benefit assessment to the justice system—and by corporate
actors—from financial offers to traffic management.
   We could argue that citizenship has been digital for decades.
Yet many different actors in society—civil society groups, governments, journalism organizations—, and legal systems struggle to
keep up with shifting the ways in which individuals might enact
their citizenship, with the impacts of increased use of digital tools,
and with questions about what is technically possible and ethically
advisable. This book outlines some of the ways in which civil society,
governments, and legal systems are being challenged by an evolving
digital context to rethink their relationships with citizens. Informed

by academic literature and empirical research, this collection of policy-focused essays puts forward a research and policy agenda providing recommendations for next steps both within and outside of academia. The aim is to help develop better policies, tools, and research. In order to do so, we need to understand how individuals enact their citizenship in digital contexts. Reflection on the uses of technology by citizens and their preferences about how technologies and digital data could or should be used is important for developing relevant responses in a digital context. While the digital context is not entirely new, it is sometimes overlooked.

Furthermore, as technology advances and as our use of technologies matures, the way we citizens are impacted by those technologies evolves. For example, at one time the "digital divide" conversation centred on who had Internet access and who did not (Paré, 2005). This was the primary concern for anyone trying to assess the most important policy issues related to digital technology. Indeed, a connected Canada certainly requires better broadband and connectivity policies (Clement et al., 2012) to minimize a digital divide related to access and to ensure equal and equitable opportunities for enacting citizenship. Particularly in remote and rural parts of Canada, there continue to be individuals with limited or no Internet access (Canadian Internet Registration Authority [CIRA], 2020) who typically pay higher rates than those in urban centres (Waterhouse, 2019). However, the problems at hand have become more complex than connectivity alone: skill, experience, social treatment, and many other factors must also be considered when we think about who is digitally enabled and who is digitally excluded (Paré, 2005; Quan-Haase et al., 2018; Robinson et al., 2015). As a host of new kinds of digital tools enter the arena—ranging from mobile apps to the Internet of Things and smart cities—many actors are faced with new digital contexts which require new skills and approaches. These technological advances, and the resulting changes as we incorporate them into our lives, have meaningful effects on our relationships with each other, with societal institutions such as government and journalism, and with the law and its frameworks.

Consequently, these changes have sparked both optimism and fear about what is next for Canadian society and how citizens will be impacted. A digital context provides the potential for innovative engagement of citizens in their political systems (Matheus et al., 2010; Haro-de-Rosario et al., 2018) as well as the potential for disinformation (Faris et al., 2017), election interference (Goldman et al., 2020), and an amplification of existing injustices (Powell et al., 2018). Similarly, unchecked development in artificial intelligence, while offering possible benefits, also raises significant challenges, such as creating uncertainty surrounding the future of work (Loewen & Stevens, 2019) causing shifts in power, and building new structures outside the control of existing and understood governance and accountability frameworks (Millar et al., 2018). This list could continue for many pages, but ultimately each opportunity or challenge offered in a digital context requires us to understand both how digital technologies are currently impacting civic life and how people feel about the various ways in which these tools are used by different actors in society.

Historically, technology and policy developments have responded unevenly to the needs of individuals and have excluded people and groups such as linguistic minorities, LGBTQ2S+, those who are differently abled, and Indigenous Peoples. But for our society to thrive in its digital context, technology and policy developments need to be intentionally inclusive and must recognize a need for decolonization and reconciliation, which call for new perspectives and policy frameworks. From a base understanding of the experiences lived by people in Canada, we can develop better policies and make better decisions about whether and how to regulate new technologies as they emerge.

Taken together, the chapters in this collection advance the argument that we need to understand how to work toward a connected Canada that maximizes equitable access to information and communication technologies, and boosts digital literacy and skills. We must be cognizant of the need to mitigate risks and take advantage of persistent and pervasive connectivity in a society that is increasingly impacted by digital tools. In order to do this, various actors within society must come together to grapple with the difficult questions related to Canada's digital future. Multi-stakeholder approaches have been leveraged in many fields and have been called for by stakeholders within digital policy development (e.g., Buell, 2019). Multi-stakeholder initiatives have been identified as the best approach to discuss and address the complex issues that implicate a wide range of actors and to ensure better representation of the different layers of society (Dentoni et al., 2018). Indeed in 2013, discussing the future role of civil society, the World Economic Forum called for such an approach, to build resilient societies with civil society, academia, industry, and government working together across their usual silos to take issues outside of their organizational boundaries.

This edited collection continues a unique conversation which stemmed from the Connected Canada initiative, launched in 2017, which embraces the ethos of this multi-stakeholder approach. We bring together scholars, activists, policy-makers, and businesses to build consensus around what a digitally connected society means for Canada. Ultimately, we aim to better understand both what it means to be a citizen in Canada in a digital context as well as the implications of such citizenship on policy-making in a digital context. Our aim in this collection is to extend and expand upon the research agenda we outlined in the *Canadians in a Digital Context* report (Dubois & Martin-Bariteau, 2018).

Defining Citizenship in a Digital Context

As we have previously articulated,[1] for us, "citizenship" describes the civic experience of individuals. In this collection, we focus specifically on those living within Canada. We intentionally take this broad definition in contrast to more narrow ones based on legal requirements of citizenship, which can be exclusionary. Defining citizenship in this way requires us to consider the various ways in which individuals enact their citizenship. Such civic experiences can include various acts from requesting government services, to submitting taxes online, to signing petitions. It also includes digitally mediated relationships between societal actors such as journalists reporting public opinion, data being collected to prioritize government resource deployment, or political parties targeting messages to potential supporters. In these and many other ways, citizenship is experienced with and through digital contexts.

Definitions of citizenship vary across sectors and disciplines, and have evolved over time, but core commonalities can guide our understanding of who is a citizen and what enacting citizenship looks like. From a legal perspective, citizenship is bound by recognition from a given nation-state: "The notion of citizenship provides people living in these nation-states with certain civil, social, political, and economic rights and responsibilities" (Choi, 2016, p. 3). Marshall (1964) describes elements of citizenship: civil (such as freedoms and rights), political (such as the ability to exercise power over elected officials and voting) and social (such as civic culture and national heritage). These are widely accepted as a base framework for understanding citizenship (Banks, 2008). Meanwhile, democratic political philosophers argue that citizens play a crucial role in selecting representatives through elections, suggesting that citizens must be, to varying extents, informed about their political system, the decisions of political leaders, and current affairs (Delli Carpini, 2000; Strömbäck, 2005). From this perspective, citizenship involves not only participating in procedural aspects of democracy but also being part of information systems and communities. However, legal definitions of citizenship may then break down because one can participate in and contribute to those systems and communities without legally being a citizen of a given nation-state. As such, legal conceptualizations of citizenship can be exclusionary, and the lines of exclusion too often fall along differences in language, religion, ethnic, or cultural groups.

Conversely, citizenship might be more usefully considered in terms of identity and belonging to a community (Banks, 2008). While there are various conceptualizations of "cultural" citizenship (Choi, 2016, pp. 4–5), these approaches all tend to define citizenship in terms of a sense of community and the construction of identity developed through shared experience and common aspirations and purpose, which are often outside legal bounds. In the Canadian context, this is particularly relevant given the many nations found within the geographic bounds of Canada.

Culture-based understandings of citizenship are even more relevant when discussing digital contexts, since these often extend beyond national borders and governments (Barlow, 1996). Overall, they allow for more fluidity in understanding who counts as a citizen within a specific context because belonging and community shift as those involved grow and change, and as social norms evolve. Ultimately, definitions of citizenship are necessarily fluid. Different perspectives on citizenship are therefore useful, depending on the *contexts* in which those definitions are employed or discussed. That notion of the context in which citizenship is enacted is most interesting for the present collection—in particular, digital contexts.

Scholarship often distinguishes experiences of online and offline citizenships, conceptualizing *digital citizenship* as distinct from traditional (offline) citizenship. Some have conceptualized digital citizenship in terms of behavioural norms online (Ribble et al., 2004) or in terms of frequency of and competence with technology use (Mossberger et al., 2008). Others focus on identifying digital versions of analog acts of citizenship in order to expand our understanding of what constitutes such an act (Bennett et al., 2011). Digital citizenship as delineated by the Council of Europe (2018) is construed as any online participation (Greffet & Wojcik, 2014). Hintz, Dencik, and Wahl-Jorgensen suggest commonalities across definitions of digital citizenship: "In most iterations it tries to understand the relation between the digital and the political, and thus the role of the digital subject as a political subject" (Hintz et al., 2019, p. 20). They argue, commenting on the role of government and business in capitalist systems, that "digital citizenship thus denotes our roles, positions and activities in a society that is organized through digital technologies" (Hintz et al., 2019, p. 144).

Problematically, many definitions of digital citizenship require active and intentional use of digital technology by individuals. Research into digital divides has shown that individuals may choose to not use digital tools for various reasons, may not have access to the Internet, or may not have the skills required to make use of the digital tools available to them (Helsper & Reisdorf, 2017; Bertot, 2003; Hadziristic, 2017; Paré, 2005). However, this does not mean that their experience of citizenship is not digital. Regardless of individual citizens' digital activity, policies and laws are developed about digital data, privacy, and other issues; data about individuals are collected and used by governments; and political information is almost always shared digitally at some point in the information system.

Given that our lives have become unavoidably impacted by digital technologies, we endeavour to examine citizenship *in a digital context*, rather than *digital* citizenship. This slight change in phrasing may seem pedantic but it draws necessary attention to the fact that, in this collection, we wish to focus on a digital context which is continually evolving. Indeed, we suggest that it is most useful for policy-makers, civil society groups, and researchers to think about the ways citizenship is enacted in increasingly digital contexts. The aim is not to think of an entirely new form of digital citizenship—as if it is something distinct from an offline citizenship—but instead to reconcile both online and offline experiences and to think about the ways in which individuals enact their citizenship in evolving digital contexts.

Of course, digital contexts have existed for many years, and what we propose is not new. However, the COVID-19 pandemic has underscored the many ways in which our lives are indeed unavoidably digital and has intensified dependence on digital tools. Due to the COVID-19 outbreak, governments, corporations, and communities all over the world shut down physical spaces almost overnight and shifted to a new online reality compatible with physical distancing. Responding to the pandemic has prompted increased digitalization of political institutions, and even of the justice system; yet the quick shift has left out a growing number of citizens. From privacy to access to news media to connectivity issues, the road is long for vulnerable people to be part of the digital conversation (Ranchordas, 2020; Bailey et al., 2020).

Now, more than ever, is an important moment to reflect on the ways in which our understandings of both citizenship and digital contexts are shifting, and the challenge this raises for building an inclusive society. Governments, journalism organizations, law- and policy-makers, and other actors are routinely faced with pressures to innovate in their uses of technologies and to respond to others making use of digital tools in new ways. Without continued reflection on these practices, it is possible to lose track of the state of the digital context and the needs of the citizens who act within it.

Exploring Citizenship in a Digital Context in Canada

Individuals have been enacting their citizenship in digital contexts for decades, but "there has been a remarkably limited discussion, let alone theorization, of the relationship between citizens and the Internet" (Isin & Ruppert, 2015, p. 6). In Canada, there is a lack of information about how Canadians interact with the Internet and related technologies and how they enact their citizenship digitally. For instance, we do not yet know how Canadians feel about the use of their digital data for digital government service delivery; in political and news information systems, which are increasingly online first (Hermida et al., 2012); or in the development of new laws and policies. However, the majority of Canadian adults are uncomfortable with governments, journalists, and political parties (among others) making use of even publicly available social media data (Gruzd et al., 2018). Similarly, if the forceful response by Canadians to the attempt by Statistics Canada to collect personal banking information in

2018 suggests that Canadians feel strongly about the ways in which governments collect and use their data (Gilmore, 2019; Press, 2018; Russell, 2018). In order for societal actors, such as civil society groups, governments, and journalism organizations, and legal systems to respond to the needs of Canadians in a digital context, we need critical reflection on the gaps in our knowledge and how to fill those gaps.

Given the dearth of knowledge, researchers in Canada often turn to studies about the United States and the United Kingdom because of shared language or similarities in culture or political systems. In these countries, large-scale surveys examine the impact of digital technology on many aspects of daily life. For example, the Pew Research Center in the United States maintains an extensive Internet and Technology program,[2] and the Oxford Internet Surveys run regular nationally representative surveys in the United Kingdom.[3] While similarities between the three do exist, Canada is unique in important ways. For example, while Silicon Valley in the United States is home to many major technology companies, very few have headquarters north of the border. Canada is a relatively small player in terms of audience size and potential profit for most large technology companies, which limits Canada's regulatory bargaining power (Centre for International Governance Innovation, 2018; Dubois et al., 2019). Furthermore, the way Canadians are likely to use digital tools may be quite different, given how geographically dispersed the population is and how limited broadband access continues to be in rural and northern communities (Broadcasting and Telecommunications Legislative Review, 2020; CIRA, 2020; House of Commons Standing Committee on Industry, Science and Technology, 2018).

Responding to this lack of information about the experiences of Canadians, in 2017 we launched Connected Canada/Canada Connecté. This pan-Canadian, multi-stakeholder, and interdisciplinary initiative aims to foster a conversation about citizenship in a digital context, with a focus on policy and, more importantly, on Canada. Up until that point, pockets of robust civil society and government departments, as well as researchers at universities and think tanks across the country, had dedicated themselves to help solve problems and develop strong policies that would be responsive to the needs of Canadians and Canada in a digital context. Yet there was little collaboration across these groups, data about citizens' Internet use and preferences related to digital technology were limited or proprietary, and policy-makers often struggled to understand the needs of citizens in a digital context.

Through the Connected Canada initiative, we aim to draw together and facilitate a network of people and organizations interested in understanding citizenship in a digital context. Our goal is to work together to develop a research and policy agenda. We set out to answer questions such as: What research and what methods of inquiry have been the most successful at creating positive change? What do we need to know about Canadians to encourage the use of new digital tools, ranging from social media to digital government services? What aspects of digital life are we forgetting about in our research and policy-making? How can we, as academics, policy-makers, or members of civil society work together to create stronger digital policies in Canada?

On October 13 and 14, 2017, we hosted the Connected Canada inaugural conference at the University of Ottawa, bringing together 150 academics, policy-makers, and technologists around the common goal of mobilizing research into what it means to be a citizen in a digital context in Canada and how we, as researchers and activists, can overcome the existing gaps in data that limit our current understanding. Using the above questions as a springboard, participants at the Connected Canada conference dove deep into our existing knowledge and our knowledge gaps related to Canadians' Internet use, comfort levels, and needs. Throughout the event, we heard many suggestions for expanding research, which we presented in *Canadians in a Digital Context: A Research Agenda for a Connected Canada* (Dubois & Martin-Bariteau, 2018).

Conference activities began with an expert's meeting to discuss the institutional barriers to sharing data about how Canadians use the Internet to engage in their communities and enable their citizenship. Next, we organized the wider conversation around four streams: Digital Rights, Government Service Design, News and Media, and Citizen Engagement. As part of the Digital Rights stream, participants discussed how to design coherent legal frameworks to protect citizens' rights in a digital context. They identified several challenges constant connectivity poses for citizens. The conversation notably focused on the role, responsibilities, and obligations of digital platforms, and concerns regarding consent to terms and conditions, especially with respect to privacy.

Through the Government Service Design discussions, participants exchanged ideas about how to help governments identify risks in deploying new digital services and the importance of learning from our mistakes. Participants made it clear that we need to create resources to help all levels of government choose between digital and analog service delivery, in recognition of the present limits of digital connectivity, as well as to promote an "Open by Design" approach to data, services, and the governance of both.

Within the News and Media Literacy stream, participants discussed the ways in which citizens access, understand, and share information about current affairs and their political system. The conversation highlighted a concern that there is a sense of disconnection between Canadian readers and news content. Many participants also expressed concern over disinformation and misinformation, as well as an interest in creating a culture that guards against over-regulation in order to future-proof Canadian news media against government interference.

Finally, with respect to Citizen Engagement, participants discussed the importance of institutional bridge building and of creating strong methods for measuring citizen engagement. The conversation highlighted the need to use existing knowledge about who is excluded from digital technologies to create concrete actions aimed to connect all Canadians. Discussants noted that to develop best practices, we need to better understand how online influencers as well as lobbyists shape government outreach and policies.

Our vision for the conference came from concern about a lack of data about Canadians' Internet use, preferences, and comfort levels. Indeed, when we began our work in 2017, there had been no detailed surveys about Internet use conducted by Statistics Canada since 2012. A report on the future of news and democracy commissioned by the Government of Canada also found there was such a lack of Canadian data, and one of the report's 12 recommendations was to establish a research institute dedicated to the topic (Public Policy Forum, 2017). However, we learned that some more recent data exists, but this is siloed and inaccessible to most researchers because of institutional and communication barriers. Despite this lack of consistent data, our motivated and active governments at all levels, civil society groups, and private sector actors are working to develop new tools and practices. Since then, on October 29, 2019, Statistics Canada published a long-awaited update of the *Canadian Internet Use Survey* (Statistics Canada, 2019). While a helpful addition which provides some much-needed data, the limited scope of the survey, an inability to compare year to year, and uncertainty about the next update have confirmed for us that more coordinated, regular, and comprehensive studies on Canadians' Internet use are needed.

The conference also confirmed that academia, civil society, and government were ready to work together but were lacking a Canadian space for such a conversation. Since then, we continued the conversation with participants and reached out to some of the missing voices from our conference.

Building on the *Canadians in a Digital Context* research agenda (Dubois & Martin-Bariteau, 2018), we invited some of Canada's pre-eminent leading and emergent voices—from academia, government, and civil society—to expand on some of the most urgent policy issues through short policy papers, informed by evidence-based research. We have organized this collection of policy-oriented essays around three building blocks for a comprehensive digital policy for a Connected Canada, reflected in this book's divisions. Part 1 examines the current landscape of digital civic participation, and notes some of the missing voices which are required to ensure an inclusive digital society. In Part 2, experts reflect on relationships between citizens and their political and democratic institutions, from government service delivery to academic and citizen engagement in policy-making. Finally, in Part 3, experts address key legal frameworks that need to be discussed and redesigned to allow for the building of an inclusive society and the strengthening of our democratic institutions.

These three components are important building blocks for digital policy in Canada, but they certainly do not represent an all-encompassing examination of all the ways in which citizenship is being enacted in a digital context. In selecting these areas of focus, and the chapters which make them up, we aim to spark discussion on some of the most pressing issues. However, readers should not consider this list to be exhaustive. As technologies, and our relationships to those technologies, continue to evolve, so too does the list of priorities. Furthermore, we intentionally did not substantially address electoral politics and participation because a recent report addressed key issues related to political uses of digital media during the 2019 Canadian federal election (Dubois & Owen, 2020).

Building an Inclusive Society in a Digital Context

As a society, we need to reflect on what it means to be a citizen in a digital context. In Part I, we have invited community-based voices to examine opportunities and challenges for digital equity and inclusion, highlighted in the *Canadians in a Digital Context* report. These chapters draw both on academic literature related to well-defined concepts as well as the experiences of community-based organizations in order to highlight some of the voices which have been missing in digital policy discussions. The chapters provide opportunities to develop more inclusive approaches to understanding and advancing a connected Canada.

In conversations about digital policy, Indigenous perspectives are too frequently excluded. In "Decolonizing Digital Spaces" (Chapter 1), Alexander Dirksen reflects on the dominant narrative of the technology sector's rise and the urgency of grounding ourselves more deeply in the current realities and complexities of citizenship in a digital context as it relates to reconciliation in Canada. Dirksen identifies ways in which the private and public sectors can begin to mobilize around a more robust definition of citizenship in a digital context in Canada that will serve and support the emergence of decolonized digital spaces.

Certainly, the new centrality of online spaces in which political discourse can take place has disrupted politics and generated questions about the robustness and sustainability of liberal democracies, and the amplification of inequalities—both on- and offline. To build inclusion and trust in this digital context, we need to learn more about how Canadians perceive themselves and their democratic institutions in the networked society. With this in mind, Adelina Petit-Vouriot and Mike Morden, in "Telling a Different Story: Canadian Citizens and Their Democracy in the Digital Age" (Chapter 2), draw on recent public opinion research to examine trends in Canadians' attitudes toward democracy and their engagement in formal and informal politics. They suggest that technological and geopolitical changes have produced concern among Canadians about the health of their democracy, yet they also illustrate how Canadians are becoming more engaged and satisfied with their democracy. The contribution also confirms some voices are missing in this crucial discussion.

Finally, Leslie Regan Shade, Jane Bailey, Jacquelyn Burkell, Priscilla Regan, and Valerie Steeves examine the digital perspectives and experiences of youth in "Framing the Challenges of Digital Inclusion for Young Canadians" (Chapter 3). Offering a critical discussion of elements of digital inclusion in a connected Canada, the authors report on findings of focus groups conducted across Canada that explore online activities and platforms used by youth, ages 13 to 17. The authors examine whether and how privacy was an essential aspect to the youths' enjoyment, online experiences where they felt unwelcome or disrespected, and their strategies to mitigate these constraints.

Building Democratic Institutions in a Digital Context

A conversation around what it means to be a citizen in Canada's digital context requires us to reflect on the impact of technology on democratic institutions and on the social fabric. Naturally, we need to discuss, assess, and reimagine government service delivery and design. We also need to examine how citizens interact with their political institutions, for example by considering news and media literacy, citizen engagement, and corporate lobbying. In Part II, we have invited academics, public servants, and activists to develop a few of the key areas highlighted in the *Canadians in a Digital Context* report as they concern digital government, the journalism industry, and technology policy lobbying.

As we have argued before, "citizens' practices, preferences, and needs must inform the extent to which services could—or should—be digitized as well as the types of data governments should gather about citizens" (Dubois & Martin-Bariteau, 2020). The digital era has created unprecedented speed and reach for citizens accessing government services or voicing their opinion about the policies behind those services. Digital tools have been developed so that citizens can sometimes directly change or circumvent government programs. Perhaps most importantly, the digital age has revealed a staggering volume of previously invisible or ignorable voices and perspectives, such as those of people in marginalized populations. In "Government in the Connected Era" (Chapter 4), Kent Aitken explores how the Canadian government is evolving, what digital government means for citizens, and what questions remain unanswered.

Discussing this new orthodoxy of digital government service delivery, Amanda Clarke examines the needs for data governance reforms in "Data Governance: The Next Frontier of Digital Government Research and Practice" (Chapter 5). Building on case studies, Clarke outlines a research and policy agenda to ensure that digital era public management reforms bolster, rather than erode, Canadians' already-precarious levels of trust in government.

Journalism and political information systems also impact our experiences of citizenship in a digital context. Political information, including journalistic content, is crucial for individuals as they learn about their communities or make decisions—about voting, for example. As argued by the authors of Chapter 6, although Canada is seeing a market failure in journalism, there is possible growth in digital journalism start-ups. In "The Conversation Canada: Not-for-Profit Journalism in a Time of Commercial Media Decline," Mary Lynn Young and Alfred Hermida assess journalism innovation in Canada through a case study of a not-for-profit start-up, The Conversation Canada. Their illustration of this case highlights opportunities and challenges for political information systems and offers a concrete case that can be a helpful starting point for discussions about how the industry might evolve and what role government, citizens, and academics might play.

A conversation about the relationships among citizens and their democratic institutions also calls for an examination of citizen engagement in policy-making. Citizens are too often far from these conversations and decisions, which will nonetheless have immense impact on their daily lives. In the Canadian context, for example, conversations about regulating technology platforms have been primarily led by technology corporations, behind closed doors and far from the public's eye. The issue, shared across the digital policy spectrum, is discussed by Megan Beretta in "Influencing the Internet: Lobbyists and Interest Groups' Impact on Digital Rights in Canada" (Chapter 7). Beretta offers recommendations to ensure that citizens are heard, as many legal frameworks need to be re-examined in a digital context.

Rethinking Legal Frameworks for the Digital Context

As digital tools permeate everyday experiences, the effectiveness of the legal system is brought into question. In particular, the increasing reliance on autonomous systems calls for a reimagination of legal frameworks. The building of an inclusive society and robust democratic institutions calls for the development of improved frameworks to ensure respect for fundamental rights in the digital space. Similarly, while the Internet offers remarkable opportunities for all Canadians to create, communicate, and engage in civic activities, policy-makers and regulators are facing several challenges to ensure

Canadian law offers adequate protection for citizens and a level playing field for all. In Part III, we invited leading Canadian legal scholars to discuss some of the key legal issues which were highlighted in the *Canadians in a Digital Context* report.

In order to be producers, creators, learners, critical thinkers, and citizens, Canadians click to agree to or sign lengthy standard-form contracts before getting access to goods and services—including government services. In "Consumers First, Digital Citizenry Second: Through the Gateway of Standard-Form Contracts" (Chapter 8), Marina Pavlović explores the relationship between consumer rights and digital citizenry, with a focus on standard-form contracts—such as the lengthy terms and conditions that one often accepts without reading—that have become the dominant regulatory mechanism of consumer relationships with goods and services, and their impact on digital civic participation. Pavlović calls for a paradigm shift to ensure proper protection of digital rights, and access to justice for citizens in a digital context.

This issue of standard-form contracts goes beyond consumer protection as it has been traditionally understood and engages with all aspects of the digital life. Building on Pavlović's approach (2016), the Supreme Court of Canada highlighted the risks such contracts present for Canadians' privacy in *Douez v. Facebook* (2017), framing privacy as a fundamental right to be protected as such. Although quite common in other parts of the world, notably in Europe, the reading of privacy rights as human rights is quite new under Canadian law. Building on the European approach, Teresa Scassa's contribution, "A Human Rights-Based Approach to Data Protection in Canada" (Chapter 9), explores the potential for such a paradigm shift and proposes models for a human rights-based approach to data and privacy.

Within the conversation around the legal and regulatory framework of Canadian digital ecosystems, few issues have proven as confusing—and divisive—as the debate over taxation of digital services and platforms. The current state of affairs leaves domestic firms disadvantaged and government missing out on important tax revenues. Michael Geist examines this digital tax policy debate, the core policy choices, and the potential to develop a fair digital policy structure in "Making Sense of the Canadian Digital Tax Debate" (Chapter 10). Another heated policy issue is the confusing and uneven Canadian framework surrounding Internet intermediaries' liability, especially as content moderation (e.g., copyrighted content, harmful speech, right of erasure, etc.) raises concerns related to freedom of expression and information. Today, Canada is at a cross-roads and faces pressure to review its framework. Consequently, we conclude this section with "Online Abuse, Chilling Effects, and Human Rights" (Chapter 11), a contribution by Jonathon W. Penney that discusses how online abuses pose significant threats to human rights. Rooted in empirical findings, the chapter analyzes the current US framework, the possible reaches of its chilling effect, and lessons for Canadian policy-makers. Penney argues that Internet speech regulations, such as online harassment laws, rather than having a chilling effect on general freedom of speech, can also have a salutary impact on the speech and engagement of victims whose voices have been typically marginalized.

*

Our concluding chapter reviews the key arguments presented in all three parts and suggests, as the chapter title says, "Next Steps for a Connected Canada." In order to develop policy that responds to the needs of citizens in a digital context, we need high-quality and rigorous research into the agenda items and policy needs highlighted across the chapters in this edited collection. This concluding chapter ends with a discussion about how we, as academics, policy-makers, and civil society members, together with private sector actors, might endeavour to continue advancing existing lines of research and policy development, while adjusting our efforts to be more inclusive of the voices and issues which are too often excluded or ignored. This collection, we hope, will serve to spark discussion, debate, and future work in order to inform policy-makers, civil society groups, legal systems, and other actors as they adapt to a digital context.

Notes

1. This section builds on the previously published "Citizens and Their Political Institutions in a Digital Context" (Dubois & Martin-Bariteau 2020).
2. See: https://www.pewresearch.org/internet/.
3. See: https://oxis.oii.ox.ac.uk/.

References

Bailey, J., Burkell, J., Regan, P., & Steeves, V. (2020, April 21). Children's privacy is at risk with rapid shifts to online schooling under coronavirus. *The Conversation Canada*. https://theconversation.com/childrens-privacy-is-at-risk-with-rapid-shifts-to-online-schooling-under-coronavirus-135787

Banks, J. A. (2008). Diversity, group identity, and citizenship education in a global age. *Educational Researcher, 37*(3), 129–139. https://doi.org/10.3102/0013189X08317501

Barlow, J. P. (1996). *A Declaration of Independence of Cyberspace*. http://homes.eff.org/~barlow/Declaration-Final.html

Bennett, W. L., Wells, C., & Freelon, D. (2011). Communicating civic engagement: Contrasting models of citizenship in the youth web sphere. *Journal of Communication, 61*(5), 835–856. https://doi.org/10.1111/j.1460-2466.2011.01588.x

Bertot, J. C. (2003). The multiple dimensions of the digital divide: More than the technology "haves" and "have nots." *Government Information Quarterly, 20*(2), 185–191. https://doi.org/10.1016/S0740-624X(03)00036-4

Broadcasting and Telecommunications Legislative Review (2020). *Canada's communications future: Time to act*. Department of Innovation, Science and Economic Development Canada. https://www.ic.gc.ca/eic/site/110.nsf/vwapj/BTLR_Eng-V3.pdf/$file/BTLR_Eng-V3.pdf

Buell, M. (2019, May 3). *Why multistakeholder policymaking works*. Policy Options. https://policyoptions.irpp.org/fr/magazines/may-2019/why-multistakeholder-policymaking-works/

Canada, House of Commons, Standing Committee on Industry, Science and Technology. (2018, April). *Broadband connectivity in rural Canada: Overcoming the digital divide*. Report no. 11. 42nd Parliament, 1st session. https://www.ourcommons.ca/Content/Committee/421/INDU/Reports/RP9711342/indurp11/indurp11-e.pdf

Canadian Internet Registration Authority [CIRA]. (2020, May 7). *Call for comments regarding potential barriers to the deployment of broadband-capable networks in underserved areas in Canada*. Submission to the CRTC Consultation 2019-406, https://www.cira.ca/sites/default/files/2020-05/CRTC%202019-406%20CIRA%20Submission.pdf

Centre for International Governance Innovation. (2018, February). *A national data strategy for Canada: Key elements and policy considerations* (CIGI Papers No. 160). Centre for International Governance Innovation. https://www.cigionline.org/sites/default/files/documents/Paper%20no.160_3.pdf

Choi, M. (2016). A concept analysis of digital citizenship for democratic citizenship education in the Internet age. *Theory & Research in Social Education, 44*(4), 565–607. https://doi.org/10.1080/00933104.2016.1210549

Clement, A. H., Gurstein, M., Longford, G., Moll, M., & Shade, L. (2012). *Connecting Canadians: Investigations in community informatics.* Athabasca University Press.

Council of Europe. (n.d.). *Digital citizenship and digital citizenship education.* https://www.coe.int/en/web/digital-citizenship-education/digital-citizenship-and-digital-citizenship-education/

Delli Carpini, M. X. (2000). In search of the informed citizen: What Americans know about politics and why it matters. *The Communication Review, 4*(1), 129–164. https://doi.org/10.1080/10714420009359466

Dentoni, D., Bitzer, V., & Schouten, G. (2018). Harnessing wicked problems in multi-stakeholder partnerships. *Journal of Business Ethics, 150,* 333–356. https://doi.org/10.1007/s10551-018-3858-6

Douez v. Facebook, Inc., 2017 SCC 33.

Dubois, E., & Martin-Bariteau, F. (2018). *Canadians in a digital context: A research agenda for a connected Canada.* SSRN. https://ssrn.com/abstract=3301352

Dubois, E., & Martin-Bariteau, F. (2020). Citizens and their political institutions in a digital context. In W. H. Dutton (Ed.), *A research agenda for digital politics* (p. 102). Edward Elgar. https://ssrn.com/abstract=3499315

Dubois, E., McKelvey, F., & Owen, T. (2019, April 10). *What have we learned from Google's political ad pullout?* Policy Options. https://policyoptions.irpp.org/magazines/april-2019/learned-googles-political-ad-pullout/

Dubois, E., & Owen, T. (2020). *Understanding the digital ecosystem: Findings from the 2019 federal election* [Report]. Digital Ecosystem Research Challenge. https://www.digitalecosystem.ca/report

Faris, R. M., Hal, R., Etling, B., Bourassa, N., Zuckerman, E., & Yochai, B. (2017). Partisanship, propaganda, and disinformation: Online media and the 2016 U.S. presidential election [Research paper]. Berkman Klein Center for Internet & Society. http://nrs.harvard.edu/urn-3:HUL.InstRepos:33759251

Gilmore, R. (2019, December 10). *StatCan didn't break the law by collecting banking data, privacy watchdog says.* CTV News. https://www.ctvnews.ca/politics/statcan-didn-t-break-the-law-by-collecting-banking-data-privacy-watchdog-says-1.4723494

Goldman, A., Barnes, J. E., Haberman, M., & Fandos, N. (2020, February 20). Lawmakers are warned that Russia is meddling to re-elect Trump. *The New York Times.* https://www.nytimes.com/2020/02/20/us/politics/russian-interference-trump-democrats.html

Greffet, F., & Wojcik, S. (2014). La citoyenneté numérique : Perspectives de recherche. *Réseaux, 184–185*(2), 125–159. https://doi.org/10.3917/res.184.0125

Gruzd, A., Jacobson, J., Mai, P., & Dubois, E. (2018). *Social media privacy in Canada* (Version: 1.0). Ryerson University Social Media Lab. https://doi.org/10.5683/SP/JVOToS

Hadziristic, T. (2017). *The state of digital literacy in Canada: A literature review* [Working paper]. The Brookfield Institute for Innovation and Entrepreneurship. https://brookfieldinstitute.ca/wp-content/uploads/ BrookfieldInstitute_State-of-Digital-Literacy-in-Canada_Literature_ WorkingPaper.pdf

Haro-de-Rosario, A., Sáez-Martín, A., & del Carmen Caba-Pérez, M. (2018). Using social media to enhance citizen engagement with local government: Twitter or Facebook? *New Media & Society, 20*(1), 29–49. https:// doi.org/10.1177/1461444816645652

Helsper, E. J., & Reisdorf, B. C. (2017). The emergence of a "digital underclass" in Great Britain and Sweden: Changing reasons for digital exclusion. *New Media & Society, 19*(8), 1253–1270. https://doi.org/10.1177/ 1461444816634676

Hermida, A., Fletcher, F., Korell, D., & Logan, D. (2012). Share, like, recommend: Decoding the social media news consumer. *Journalism studies, 13*(5–6), 815–824.

Hintz, A., Dencik, L., & Wahl-Jorgensen, K. (2019). *Digital citizenship in a datafied society.* Polity Press.

Isin, E., & Ruppert, E. (2015). *Being digital.* Rowman and Littlefield.

Loewen, P., & Stevens, B. A. (2019, July). *Automation, AI and anxiety: Policy preferred, populism possible.* Public Policy Forum. https://ppforum.ca/wp-content/uploads/2019/07/AutomationAIandAnxiety-PPF-July2019-EN1. pdf

Marshall, T. H. (1964). *Class, citizenship, and social development: Essays of T. H. Marshall.* Greenwood.

Matheus, R., Ribeiro, M. M., Vaz, J. C., & de Souza, C. A. (2010). Case studies of digital participatory budgeting in Latin America: Models for citizen engagement. In J. Davies & T. Janowski (Eds.), *ICEGOV '10: Proceedings of the 4th international conference on theory and practice of electronic governance* (pp 31–36). Association for Computing Machinery. https://doi. org/10.1145/1930321.1930328

Millar, J., Barron, B., Hori, K., Finlay, R., Kotsuki, K., & Kerr, I. (2018, December 6). Accountability in AI: Promoting greater societal trust [Discussion paper for breakout session]. G7 Multistakeholder Conference on Artificial Intelligence, Montréal, QC, Canada. https://www.ic.gc.ca/eic/site/133.nsf/vwapj/3_Discussion_Paper_-_ Accountability_in_AI_EN.pdf/$FILE/3_Discussion_Paper_-_ Accountability_in_AI_EN.pdf

Mossberger, K., Tolbert, C. J., & McNeal, R. S. (2008). *Digital citizenship: The Internet, society, and participation.* MIT Press.

Paré, D. (2005). The digital divide: Why the "the" is misleading. In A. Murray & M. Klang (Eds.), *Human rights in the digital age* (pp. 85–97). Cavendish Publishing.

Pavlović, M. (2016). Contracting out of access to justice: Enforcement of forum-selection clauses in consumer contracts. *McGill Law Journal*, 62(2), 389–440.

Powell, A., Scott, A. J., & Henry, N. (2018). Digital harassment and abuse: Experiences of sexuality and gender minority adults. *European Journal of Criminology*, 17(2), 199–223. https://doi.org/10.1177/1477370818788006

Press, J. (2018, November 1). *Bank data furor threatens ability to compile accurate data: chief statistician*. CBC News. https://www.cbc.ca/news/politics/statistics-canada-private-information-1.4888462

Public Policy Forum. (2017, January). *The shattered mirror: News, democracy and trust in the digital age*. https://shatteredmirror.ca/wp-content/uploads/theShatteredMirror.pdf

Quan-Haase, A., Williams, C., Kicevski, M., Elueze, I., & Wellman, B. (2018). Dividing the grey divide: Deconstructing myths about older adults' online activities, skills, and attitudes. *American Behavioral Scientist*, 62(9), 1207–1228. https://doi.org/10.1177/0002764218777572

Ranchordas, S. (2020, May 13). We teach and learn online. Are we all digital citizens now? Lessons on digital citizenship from the lockdown. *I-CONnect: Blog of the International Journal of Constitutional Law*. http://www.iconnectblog.com/2020/05/we-teach-and-learn-online-are-we-all-digital-citizens-now-lessons-on-digital-citizenship-from-the-lockdown/

Ribble, M. S., Bailey, G. D., & Ross, T. W. (2004). Digital citizenship: Addressing appropriate technology behavior. *Learning & Leading with Technology*, 32(1), 6–11.

Robinson, L., Cotten, S. R., Ono, H., Quan-Haase, A., Mesch, G., Chen, W., Schulz, J., Hale, T. M., & Stern, M. J. (2015). Digital inequalities and why they matter. *Information, Communication & Society*, 18(5), 569–582.

Russell, A. (2018, October 29). *Trudeau defends Statistics Canada move to collect banking info of 500,000 Canadians*. Global News. https://globalnews.ca/news/4608105/trudeau-defends-statistics-canada-move-to-collect-banking-info-of-500000-canadians/

Statistics Canada. (2019). *Canadian Internet use survey*. https://www23.statcan.gc.ca/imdb/p2SV.pl?Function=getSurvey&SDDS=4432

Strömbäck, J. (2005). In search of a standard: Four models of democracy and their normative implications for journalism. *Journalism Studies*, 6(3), 331–345. https://doi.org/10.1080/14616700500131950

Waterhouse, R. (2019). Addressing Rural & Northern Internet Connectivity. https://www.cengn.ca/rural-northern-internet-connectivity/

World Economic Forum. (2013, January). *The future role of civil society* (World Scenario Series). http://www3.weforum.org/docs/WEF_FutureRoleCivilSociety_Report_2013.pdf

PART I

BUILDING AN INCLUSIVE
SOCIETY IN A DIGITAL CONTEXT

CHAPTER 1

Decolonizing Digital Spaces

Alexander Dirksen

Abstract

Power without purpose. Aspiration without intention. Ubiquity without diversity. For too long, we have been enraptured by the promise of the digital age, failing to critically examine the roots, intentions, and impact of an increasingly small number of for-profit firms. In a world where digital spaces play such an integral role in all aspects of our lives, this accumulation of reach, power, and influence poses critical questions and concerns relating to citizenship in a digital context, and in particular within the context of Canada as a colonial state articulating a commitment to reconciliation. In this chapter, I will provide a brief overview of the history of digital spaces through a decolonized lens, a critical step toward grounding ourselves in the current realities and complexities around citizenship in a digital context. Focus will then shift with an eye to the future, identifying potential next steps for researchers and policy-makers so that the private and public sectors can begin to mobilize around a more robust definition of citizenship in a digital context in Canada, one that will serve and support the emergence of decolonized digital spaces.

From Alexa to Siri, we are asking more questions of our devices than ever before. Their soothing mechanical voices are a far cry from the jarring tones of dial-up modems, revealing how seamlessly ubiquitous technology has become in the ensuing decades. We now exist in an era in which an entire digital world is being integrated into our physical spaces.

Yet as we ask more of our devices, the time has come to also ask more of our governing and regulatory bodies regarding digital access, agency, equity, and rights. For too long, for-profit corporations have dictated the terms by which we engage with digital spaces, and have enjoyed largely unfettered reign over these spaces, which have become so foundational to our lives as hubs of commerce, connection, and knowledge exchange. An emphasis on consumers over citizens carries with it considerable implications, particularly for those for whom capitalist-colonial systems were engineered to marginalize or exclude.

While privacy breaches and the spread of misinformation are forcing governments around the world to grapple with such realities, these conversations carry particular weight here in Canada, a colonial construct built forcibly atop the many Indigenous Nations of Turtle Island.[1] In an age of commitments to Nation-to-Nation relationships (Wilson-Raybould, 2017), what does it mean to have such a small set of corporations—whose reach and influence are beginning to transcend that of the colonial nation-state—able to exert such unfettered control and influence? It is clear that we cannot discuss citizenship in a digital age without discussing the ways in which the privatization of the web, data sovereignty, lack of regulatory oversight, and the demographics of the sector itself relate to reconciliation in Canada. How can we begin to meaningfully decolonize digital spaces? And what is the role of policy-makers in these efforts?

We are at a critical juncture in regard to these conversations. If we move forward rooted in recognition and respect of Indigenous rights and in a shared spirit of reconciliation, we can amplify the work of Indigenous innovators across Turtle Island, and, in turn, craft a vibrant digital domain for all. To realize this promise, policy-makers must become more actively engaged in the digital domain, countering market forces that claim neutrality in a complex and unequal world.

In this chapter, I provide a brief overview of the history of digital spaces that decentres its dominant narrative—a critical step toward grounding ourselves in the current realities and complexities around citizenship in a digital context. Focus then shifts to the future, and I identify potential next steps for researchers and policy-makers to take to private and public sectors to mobilize them around a more robust definition of citizenship in a digital context[2] in Canada. This will serve and support the emergence of decolonized digital spaces.

From Defence to Dominance

Technology is never a neutral force. Behind the sleek glass and metal enclosures of our lithium-charged lifelines are *people*: the technology sector's evolution (from its militarized roots to today's growing surveillance state) reflects the values and beliefs of those people who craft the code that powers our digital age. Meaningfully assessing our current context and potential paths forward requires us to first re-examine the dominant narrative of our electronic evolution with a more critical lens, exposing how the forces of colonialism, patriarchy, and Whiteness have shaped the sector and its offerings.

While Canadian firms have played a key role in the development of what is now the technology sector—from the companies that would become Nortel Networks Corporation (commonly known as Nortel) to the dominance of Research in Motion (RIM) in smartphone development—a more comprehensive understanding of the patterns and trends in tech development comes from an exploration of what's commonly called Silicon Valley, a small geographic area in Northern California with a disproportionate impact as the home of the world's largest and most influential technology firms.

How have the specific roots and current realities of Silicon Valley shaped the approach to an general engagement with digital spaces? And what do these trends reveal about the role of policy-makers in ensuring digital spaces are equitable for all?

Silicon Valley: A Case Study

The lands now known as Silicon Valley (loosely defined as the San Francisco Bay area) knew innovation long before the emergence of electronics. The Ohlone Peoples (a modern grouping of a number of distinct Indigenous tribes and language groups) had a deep relationship with the lands and waters of the region prior to the arrival of the Spanish (Spencer, 2018). With colonization came measles and missions—Keith Spencer (2019) notes a drop in the Indigenous population of what is now California from 310,000 to 100,000 people.

This disruption and destruction set the tone for the technological "progress" that would follow in future generations. As Spencer (2019) notes:

> The differences between the Ohlone and the Spanish ways of life reveal the contradictions inherent to our present-day idea of "technology." To borrow the Silicon Valley business-speak of today, who possessed more advanced technology? The Ohlone or the Spanish? Who was more innovative? The deep knowledge of the maintenance of the landscape, and the communal lifestyles enjoyed by the Ohlone, meant that the Bay Area remained in a relatively stable ecological state for a thousand years. The incursion of the colonizers disrupted this; they imposed their technological whims and their agricultural logic on the landscape and enslaved and exploited the Ohlone. (para. 11)

European agricultural practices were forcibly imposed upon the region and its peoples at the turn of the eighteenth century, stripping the region of its abundance of plant and animal life and replacing it with farmland and orchards (Spencer, 2018). A second ecological disruption would come as the region shifted from apple orchards to Apples of a different variety, a concrete densification that came in part through military-defence spending in the mid 1950s—ARPANET (the forerunner of today's Internet) was supported by the Defense Advanced Research Projects Agency (Balachander, 2017; Dembosky, 2013; O'Mara, 2018; Tarnoff, 2016). The first transistors produced by Fairchild Semiconductor (one of the earliest and most prominent semiconductor companies in Silicon Valley) were used in the computer of the B-70 bomber, with others used to form the guidance system for the Minuteman II ballistic missile (Laws, 2017; *1958: Silicon Mesa Transistors*, n.d.). And the first tenant of the technology park Stanford Research Park was Varian Associates (Findlay, 1992, p. 136), a company whose roots were tied to creating military radar components, including the development of the fuse for the atomic bomb (Lécuyer, 2006, p. 102).

Whether it focuses on Steve Jobs's garage or Mark Zuckerberg's dorm room, the mainstream narrative about technological development emphasizes human ingenuity, creativity, and innovation as its roots. But without active investment from military institutions for imperialistic purposes (aggravating colonial tensions and solidifying colonial borders abroad), what we now know as our digital age would look markedly different. We cannot extricate the online spaces of today from these troubling roots, and instead must recognize both the harm caused by these efforts as well as the precedent it set for the future of the technology sector.

For as the pace of technological progress in Silicon Valley steadily increased, perceptions around technology began to shift. No longer a niche product for military or academic applications, young upstarts such as Bill Gates had high aspirations for the sector's potential. It became about more than the mere selling of keyboards and mice; there was a belief that technology had the power to fundamentally transform all aspects of our lives, far beyond the reach of the first Netscape computer browser (Beaumont, 2008). These early aspirations (which have now solidified into a pervasive ideology in Silicon Valley) were evidenced by Apple's "Here's to the crazy ones" ad, which posited that "the ones who are crazy enough to think they can change the world are the ones who do" (Dormehl, 2018). But lost in this clever catchphrase is a deeper truth: that despite a utopian dream of borderless and democratized digital spaces, social inequities and injustices continue to inexplicably determine whether your crazy, world-changing idea will even be heard or resourced. The sector continues to disproportionately attract, promote, and follow the leadership of the most privileged segments of our society. Of its five dominant firms (Amazon, Apple, Facebook, Microsoft, and Google) over 70 percent of their senior leadership teams identify as white, over 73 percent of all staff (in the case of Microsoft) are male, and none have more than 1 percent of their workforce who identify as Indigenous, Native American, Native Hawaiian, or Pacific Islander (Brown & Parker, 2019; Apple, 2019; Microsoft, 2018; Facebook, 2018; Our workforce data, 2018).[3] As noted by Harris (2018) of Code2040 (a non-profit dedicated to increasing Black and Latinx representation and leadership in the technology sector), this is more than mere under-representation; it is systematic exclusion.

This systematic exclusion and the homogeneity of the sector have critical implications for the digital landscape. The fact that so many Indigenous communities continue to face the effects of the digital divide, which is "the division between those who are able to access and use the internet and those who are not" (Cañares et al., 2018, p. 6) is the type of reality that often exists outside of the lived experiences of those most actively involved in shaping the tools and technologies of our digital age.

Within the context of rights and citizenship in the digital environment, governments must come to play a more active and central role in the technology sector's continued growth and evolution, as "self-regulation" has proven insufficient to ensure equitable and just access and engagement with digital tools and platforms. Policy-makers can and must begin to address structural inequities, support the emergence of new digital spaces, and establish a form of citizenship in a digital context that is rooted in the realities of the Canadian colonial state. Such shifts will help to facilitate broader changes within a sector whose roots and history have largely failed to represent, reflect, or respect the diversity of its user base.

Decolonizing Citizenship in a Digital Context

The critical conversation on decolonizing citizenship in a digital context comes at a time of increasing complexity and change in the policy landscape as it relates to issues of technology. From rapid e-commerce growth (soon to account for 10 percent of Canadian retail purchases) to the ubiquity of social media platforms (with 94 percent of Canadians who use the Internet on at least one platform), the implications of the rapidly evolving digital landscape are inescapable (Gruzd et al., 2018; Mohammad, 2018). As the pervasiveness of digital technologies has grown, so too has the power and influence of the technology sector, placing policy-makers in the position of a seeming need to choose between the economic growth of the future and citizens' rights. To date, the pendulum has swung in favour of tech monopolies—whether in the types of government incentives offered for Amazon's second headquarters,[4] the wish to embrace Sidewalk Labs in Toronto, or the lack of a proportional response to the revelations of the Cambridge Analytica scandal, governments appear reluctant to take on a sector with such vast reach and influence (Dayen, 2018; Gruzd et al., 2018; Wylie, 2018).

The crucial questions are worth repeating: How can policy-makers support the emergence of a form of decolonized digital spaces? And what is the role of citizenship in a digital context in ensuring such spaces are able to thrive?

As we explore tangible steps that can be undertaken at the federal level to support such efforts, it is critical to reaffirm that all steps forward must be rooted in recognition, respect, and embodiment of Nation-to-Nation relationships. Only through such relationships and partnerships can progress be made in a way which addresses issues of sovereignty and jurisdiction, rights and oversight, and regulation. Such dialogue and collaboration must take differing forms in recognition of the diversity of Indigenous Nations and Peoples.

A Continued Commitment

A strong foundation for a decolonized digital landscape demands broader societal shifts. As the result of a fundamentally human endeavour, digital spaces mirror, replicate, and at times exacerbate the real and pressing realities faced by Indigenous Peoples and other racialized communities in physical spaces. Eliminating the digital divide faced by rural and remote Indigenous communities (Howard et al., 2010; McMahon, 2014) demands an examination of the historic and continued underfunding of Indigenous Nations. At the same time, levels of hate speech experienced by Indigenous voices online (Chapin, 2015; Kassam, 2017) require reflection on the intentional marginalization and minimization of Indigenous world views and perspectives across school curricula, mainstream media, and social media. Growing awareness, advocacy, and action across these tangible and material fronts is critical to crafting digital spaces that are equitable for all. While potential policy interventions to support these shifts are too numerous to note exhaustively in this chapter, they include sustained investments in Indigenous communities to counter a decade-long 2 percent funding cap (Fontaine, 2015), and concrete commitments to the realization of the Calls to Action of the Truth and Reconciliation Commission (2015) and the Calls to Justice of the National Inquiry into Missing and Murdered Indigenous Women and Girls (2019).

Eliminating the Digital Divide

As long advocated for by the First Nations Technology Council and other digital rights groups (Williams, 2018), decolonized digital rights begin with addressing basic issues of access. Despite a 2016 ruling by the Canadian Radio-television and Telecommunications Commission that access to broadband Internet was a basic service for all Canadians, far too many Indigenous Nations are grappling with a complete lack of connectivity, or connectivity far below the speeds which so many of us take for granted (Kupfer, 2016; Williams, 2018).

Investments in the necessary connectivity infrastructure is critical to ensuring full and equitable access to digital spaces. How this work is undertaken (and by whom) represents a tangible opportunity to engage in economic reconciliation by working in partnership with Indigenous-led broadband initiatives and continuing efforts to increase the number of federal procurement opportunities awarded to Indigenous-led businesses.

UNDRIP Implementation

Strengthened digital rights are dependent upon strengthened rights overall, which gives increased urgency to the full implementation of legislation incorporating the articles of the *United Nations Declaration on the Rights of Indigenous Peoples* (UNDRIP 2017) into federal law.

In the absence of action on easing the digital divide, the enshrinement of these rights and protections in federal jurisdiction would provide another avenue (via Articles 5, 21, and 23) with which to advocate for the necessary investments to eliminate the digital divide faced by remote communities.[5] Such advocacy efforts are already underway within the province of British Columbia following the passage of Bill 41 in November 2019 (Jang, 2019; Khelsilem, 2019).

Sustained Investments

Countering current trends across the technology sector requires sustained investments in the service of the emergence of a decolonized digital future. From the provision of digital skills training opportunities in remote communities to supporting Indigenous innovators leveraging digital tools for cultural revitalization and resurgence, meaningful, long-term resources will accelerate the transformative work that is already taking place across Indigenous communities.

A Digital Bill of Rights

Amid data breaches, privacy violations, and manipulative practices by technology firms, there has been a renewed interest and attention in the crafting of a "digital bills of rights" for citizens (Swisher, 2018; Tisne, 2018). The *Canadian Bill of Rights* (1960) and the *Canadian Charter of Rights and Freedoms* (1982) reflect an understanding of government as the protector of citizenship rights that transcended all other (e.g., market) pressures or incentives. We need the same now within the digital realm.

While of critical importance for all Canadians, such a framework would carry particular weight and significance for marginalized communities, who are disproportionately targeted by digital surveillance, biases in algorithms, and online hate crime (Buolamwini, 2019; Massey, 2018; Small, 2019; Tahir, 2019). The European Union's *General Data Protection Regulation* (GDPR) represented a tangible advancement toward more robust data privacy protections for citizens, but a broader scope needs to be considered (Shull, 2018). The Digital Rights Now coalition has called for the federal government to establish a strategy that includes a focus upon "data collection, ownership, use, and rights; privacy as a public good; consent; equitable internet access; fair competition and future prosperity"[6] (Tech Reset Canada, the Digital Justice Lab, and the Centre for Digital Rights, 2018).

Canada's *Digital Charter*, first introduced in 2019, represents a first step within the Canadian context. It remains to be seen how these principles will translate into legislation and oversight, including whether (and how) such efforts will be grounded in a commitment to reconciliation and Indigenous rights.

Establishing New Regulatory Bodies

Such concerns raise another critical area of focus for policy-makers. Election interference and the spread of extremist content online has raised serious questions around the "self-regulation" approach the technology sector currently enjoys as it pertains to their platforms—a privileged position of low accountability to users or to governments. Furthermore, these platforms are ill-equipped to self-regulate. Reporting by Angwin and Grassegger (2017), Hopkins (2017), and Koebler and Cox (2018) based upon leaked content moderation guides revealed these platforms' acceptance of white nationalist and separatist sentiments, as well as a reliance upon Wikipedia to articulate the distinction between them and white supremacy.

Tisne (2018, para. 2) notes that "a new set of institutions and legal instruments to safeguard the rights it lays out" will be required to strengthen and support a digital bill of rights, which could take the form of a series of robust, sector-wide regulatory frameworks, as well as enforcement mechanisms. These will need to go considerably further than Canada's current *Privacy Act, Access to Information Act,* and *Personal Information Protection and Electronic Documents Act,* which are largely "premised on informed consent" (Shull, 2018, para. 6) The recent Public Policy Forum report "Poisoning Democracy: How Canada Can Address Harmful Speech Online" (Tenove et al., 2018), included a recommendation to create a "Moderation Standards Council" (which would establish a digital equivalent to the Canadian Broadcast Standards Council), while Change the Terms (Center for American Progress et al., 2019), a coalition of organizations committed to the online rights of marginalized communities, is advocating for more stringent efforts to combat hate in digital spaces.

Breaking Up Tech Monopolies

Staltz (2017) suggests that we are moving rapidly from an Internet to a Trinet—in essence, a trio of companies (Amazon, Facebook, and Google) complicit in the carving up of cyberspace into domains of power and influence. Amid this e-imperialism have arisen growing calls to splinter the tech monopolies, curbing the influence of their respective CEOs, Jeff Bezos, Mark Zuckerberg, and Sundar Pichai, as we did at the turn of the twentieth century with the Carnegies and Rockefellers. These calls may begin to be answered—the US Federal Trade Commission and Justice Department are each launching antitrust and anti-competitive investigations into Facebook, Amazon, Apple, and Google, while a number of 2020 presidential candidates (Elizabeth Warren, Bernie Sanders, and Amy Klobuchar) expressed a desire to break up the largest firms in part through a re-examination of recent mergers and acquisitions (Herndon, 2019). While Canadian policy-makers clearly cannot play a direct role in breaking up American firms, they can play a much more active role in influencing and advocating for such changes in response to recent developments.

Conclusion

The commodification and corporatization of digital spaces have a significant impact upon the real and urgent decolonization efforts we have committed to as a country. In this chapter, I have sought to outline the ways in which patterns of power, influence, and ideology in physical spaces have manifested in the digital realm, and offer some reflections as to potential paths forward for policy-makers to help counter these trends. Companies are not governments—they are driven not by public good nor public accountability but by profit and market dominance. Market demands and citizen rights are two very different calculations, producing markedly different outcomes. Technology companies have no obligation toward diverse or historically marginalized communities outside of those that are provided to its entire (paying) user base. In the absence of more concerted leadership of governments in these conversations, we run the risk of replicating the failings of our current conceptualizations of citizenship in this new, uncharted domain.

Advancing the decolonization of digital spaces will require a thoughtful and significant shift in how we approach efforts to democratize and decolonize digital spaces. The value of "nothing about us without us" must be respected and upheld by policy-makers by centring the voices of Indigenous Peoples in these conversations. This can—and should—take many forms, but must include representation and resources. The federal commitment to Nation-to-Nation relationships must be reflected in who is at the table in a leadership capacity as a digital rights framework takes shape, and investments must be made in Indigenous-led initiatives and in spaces that are already actively exploring the questions raised by this work. Truly decolonizing digital spaces demands that Indigenous Nations and Peoples are able to determine, on their own terms, what their visions are around their own digital futures, providing a counterpoint to the dominant voices currently amplified in the digital technology sector.

Citizenship in a digital context, like all forms of citizenship, is only as strong as the rights, protections, and agency contained within it that are accessible to *all its people*. From the *Indian Act* to ongoing acts of genocide against Indigenous Peoples across these unceded territories, it is clear that Canadian citizenship continues to fail in this regard. As Canada begins to reckon more meaningfully with its past and current realities (most recently in the form of the final report of the National Inquiry into Missing and Murdered Indigenous Women and Girls [2019]), there is an opportunity to articulate a form of citizenship in a digital context that reflects a deepened understanding and commitment to inherent Indigenous rights.

Digital spaces hold such incredible promise—an opportunity to reimagine, with each line of code, a different way of engaging with each other and with the world around us. Yet while current constraints, barriers, and inequities have been unable to halt Indigenous innovation, creativity, resiliency, or resistance in digital spaces, they continue to perpetuate patterns of power and dominance. Thus, as we work to decolonize our physical spaces, we must also turn our attention to digital spaces, decolonizing current platforms and products while ensuring that Indigenous voices actively lead those that are just beginning or have yet to emerge. In doing so, we can begin to realize a digital future and citizenship in a digital context for Canada that is just and equitable for all.

Acknowledgements

This work would not be possible without the advocacy, effort, and vision of those at the front lines of these conversations and movements. I am grateful for the efforts of (and my experience with) the First Nations Technology Council, and remain inspired by Animikii Indigenous Technology and other Indigenous-led digital initiatives embodying decolonized approaches in their work. This chapter is dedicated to all these Indigenous innovators and to the Indigenous innovators of tomorrow.

Notes

1. Turtle Island is used in this work to refer to the unceded territories of Indigenous Nations that transcend colonial borders. More on its origins and significance can be explored here: https://www.thecanadianency-clopedia.ca/en/article/turtle-island.
2. In discussing a more robust definition of citizenship in a digital context, I wish to acknowledge the inherent tensions, complexities, and challenges posed by the concept of citizenship within a settler-colonial state. I also wish to acknowledge those for whom citizenship refers to membership within their Indigenous Nation and not to citizenship in a Canadian context.
3. Data has been sourced from the five firms' most recent diversity and inclusion reports, which are included in the references list for this chapter.
4. While much of the coverage of Amazon's "HQ2" focused on the bids of American cities, Toronto's bid proposal opened with a letter from Prime

Minister Trudeau, pledging that "the full support of our government stands behind" those submitting the proposal (Toronto Global, 2017.)

5. Of 292 communities identified as remote in Canada, 170 are Indigenous: https://www.nrcan.gc.ca/sites/www.nrcan.gc.ca/files/canmetenergy/files/pubs/2013-118_en.pdf.

6. This direct quote appeared in the online petition, which is no longer accessible online.

References

1958: Silicon mesa transistors enter commercial production. (n.d.) Computer History Museum. https://www.computerhistory.org/siliconengine/silicon-mesa-transistors-enter-commercial-production/

Amazon (2018). *Our workforce data.* Retrieved May 5, 2020, from https://www.aboutamazon.com/working-at-amazon/diversity-and-inclusion/our-workforce-data

Angwin, J., & Grassegger, H. (2019, March 9). *Facebook's secret censorship rules protect white men from hate speech, but not black children.* ProPublica. https://www.propublica.org/article/facebook-hate-speech-censorship-internal-documents-algorithms

Apple (2019). *Different together.* Retrieved May 5, 2020, from https://www.apple.com/diversity/

Balachander, S. (2017, December 21). *Historians weigh forces that shaped Silicon Valley.* Stanford. https://west.stanford.edu/news/historians-weigh-forces-shaped-silicon-valley

Beaumont, C. (2008, June 27). Bill Gates's dream: A computer in every home. *The Telegraph.* https://www.telegraph.co.uk/technology/3357701/Bill-Gatess-dream-A-computer-in-every-home.html

Brown, D., & Parker, M. (2019). *Google diversity annual report 2019.* Google. https://diversity.google/annual-report/#!#_this-years-data

Buolamwini, J. (2019, February 7). Artificial intelligence has a racial and gender bias problem. *Time.* https://time.com/5520558/artificial-intelligence-racial-gender-bias/

Cañares, M., Thakur, D., Alonso, J., & Potter, L. (2018). *The case #ForTheWeb.* Web Foundation. https://webfoundation.org/research/the-case-for-the-web/

Center for American Progress, Color of Change, Free Press, Lawyers' Committee for Civil Rights Under Law, National Hispanic Media Coalition, & Southern Poverty Law Center. (2019). *Change the terms.* Change the Terms. https://www.changetheterms.org

Chapin, A. (2015, December 4). CBC's racist comment sections spark debate on Canada's prejudice problem. *The Guardian.* https://www.theguardian.com/world/2015/dec/04/cbc-racist-comment-section-canada-prejudice-indigenous-people

Dayen, D. (2018, November 9). *The HQ2 scam: How Amazon used a bidding war to scrape cities' data*. In These Times. http://inthesetimes.com/article/21571/the-hq2-scam-how-amazon-used-a-bidding-war-to-scrape-cities-data

Dembosky, A. (2013, June 9). *Silicon Valley rooted in backing from US military*. Financial Times. https://www.ft.com/content/8c0152d2-d0f2-11e2-be7b-00144feab7de

Dormehl, L. (2019, September 28). *Today in Apple history: "Here's to the crazy ones" who "think different."* Cult of Mac. https://www.cultofmac.com/447012/today-in-apple-history-heres-to-the-crazy-ones/

Facebook (2018). *Facebook diversity update*. Retrieved May 5, 2020, from https://www.facebook.com/careers/diversity-report

Findlay, J. M. (1992). *Magic Lands: Western Cityscapes and American Culture After 1940*. University of California Press.

Fontaine, T. (2015, December 12). *First Nations welcome lifting of despised 2% funding cap*. CBC News. https://www.cbc.ca/news/indigenous/first-nations-funding-cap-lifted-1.3359137

Gruzd, A., Jacobson, J., Mai, P., & Dubois, E. (2018). *The state of social media in Canada 2017*. Ryerson University Social Media Lab. http://dx.doi.org/10.5683/SP/AL8Z6R

Harris, C. (2018, September 18). *Changing the narrative: What's missing from the conversation on equity in tech?* Medium. https://medium.com/racial-equity-in-tech/changing-the-narrative-whats-missing-from-the-public-conversation-on-equity-in-tech-eb5f00c5b829

Herndon, A. W. (2019, October 1). *Elizabeth Warren Proposes Breaking Up Tech Giants Like Amazon and Facebook*. https://www.nytimes.com/2019/03/08/us/politics/elizabeth-warren-amazon.html

Hopkins, N. (2017, May 21). Revealed: Facebook's internal rulebook on sex, terrorism and violence. *The Guardian*. https://www.theguardian.com/news/2017/may/21/revealed-facebook-internal-rulebook-sex-terrorism-violence

Howard, P., Busch, L., & Sheets, P. (2010). Comparing digital divides: Internet access and social inequality in Canada and the United States. *Canadian Journal of Communication, 35*(1), 109–128. https://doi.org/10.22230/cjc.2010v35n1a2192

Innovation, Science and Economic Development [ISED]. (2019). *Canada's digital charter: Trust in a digital world*. https://www.ic.gc.ca/eic/site/062.nsf/eng/h_00108.html

Jang, T. (2019, November 30). *Indigenous people seeking digital equity as BC enshrines UN Declaration into provincial law*. First Nations Technology Council. https://technologycouncil.ca/2019/11/30/indigenous-people-seeking-digital-equity-as-bc-enshrines-un-declaration-into-provincial-law/

Kassam, A. (2017, July 27). First Nations leader urges Canada to prosecute "out of hand" hate speech. *The Guardian.* https://www.theguardian.com/world/2017/jul/27/canada-first-nations-hate-speech-bobby-cameron

Khelsilem, T. (2019, November 9). *BC's Declaration Act explained.* The National Observer. Retrieved April 9, 2020, from https://www.nationalobserver.com/2019/11/08/opinion/bcs-declaration-act-explained

Koebler, J., & Cox, J. (2018, August 23). *Here's how Facebook is trying to moderate its two billion users.* Vice. https://www.vice.com/en_us/article/xwk9zd/how-facebook-content-moderation-works

Kupfer, M. (2016, December 22). *Canada's telecom regulator declares broadband internet access a basic service.* CBC News. https://www.cbc.ca/news/politics/crtc-internet-essential-service-1.3906664

Laws, D. (2017, September 19). *Fairchild semiconductor: The 60th anniversary of a Silicon Valley legend.* Computer History. https://www.computerhistory.org/atchm/fairchild-semiconductor-the-60th-anniversary-of-a-silicon-valley-legend/

Lécuyer, C. (2006). *Making Silicon Valley: Innovation and the Growth of High Tech, 1930-1970.* MIT Press.

Massey, K. (2018, September 7). *#DefendOurMovements: What is movement security?* Medium. https://medium.com/defendourmovements/defendourmovements-what-is-movement-security-d1484ac7404b

McMahon, R. (2014). From digital divides to the first mile: Indigenous peoples and the network society in Canada. *International Journal of Communication, 8,* 2002–2026. http://firstmile.ca/wp-content/uploads/2014-McMahon-From-Digital-Divides-to-the-First-Mile-Indigenous-Peoples-and-the-Network-Society-in-Canada.pdf

Microsoft. (2018). *Diversity within Microsoft.* Retrieved May 5, 2020, from https://www.microsoft.com/en-us/diversity/inside-microsoft/default.aspx#coreui-contentrichblock-9se7qru

Mohammad, Q. (2018, July 10). Canada's e-commerce ecosystem continues its rise. *The Globe and Mail.* https://www.theglobeandmail.com/business/commentary/article-canadas-e-commerce-ecosystem-continues-its-rise/

National Inquiry into Missing and Murdered Indigenous Women and Girls. (2019). Calls for justice. In *Reclaiming Power and Place: The Final Report of the National Inquiry into Missing and Murdered Indigenous Women and Girls.* https://www.mmiwg-ffada.ca/wp-content/uploads/2019/06/Calls_for_Justice.pdf

O'Mara, M. (2018, October 26). Silicon Valley can't escape the business of war. *The New York Times.* https://www.nytimes.com/2018/10/26/opinion/amazon-bezos-pentagon-hq2.html

Shull, A. (2018, August 16). *The Charter and human rights in the digital age.* Centre for International Governance Innovation. https://www.cigion-line.org/articles/charter-and-human-rights-digital-age

Small, T. (2019, April 25). *Technology has a race problem.* Flare. https://www.flare.com/identity/technology-bias-racism-airport-scanners/

Spencer, K. A. (2018, December 21). *In the Bay Area, technology has gone hand in hand with imperialism for 500 years.* Salon. https://www.salon.com/2018/12/09/in-the-bay-area-technology-has-gone-hand-in-hand-with-imperialism-for-500-years/

Spencer, K. A. (2019, January 8). Long before tech bros, Silicon Valley had a highly developed society. *The Guardian.* https://www.theguardian.com/technology/2019/jan/08/silicon-valley-history-society-book-ohlone-native-americans

Staltz, A. (2017, October 30). *The web began dying in 2014—Here's how.* Staltz. https://staltz.com/the-web-began-dying-in-2014-heres-how.html

Swisher, K. (2018, October 5). *Introducing the Internet Bill of Rights.* The New York Times. https://www.nytimes.com/2018/10/04/opinion/ro-khanna-internet-bill-of-rights.html

Tahir, O. (2019, March 2). *When machines know sin: The algorithmic bias of technology.* Hacker Noon. https://hackernoon.com/when-machines-know-sin-the-algorithmic-bias-of-technology-82402b70dfd0

Tarnoff, B. (2016, July 15). How the internet was invented. *The Guardian.* https://www.theguardian.com/technology/2016/jul/15/how-the-internet-was-invented-1976-arpa-kahn-cerf

Tech Reset Canada, Digital Justice Lab, & Centre for Digital Rights. (2018). *About Digital Rights Now.* Digital Rights Now. https://digitalrightsnow.ca/about/

The United Nations. *United Nations Declaration on the Rights of Indigenous Peoples* [UNDRIP]. (2007). https://www.un.org/development/desa/indigenouspeoples/wp-content/uploads/sites/19/2018/11/UNDRIP_E_web.pdf

Tisne, M. (2018, December 18). *It's time for a bill of data rights.* MIT Technology Review. https://www.technologyreview.com/s/612588/its-time-for-a-bill-of-data-rights/

Tenove, C., Tworek, H., & McKelvey, F. (2018). *Democracy divided: Countering disinformation and hate in the digital public sphere.* Public Policy Forum. https://ppforum.ca/publications/social-marketing-hate-speech-disinformation-democracy/

Toronto Global. (2017). *Toronto Amazon HQ2 Proposal.* https://www.document-cloud.org/documents/5411002-Toronto-Amazon-HQ2-Proposal.html

Truth and Reconciliation Commission of Canada. (2015). *Truth and Reconciliation Commission of Canada: Calls to action.* http://trc.ca/assets/pdf/Calls_to_Action_English2.pdf

Williams, D. (2018). *Digital equity*. Indian Horse. https://next150.indianhorse.ca/challenges/digital-equity

Wilson-Raybould, J. (2017, July 3). *Realizing a nation-to-nation relationship with the Indigenous peoples of Canada* [Speech]. Cambridge Lectures, Cambridge, UK. https://www.canada.ca/en/department-justice/news/2017/07/realizing_a_nation-to-nationrelationshipwiththeindigenouspeoples.html

Wylie, B. (2018, May 9). *Sidewalk Toronto has yet to give us a reason to trust its smart city experiment*. Huffington Post. https://www.huffingtonpost.ca/bianca-wylie/sidewalk-labs-toronto-plans-transparency_a_23428379/

Telling a Different Story: Canadian Citizens and Their Democracy in the Digital Age

Adelina Petit-Vouriot and Mike Morden

Abstract

The new centrality of the digital public sphere has disrupted politics and generated questions about the robustness and sustainability of liberal democracies. This chapter draws on recent public opinion research to examine trends in Canadians' attitudes toward democracy and their engagement in formal and informal politics. The data suggests that technological and political changes both in Canada and abroad have produced concern among Canadians about the health of their democracy. But longitudinal comparison reveals that, despite these disruptions and contrary to prevailing public narratives, Canadians have become more engaged and more satisfied with their democracy in recent years.

What Is the Digital Public Sphere Doing to Democracy?

Throughout the liberal democratic world, it appears as though we have entered a new era of democratic anxiety. There are several sources of this anxiety. They include a longer-term global democratic recession; resurgent and more activist anti-democratic actors in the world, specifically aiming to devalue, discredit, disrupt, and demoralize liberal democracies; increasing political polarization—or the perception thereof; and the electoral success of several populist extremist candidates and parties (such as Donald Trump in the United States, Viktor Orbán in Hungary, Narendra Modi in India, and Jair Bolsonaro in Brazil), who threaten democratic norms like political tolerance and respect for institutions. This confluence of forces has led thoughtful observers in some of the world's oldest democracies to ask serious questions about the sustainability of democracy as we know it (Freedom House, 2018; Levitsky & Ziblatt, 2018; Mounk, 2018).

All of these phenomena are associated, rightly or wrongly, and to greater or lesser degrees, with the new centrality of the digital public sphere. Social media, in particular, can be regarded as a tool for autocratic monitoring and control (Diebert, 2019); a facilitator of foreign interference by malicious actors; a soapbox for radicalized citizens and extremist groups; a site which is contributing to affective polarization and the coarsening of democratic politics; and a vehicle propelling transgressive populist politicians to power. Add to this the distinct but often confluent, usually conflated concerns over the collection and use of our personal data, the practices of "surveillance capitalism" (Zuboff, 2019), and the still-nascent platform governance, and we can confirm the digital public sphere as a central player in the current democratic drama. In this context of digitally driven democratic anxiety, how are Canadians actually feeling about their democracy? This was one of the questions the Samara Centre for Democracy asked in the 2019 iteration of our Citizens' Survey, which forms the basis for Democracy 360, a biennial report card on the health of Canadian democracy (Petit-Vouriot et al., 2019). The findings are at times surprising and broadly, though not universally, positive. Canadians have actually grown more satisfied with their democracy in recent years, as well as incrementally more engaged in their politics. They continue to view politicians and institutions with suspicion, but there is little evidence to suggest this suspicion has grown or deepened. All of this should be cause to revisit some of the public narrative about the state of our democracy and politics, which is casually and uncritically accepted—like the suggestion that, due to digital and economic disruption, we're cresting toward a populist revolt.[1] But while there are some positive indicators, there is also evidence that Canadians are anxious about their democratic future: a significantly greater number of Canadians perceive our democracy as becoming weaker, not stronger.

A Note on the Project and the Data

The public opinion data in this chapter come from the Samara Centre for Democracy's Citizens' Surveys. As noted above, the surveys support the production of Democracy 360, with citizens acting as the evaluators. The Samara Centre is a non-partisan charity with a mandate to work to strengthen Canada's democracy. Alongside research on institutions and political leadership, Democracy 360 is one of the centre's major ongoing research projects. It was founded on an assessment that it would be desirable to have some objective, empirical measures for examining changes in how our democracy is broadly experienced. Existing international democracy measures and ratings are useful for cross-national comparison, but not sufficiently tailored to the Canadian context to permit us to observe fine gradations of change in citizens' perceptions of democracy.

The surveys ask a series of questions about how Canadians feel about democracy generally, the myriad formal and informal ways in which they participate, and how they evaluate their political leadership. By repeating the questions and the basic survey design every two years, the hope is that survey effects can be controlled for and that change can be meaningfully observed. In addition to the core Democracy 360 questions, the 2019 survey also included some questions borrowed from the Canadian Election Study and major international surveys, enabling us to probe new areas while retaining some basis for comparing data and examining trends. The 2019 survey was conducted in English and French in January and February 2019, using an online sample of 4,054 Canadian residents over 18 years of age living in all ten provinces.

This chapter looks mostly at the aggregate picture of Canadians' democratic participation and satisfaction, along with important age effects. Obviously, these values differ from community to community in significant ways. In this respect, our measures are limited. While our tool allows for comparison across broad demographic categories like "visible minorities," those categories can often obscure more than they illuminate. It does not provide the necessary lens to examine the responses of those who may experience citizenship very differently than the majority—Indigenous Peoples, newcomers from particular communities, LGBTQ2S+, and others. Nor does it closely explore alternative democratic spaces, such as grassroots or community organizations, Indigenous governments, workers' unions, etc. Rather, its focus is on aggregate experiences of the dominant narrative of politics in Canada.

General Attitudes Toward Democracy and Politics

Despite the pervasive narrative of global democratic decline, public opinion data collected from the last three Citizens' Surveys show that a growing majority of Canadians view our democracy favourably. In 2014, 65 percent of Canadians reported that they were either satisfied or very satisfied with the way democracy worked in Canada, and by 2019, this number had increased to 75 percent (see Table 2.1). In 2019, only 6 percent were not satisfied at all—a figure which has also dropped compared to previous years. Over the same period, the same question asked in public opinion studies in the United Kingdom, the United States, France, and Australia (for example) have tended to find a precipitous decline in satisfaction with democracy—suggesting that the recent Canadian experience is different in important ways from that of other democracies that Canadians tend to watch close-ly.[2] Regardless of whether or not this satisfaction is warranted, and whatever its causes (and indeed, it may itself be a reaction to trends in other democracies), it suggests a relatively positive orientation in Canada toward the machinery of democracy.

Table 2.1: Satisfaction with Canadian Democracy[3]

On the whole, how satisfied are you with the way democracy works in Canada?

	2014	2016	2019
Very satisfied	12.3%	16.3%	20.1%
Fairly satisfied	52.7%	54.7%	55.1%
Not very satisfied	25.2%	20.1%	19.2%
Not satisfied at all	9.8%	8.9%	5.6%
n	2238.1	3722.3	3898.4

Sources: The Samara Centre for Democracy, 2019, "The 2019 Samara Citizens' Survey," https://www.samaracanada.com/research/resourcesanddata/2019-citizens-survey/, The Samara Centre for Democracy; The Samara Centre for Democracy, 2016, "The 2016 Samara Citizens' Survey," https://www.samaracanada.com/research/resourcesanddata/2016-citizens-survey, The Samara Centre for Democracy; The Samara Centre for Democracy, 2014, "The 2014 Samara Citizens' Survey," https://www.samaracanada.com/research/resourcesanddata/2014-citizens-survey, The Samara Centre for Democracy.

General interest in politics has also remained stable, if not risen slightly, since the Samara Centre began studying Canadian public opinion trends in 2014. The 2019 results indicate that two-thirds of Canadians are either very or fairly interested in local and international politics, while three quarters reported this same level of interest for provincial/regional and national politics (see Table 2.2). Previous iterations of the Citizens' Survey did not disaggregate interest by level, and so do not offer directly comparable measures, but the 2016 survey found that approximately 64 percent of Canadians were interested in politics generally. In other words, at every level of politics, Canadians are as interested or more interested in 2019 than they were in politics in the abstract three years before. Politics also is not generally seen as remote or abstract. When asked in 2019 how much of an impact politics had on their daily life, 64 percent reported it as a 6 or higher on a scale of 1 to 10 (with 1 representing no impact whatsoever and 10 representing extremely high impact).

Table 2.2: Interest in Politics[4]

How interested would you say you are in politics?

	2016	2019			
		Local	Provincial/Regional	National	International
Very interested	17.8%	20.6%	28.6%	32.8%	22.8%
Fairly interested	46.0%	45.7%	48.0%	43.9%	43.6%
Not very interested	25.2%	25.5%	17.7%	17.7%	25.0%
Not at all interested	11.0%	8.2%	5.7%	5.6%	8.6%
n	3916.6	4018.7	4032.3	4017.7	3994.5

Sources: The Samara Centre for Democracy, 2019, "The 2019 Samara Citizens' Survey," https://www.samaracanada.com/research/resourcesanddata/2019-citizens-survey/, The Samara Centre for Democracy; The Samara Centre for Democracy, 2016, "The 2016 Samara Citizens' Survey," https://www.samaracanada.com/research/resourcesanddata/2016-citizens-survey, The Samara Centre for Democracy.

In short, Canadians are (relative to the recent past) interested in politics and satisfied with how their democracy works. The increased satisfaction in democracy has been observed across the partisan spectrum. To this point, Canada has avoided the fast slide into dissatisfaction that has captured several peer democracies. But not all indications are positive. Canadians have, perhaps, also been affected by the discourse of democratic recession. When asked about the direction of Canada's democracy, 46 percent are under the impression that it is becoming weaker; a much smaller share (31 percent) perceive it getting stronger; and the smallest share (23 percent) say they don't know. However, it is perhaps notable that party affiliation has a strong effect on this perception: for example, those who identify with the Liberal Party of Canada are more likely to say that democracy is getting stronger, not weaker.

Populism and Attitudes Toward Political Elites

Populism is central to much of the public narrative about democracy, in Canada and elsewhere. It is perceived as a driving force behind some of the major political outcomes of recent years, including the election of Donald Trump in the United States (November 2016), and the Brexit referendum in the United Kingdom (June 2016). It is sometimes thought that the digital public sphere is causally important in the rise of populism—for example, by giving populist politicians opportunities to transmit a norms-transgressive message to the public without relying on traditional intermediaries, or by creating avenues for new kinds of organizing and coalition building, from which populists can benefit (Krämer, 2017; Schaub & Morisi, 2019).

   A long line of Canadian commentators have asserted that populism is also present here, that Canada is a "tinderbox for populism" (Graves & Valpy, 2018), that populism is redrawing the basic political cleavages of the country (Harper, 2018), or creating opportunities for the ascendancy of previously marginal political traditions (Broadbent, 2019). Is this the case?

   The Citizens' Survey provides Canadians opportunities to evaluate their political leadership. The 2019 iteration also included some additional questions meant to measure aspects of populist thought, and for which there was some basis for longitudinal comparison.[5] The study adopts a definition of populism that is conventional in the scholarship but sometimes confused in the popular discourse: it treats populism as the belief that society is divided into two camps, elites and the real people, and that legitimate governance must reflect the uninhibited will of the people (Mudde & Kaltwasser, 2013).[6]

The overall finding is strong: there is scant evidence of a movement toward populism in Canadian public opinion (Morden & Anderson, 2019). Instead, Canadians have grown modestly more trusting of and satisfied with their political leadership. Attitudes toward MPs are markedly improved in the 5 years leading to 2019; for example—51 percent of Canadians trust MPs to do what is right, up from 40 percent in 2014, and 53 percent of Canadians are satisfied with MPs, compared with 46 percent in 2014. Attitudes toward political parties have held steady or softened slightly; for example, the share of Canadians who trust political parties has increased to 45 percent, from 42 percent in 2014. The Citizens' Survey also replicates questions asked in past Canadian Election Studies (CES). The results are not directly comparable for several reasons, including likely polling effects due to inconsistency in how the questions were asked over time. They are nevertheless strongly suggestive of a general decline in anti-establishment feeling since the 1990s. For example, in 2019, 60 percent of Canadians agreed that the government does not care what people like them think, compared with 75 percent of Canadians asked in the 1993 CES. Similarly, in 2019, 63 percent of Canadians agreed that those elected to Parliament soon lose touch with the people, down from the 85 percent who thought that in 1993.

These measures admittedly exclude some aspects of populist thought, or populism-adjacent tendencies. For example, they do not probe Canadians' inclination toward authoritarian leadership in the interest of the people. Nevertheless, what is manifestly absent here is any hint that Canadians are turning away from elites in some dramatic fashion. They show high levels of dissatisfaction and cynicism relative to appropriate aspirations for our democracy—but this is enduring dissatisfaction, rather than sea change. And indeed, consistent with the rise in democratic satisfaction and interest in politics, they suggest that change that has occurred has been in a mostly positive direction.

Reported Participation in Politics and Community

The consistency and even modest improvement in attitudes toward democratic politics are reflected, in some ways, in reported participation. The rise in voter turnout in the 2015 federal election, especially pronounced in several groups that are typically among the least engaged in politics (youth and Indigenous Peoples), offered some hope that Canadians are not turned off formal politics altogether. In fact, 2015 saw voter turnout rise for the second election in a row—the first time that has happened since 1972. Turnout fell slightly in 2019, but early indications are that some of the important 2015 turnout gains were sustained. In a major Statistics Canada survey, self-reported turnout among young Canadians in 2019 was at roughly the same level as in 2015 (Statistics Canada, 2020).

But as noted above, the Citizens' Survey seeks to capture the full spectrum of forms of political engagement beyond voting, the proxy that is often relied upon. The CES is the most comparable alternative data source—though the fact that CES has (previous to this point) only collected in election years makes comparison with recent data impossible. Nevertheless, it is notable that, compared to the CES, the Citizens' Survey has returned slightly higher rates of reported participation in some activities. It is therefore difficult to reach firm conclusions about whether the Citizens' Survey over-reports participation more than is typical of other instruments. New research does suggest that simply presenting our survey to prospective respondents during the recruitment phase as being "democracy focused" could yield a disproportionately engaged respondent pool (McGregor et al., 2020). It is because of these uncertainties that we regard the change over time within the (roughly) same survey administered the same way as most analytically useful.

The 2019 results find that rates of formal political participation have remained relatively stable during the last five years, with a small rise in participation most evident when using a composite index of several indicators (see Table 2.3). Although the number of people who report that they are a member of a federal political party has dipped slightly, more Canadians have recently donated or volunteered for a political party or candidate than in previous years.

On the other hand, rates of activism have fluctuated from year to year. Significantly fewer respondents reported that they had signed a petition or taken part in a protest in 2019 compared to 2014, while those choosing to boycott/"buycott" increased. There is some suggestion in this that activism may be more context- and event-driven than conventional political engagement.

Table 2.3: Formal Political Participation

In the past 12 months, have you participated in the following activities? (affirmative responses only)

	2014	2016	2019
Been a member of federal political party	8.8%	8.2%	7.7%
Attended political meeting/speech	28.5%	30.1%	31.5%
Donated money to candidate/party	18.8%	18.6%	21.0%
Volunteered for candidate/party	16.7%	15.3%	18.8%
Composite index (those who participated in at least one of the above activities)	35.5	37.1	41.4
n (of composite index)	2330.0	3864.0	3925.0

Sources: The Samara Centre for Democracy, 2019, "The 2019 Samara Citizens' Survey," https://www.samaracanada.com/research/resourcesanddata/2019-citizens-survey/, The Samara Centre for Democracy; The Samara Centre for Democracy, 2016, "The 2016 Samara Citizens' Survey," https://www.samaracanada.com/research/resourcesanddata/2016-citizens-survey, The Samara Centre for Democracy; The Samara Centre for Democracy, 2014, "The 2014 Samara Citizens' Survey," https://www.samaracanada.com/research/resourcesanddata/2014-citizens-survey, The Samara Centre for Democracy.

Table 2.4: Activism

In the past 12 months, have you participated in the following activities? (affirmative responses only)

	2014	2016	2019
Signed petition in person or online	64.3%	58.8%	56.5%
Boycotted or bought products for political reasons	37.0%	39.8%	47.5%
Protested or demonstrated	21.6%	21.2%	16.5%
Composite index (those who participated in at least one of the above activities)	69.4%	67.6%	67.6%
n (of composite index)	2321.0	3812.0	3938.0

Sources: The Samara Centre for Democracy, 2019, "The 2019 Samara Citizens' Survey," https://www.samaracanada.com/research/resourcesanddata/2019-citizens-survey/, The Samara Centre for Democracy; The Samara Centre for Democracy, 2016, "The 2016 Samara Citizens' Survey," https://www.samaracanada.com/research/resourcesanddata/2016-citizens-survey, The Samara Centre for Democracy; The Samara Centre for Democracy, 2014, "The 2014 Samara Citizens' Survey," https://www.samaracanada.com/research/resourcesanddata/2014-citizens-survey, The Samara Centre for Democracy.

A Snapshot of Youth

Younger people may or may not be more affected by the emerging centrality of the digital sphere, but they inarguably are most likely to occupy it. It is therefore particularly interesting, in a digital context, to observe the ways in which young people differ in how they regard or engage in democratic politics. Looking at 18- to 29-year-olds in comparison with older demographics, the Citizens' Survey finds some consistencies and interesting differences.

A common public narrative is that young people lack trust in our institutions and elites, or that they only see politics as remote from themselves, but this is often disputed in public-opinion research (O'Neill, 2007; Norris, 2002). The Citizens' Survey is no exception. It finds that young people, for example, are equally or slightly more satisfied than older demographics with how democracy works. They are also equally likely to believe that politics has an influence on their everyday lives.

Young people tend to evaluate our political leadership more positively, too. More young people are satisfied with MPs (60 percent of ages 18–29 versus 50 percent of ages 56+), trusting of MPs (57 percent of 18–29 versus 50 percent of 56+), satisfied with political parties (56 percent of 18–29 versus 44 percent of 56+), and trusting of parties (53 percent of 18–29 versus 42 percent of 56+). And while young people are less likely to belong to a political party, they are considerably more likely to consider joining one in the future. It is difficult to conclude that youth lack trust, at least in the abstract. Moreover, more young people hold an optimistic outlook for our democracy. It is true that just as in the aggregate, more youth perceive our democracy as getting weaker than stronger. But the gap between those groups is relatively small (5 percentage points for ages 18–29, compared with a 16-percentage-point gap among ages 30–55, and a 22-percentage-point gap among those 56+). We cannot reach causal conclusions, but it is nonetheless notable that so-called digital natives appear least affected by the democratic anxiety of the moment.

In other respects, young people present some familiar paradoxes. They are much less likely to regard living in a democracy as very important (55.9 percent versus 75.8 percent for those 56+)—a relationship that is enduring and consistent across most established democracies (Foa & Mounk, 2017). They report being less interested in politics across all levels of government and politics; the interest gap between younger and older voters is greatest for local politics (53 percent of 18–29 versus 77 percent of 56+), and smallest for international politics (62 percent of 18–29 versus 72 percent of 56+). But across the vast majority of forms of participation—other than voting—youth are most likely to participate. It is likely no surprise that young people are more likely to engage in activism, for example, but striking that they are also more likely to discuss politics—in any venue, online or offline—than are those from older cohorts.

Conclusion: Holding Steady, but Worried

While the Citizens' Survey does not allow us to directly measure the effects of the expanding digital sphere on Canadian politics, it does permit a snapshot of ordinary Canadians as democratic actors in this historical moment. The picture it reveals is complex, but there is much in here to challenge some familiar narratives about change in our democracy. A significant segment of Canadians are dissatisfied with democracy in general, and most are dissatisfied with the state of our politics. Participation is uneven, and far too many Canadians remain on the sidelines of our civic and political life. These are hugely consequential problems, and they demand solutions. But they should be understood as long-term, structural problems rather than some new crisis that has suddenly descended upon us.

There are important suggestions in the data that the democratic experience in Canada of recent years is meaningfully different than that of several of the democracies closest to our own. And while we should guard against complacency and self-satisfaction, we should also avoid uncritically copying and pasting foreign narratives onto our own democracy.

The long-term structural problems facing our democracy are well known, and include the weakness of Parliament and the legislature, and a concentration of power within political parties. This study is a reminder to address these to make our democratic institutions more responsive, accessible, and representative, rather than defending a status quo which is not good enough, against threats that have not yet completely materialized.

These findings are not predictive. It may be that our slide into dissatisfaction is coming, and that our populist moment will follow. There are at least some indicators that there is a qualitatively and quantitatively different polarization underway here (see, for example, Cochrane 2015; Kevins & Soroka, 2019), which could facilitate some of those forces. It may be that the new digital public sphere will meaningfully change how we perceive and engage our democracy, and in negative ways. Indeed, Canadians perceive a risk here; in a recent 54-country study, Canadians were found to be most likely to regard social media as a threat to their democracy (Dalia Research & Rasmussen Global, 2019). But in the meantime, scholars and students of Canadian politics should remain critical consumers of public narratives, and should work to expand the existing evidence basis to empirically probe the democratic implications of our connected age.

Acknowledgements

As a charity, the Samara Centre for Democracy relies on the generous support of donors. We are very grateful to all of our individual donors as well as BMO, Bennett Jones LLP, and Your Canada, Your Constitution, for their continued support of the Democracy 360 project. Thank you also to Peter Loewen, Daniel Rubenson, and Benjamin Allen Stevens, who collected the 2019 Samara Centre Citizens' Survey data. The data is available at https://www.samaracanada.com/research/resourcesanddata/2019-citizens-survey/.

Notes

1. For example the argument has been made by Frank Graves and Michael Valpy (2019) in *The Toronto Star*, Ed Broadbent (2019) in *The Globe and Mail*, and Jeff Rubin (2019) in *The New York Times*.
2. For example, the percentage of Australians satisfied with their democracy went from 72 percent in 2013 to 41 percent in 2018. Similarly, satisfaction rates among the French was 64 percent in 2012, then declined to 34 percent in 2017, and the United States saw a drop in satisfaction from 80 percent to 46 percent during that same time period. For more comparative data, see Pew Research Center (Wike et al. 2017), modules 1 to 4 in The Comparative Study of Electoral Systems (2015a, 2015b, 2015c, and 2015d), and the Museum of Australian Democracy and the Institute for Governance and Policy Analysis at the University of Canberra (2018).
3. All figures cited in this chapter have been weighted against census values for age, gender, language, region, and immigration status. In Table 2.2: Interest in Politics, chi-square test = 121.1778; P-value = <0.00001.

4. Data from 2014 is not available.

5. For example, respondents were asked whether they agreed or disagreed with the following statements: "I don't think the government cares much what people like me think," "Those elected to Parliament soon lose touch with the people," "Ordinary people would do a better job of solving the country's problems than elected officials," and "The will of the majority should always prevail, even over the rights of minorities." See Michael Morden and Kendall Anderson (2019) for an analysis of these populist themes.

6. Adopting such a definition of populism made it possible to measure the prevalence of populist views over time in the Canadian adult population, something which would not lend itself well to an analysis based on a rhetorical or political-strategy lens. For an overview of different approaches to studying populism and their methodological implications, see Noam Gidron and Bart Bonikowski (2013).

References

Broadbent, E. (2019, March 22). Populism isn't a bad word—and progressives should take it back. *The Globe and Mail.* https://www.theglobeandmail.com/opinion

Cochrane, C. (2015). *Left and right: The small world of political ideas.* McGill-Queens University Press.

Dalia Research & Rasmussen Global. (2019). *The democracy perception index.* Dalia Insights Report. https://daliaresearch.com/democracy

Diebert, R. (2019). The road to digital unfreedom: Three painful truths about social media. *Journal of Democracy, 30*(1), 25–39. https://doi.org/10.1353/jod.2019.0002

Foa, R. S., & Mounk, Y. (2017). The signs of deconsolidation. *Journal of Democracy, 28*(1), 5–16. https://doi.org/10.1353/jod.2017.0000

Freedom House. (2018). *Freedom in the world 2018: Democracy in crisis.* https://freedomhouse.org/report/freedom-world/2018/democracy-crisis

Gidron, N., & Bonikowski, B. (2013). Varieties of populism: Literature review and research agenda. *Weatherhead Working Paper Series, 13*(4). https://doi.org/10.2139/ssrn.2459387

Graves, F., & Valpy, M. (2018, December 3). Canada is a tinderbox for populism. The 2019 election could spark it. *Macleans.* https://www.macleans.ca/politics/canada-is-a-tinderbox-for-populism-the-2019-election-could-spark-it/

Graves, F., & Valpy, M. (2019, July 10). Why Canadians need to wake up about populism. *The Toronto Star.* https://www.thestar.com/opinion/contributors/2019/07/10/why-canadians-need-to-wake-up-about-populism.html

Harper, S. (2018). *Right here, right now: Politics and leadership in the age of disruption.* McClelland and Stewart.

Kevins, A., & Soroka, S. (2019). Growing apart? Partisan sorting in Canada, 1992–2015. *Canadian Journal of Political Science, 51*(1), 103–133. https://doi.org/10.1017/S0008423917000713

Krämer, B. (2017). Populist online practices: the function of the Internet in right-wing populism. *Information, Communication & Society, 20*(9), 1293–1309. https://doi.org/10.1080/1369118X.2017.1328520

Levitsky, S., & Ziblatt, D. (2018). *How democracies die.* Broadway Books.

McGregor, M., Prusyers, S., Goodman, N., & Spicer, Z. (2020). Survey recruitment messages and reported turnout—an experimental study. *Journal of Elections, Public Opinion and Parties.* https://doi.org/10.1080/1745728.2020.1730380

Morden, M., & Anderson, K. (2019). *Don't blame "the People": The rise of elite-led populism in Canada.* The Samara Centre for Democracy.

Mounk, Y. (2018). *The people vs. democracy: Why our freedom is in danger and how to save it.* Harvard University Press.

Mudde, C., & Kaltwasser, C. R. (2013). Populism. In M. Freeden & M. Stears (Eds.), *The Oxford handbook of political ideologies* (pp. 493–510). Oxford University Press.

Museum of Australian Democracy and the Institute for Governance and Policy Analysis at the University of Canberra. (2018, December). *Democracy 2025: Trust and democracy in Australia.* https:// www.democracy2025.gov.au/documents/Democracy2025-report1.pdf

Norris, P. (2002). *Democratic phoenix: Reinventing political activism.* Cambridge University Press.

O'Neill, B. (2007). *Indifferent or just different? The political and civic engagement of young people in Canada.* Canadian Policy Research Networks Inc. and Elections Canada.

Petit-Vouriot, A., Morden, M., & Anderson, K. (2019). *2019 Democracy 360: The third report card on how Canadians communicate, participate, and lead in politics.* The Samara Centre for Democracy.

Rubin, J. (2019, October 21). Canada isn't so different. It could go populist too. *The New York Times.* https://www.nytimes.com/2019/10/21/opinion/canada-free-trade-populism.html

Schaub, M., & Morisi, D. (2019). Voter mobilisation in the echo chamber: Broadband internet and the rise of populism in Europe. *European Journal of Political Research.* https://doi.org/10.1111/1475-6765.12373

Statistics Canada. (2020, February). *Reasons for not voting in the federal election, October 21, 2019.* https://www150.statcan.gc.ca/n1/en/daily-quotidien/200226/dq200226b-eng.pdf?st=dgTUEZSM

The Comparative Study of Electoral Systems (2015a). CSES module 1 full release [Data set]. The CSES Secretariat. doi:10.7804/cses.module1.2015-12-15

The Comparative Study of Electoral Systems (2015b). CSES module 2 full release [Data set] The CSES Secretariat. doi:10.7804/cses.module2.2015-12-15

The Comparative Study of Electoral Systems (2015c). CSES module 3 full release [Data set] The CSES Secretariat. doi:10.7804/cses.module3.2015-12-15

The Comparative Study of Electoral Systems (2015d). CSES module 4 full release [Data set] The CSES Secretariat. doi:10.7804/cses.module4.2018-05-29

Wike, R., Simmons, K., Stokes B., & Fetterolf, J. (2017, October 16). *Globally, broad support for representative and direct democracy.* Pew Research Center. https://www.pewresearch.org/global/2017/10/16/globally-broad-support-for-representative-and-direct-democracy/

Zuboff, S. (2019). *The age of surveillance capitalism: The fight for a human future at the new frontier of power.* Hachette Books.

CHAPTER 3

Framing the Challenges of Digital Inclusion for Young Canadians

Leslie Regan Shade, Jane Bailey, Jacquelyn Burkell,
Priscilla Regan, and Valerie Steeves

Abstract

This paper reports on The eQuality Project's initial findings from focus groups conducted in the fall of 2018 and winter of 2019 with a diversity of youth (ages 13–17) in three Canadian cities about their perspectives and experiences of privacy and equality in networked spaces. Focus groups explored online activities and platforms used by participants, whether and how privacy was an essential aspect to their enjoyment, online experiences where they felt unwelcome or disrespected, and their strategies to mitigate these constraints. We use a modified version of the Institute of Museum and Library Services' digital inclusion framework to link the perspectives and apprehensions of the young people we interviewed to emerging digital policy questions. These include access (availability, affordability, inclusive design, and public access), application (across various sectors and uses like education, workplaces, employment, economic development, health, public safety, and civic engagement), and adoption (uptake and relevance, privacy and data rights, safety, and digital literacy). We conclude with several policy suggestions, including holding platform companies accountable and transparent about their data collection and privacy protection practices through producing coherent and well-designed terms of service; ensuring funding for enriched digital literacy programming for schools, parents, and young people in order to strengthen digital skills and knowledge about the dynamic nature of datafication; and bringing the voices of diverse Canadian youth into policy-making to ensure that intersectional perspectives and digital justice are core components for a rights-respecting networked environment.

In May 2019, Canada's House of Commons Standing Committee on Access to Information, Privacy and Ethics (ETHI) hosted the second International Grand Committee (IGC) on Big Data, Privacy and Democracy. The meeting brought together politicians from Canada, the United Kingdom, the European Union, Morocco, Argentina, Brazil, Singapore, Mexico, Ecuador, and Trinidad and Tobago to discuss heightened concerns surrounding big tech regulation and the need to reaffirm domestic policy commitments. Parliamentarians signed the Ottawa Declaration, which supported an "unwavering commitment to foster market competition, increase the accountability of social media platforms, protect privacy rights and personal data, and maintain and strengthen democracy" (ETHI, 2019, p. 7). The declaration also called on digital platforms to "follow applicable competition and antitrust laws, to strengthen their practices regarding privacy and data protection, to increase their algorithmic accountability, and to improve the manner in which these platforms prevent digital activities that threaten social peace or interfere in the open and democratic processes around the world" (ETHI, 2019, p. 7).

At the conclusion of the three-day hearing, ETHI Chair Bob Zimmer remarked that policy-makers should protect children from the "surveillance capitalism" business model of the major high-tech companies. Stated Zimmer, "the whole drive, the whole business model is to keep them glued to that phone despite the bad health that brings to those children—our kids. It's all for a buck. We're responsible to do something about that. We care about our kids. We don't want to see them turned into voodoo dolls, to be controlled by the almighty dollar and capitalism" (Blanchfield, 2019, para. 6).

As evoked by Zimmer, "surveillance capitalism" referred to testimony by scholar Shoshana Zuboff, who detailed its attributes in her magisterial 2019 book of the same title, subtitled "The Fight for a Human Future at the New Frontier of Power." In her written testimony to the IGC, Zuboff wrote that surveillance capitalism "declares private human experience as free raw material for translation into production and sales. Once private human experience is claimed for the market, it is rendered as behavioral data for computation and analysis. While some of these data may be applied to product or service improvements, the rest is declared as a proprietary behavioral surplus. This surplus is defined by its rich predictive value" (ETHI, 2019, p. 5).

With respect to children and youth, Zuboff (2019) describes in her book how "young life now unfolds in the spaces of private capital, owned and operated by surveillance capitalists, mediated by their 'economic orientation,' and operationalized in practices designed to maximize surveillance revenues. These private spaces are the media through which every form of social influence—social pressure, social comparison, modelling, subliminal priming—is summoned to tune, herd, and manipulate behavior in the name of surveillance revenues" (p. 456). The suggestion that the commercial model of big tech should be constrained because of its impact on the well-being of children signifies an important potential shift in Canadian policy-making. From the early days of the web, children have been mobilized to support the relatively unregulated growth of networked technologies: typically presenting children as naturally facile with technology, policy-makers have been both enthusiastic about connecting young Canadians so they can become the information innovators of the future, and loath to regulate tech companies because it might stifle that innovation (Shade et al., 2005). As problems such as access to pornography and cyberbullying have been identified, legislators have stopped short of interrogating how the commercial model that drives networked spaces sets young people up for conflict and erodes their privacy. Instead, they almost universally have responded by placing children under "protective" surveillance that further erodes that privacy (Bailey, 2015; Steeves, 2016). To explore policy options that better reflect the perspectives and experiences of young people, we conducted a study in the fall of 2018 and winter of 2019 called *This Is What Diversity Looks Like: What Young People Need to Enjoy Privacy and Equality in Networked Spaces*, which aimed to explore youth experience of online privacy and equality, including their experiences of what is afforded them and what constrains them in networked activities and platforms.[1] To examine the relationship between social location, privacy, and equality, we adopt an intersectional approach designed to support young people in creating networked spaces where they feel included and able to participate fully (Bailey & Steeves, 2015;

Bailey et al., 2019). For this study, our focus groups included LGBTQ, Indigenous, racialized, and general population youth (ages 13–17) from diverse geographic locations: a mid-sized central Canadian city, a large central Canadian city, and a mid-sized western Canadian city.

In the study, we asked young people about the various elements and opportunities they felt ensured their inclusion in online spaces, and whether privacy played a key role in their enjoyment of their activities and platforms. We also asked youth whether and how schools, government, and tech companies could make online spaces more welcoming and inclusive of youth. This chapter discusses our preliminary findings. We organize our discussion around a modified version of the Institute of Museum and Library Services' (IMLS) digital inclusion framework (the IMLS Framework) to connect the perspectives and concerns of the young people we interviewed to emerging policy questions about a range of online issues, including access (availability, affordability, inclusive design, and public access), application (across various sectors and uses like education, workplaces, employment, economic development, health, public safety, and civic engagement), and adoption (uptake and relevance, privacy and data rights, safety, and digital literacy) (PPF, 2018, pp. 2–3).

Moving from Surveillance Capitalism to Digital Inclusion

A plethora of social scientists have provided evidence that networked environments are complicated ones for children. Although young people report that they enjoy the easy sense of connectedness with friends and family, and have incorporated devices into a variety of daily tasks, they have also consistently raised concerns about the surveillance they experience at school, at home, and in the marketplace (Steeves, 2005, 2014). As Kathryn Montgomery (2015) notes, this surveillance is rooted in the "economic imperatives and powerful e-commerce business models" designed to "monitor and monetize [young people's] behaviors as well as their interactions with friends and acquaintances" (pp. 772–773).

Policy-makers have typically responded to these concerns by enacting consent-based data protection legislation that purports to give young people (and their parents) a degree of control over the ways in which young people's information is collected, used, and disclosed (e.g., in the United States, the *Children's Online Privacy Protection Act* [COPPA], and in Canada, the *Personal Information*

Protection and Electronic Documents Act [PIPEDA]). However, data protection has been an incomplete corrective, primarily because young people have a different conception of privacy. From their perspective, they are required to disclose information about themselves in order to participate in the online world. But this does not mean that they are comfortable with others collecting and using that information (Marwick & boyd, 2014; Steeves, 2015). For example, it is remarkable that 95 percent of young Canadians surveyed in 2013 reported that marketers should not be allowed to see what they post on social media, in spite of the fact that the young people have technically consented to their posts' disclosure to the public (Steeves, 2014).

Because of this, numerous policy organizations are incorporating human rights-based approaches to more fully protect children in networked environments. For example, the European Union's *General Data Protection Regulation* (GDPR) has supplemented children's general data protection rights with age-specific provisions that restrict profile-based marketing and prohibit algorithmic decision-making that significantly affects a child's rights (Steeves & Macenaite, 2019). And, for its part, the UN Committee on the Rights of the Child (CRC) is developing a "General Comment" on children's rights in relation to the digital environment (2019) to support states and NGOs to interpret the 30-year-old Convention on the Rights of the Child (CRC) for the digital age and to outline the types of policy responses that are needed to ensure that young people can fully participate in online life.

The IMLS Framework is a useful tool in this process because it goes beyond informational control and aims to identify "interventions which seek to increase access, remove barriers, develop digital skills, and empower people who might be otherwise marginalized and excluded from the design and use of digital technologies" in order to "ensure that everyone can benefit from digital technologies in their lives" (*Ontario Digital Service*, 2017). We suggest that a modified version of the IMLS Framework will enable policy-makers to begin to ask the right questions that will help inform the development of a rights-respecting networked environment in which young people from diverse social backgrounds can meaningfully access networked technologies and thrive online without fear of discrimination. In Table 3.1 we provide questions that we deem to be relevant and merit further research and analysis, even though not all of these were addressed by participants in our focus groups.

Table 3.1: Some Policy Questions on IMLS Framework

Elements	Policy Questions
Access: Availability Affordability Inclusive design Public access	Do young people and their families have access to affordable high-speed broadband in their homes? Are there sufficient, affordable, and accessible spaces for young people to gain public access to digital technologies? Are digital technologies inclusively designed so everyone can use them effectively and safely? Are school-based technologies implemented in ways that promote inclusion and respect privacy?
Application: Across various sectors and uses: - education - workplaces - economic development - health - public safety - civic engagement	Are all young people able to equally benefit from the use of digital technologies? Can digital technologies enhance educational, economic, healthy, and civic engagement for all young people in ways that enhance their privacy and enable them to participate in decisions about their lives?
Adoption: Uptake and relevance Privacy and data rights Safety Digital literacy	How can young people gain the knowledge and skills to effectively use digital technologies, including cell phones, smart tablets, and laptop computers? Do teachers and parents have the support they need to help young people become digitally literate? Are tech companies being held accountable to ensure they design technologies that respect young people's needs for privacy and participation?

Adapted from: PPF (2018).

Young Canadians' Perspectives of Digital Inclusion: A View from the e-Trenches

Our study asked a central research question: What factors enable youth from diverse social locations to participate fully in networked spaces and activities, and enjoy a lived equality online? Using the IMLS Framework of access, application, and adoption, we present preliminary findings from our focus groups.

Access

Cell phones were the primary means of accessing the Internet for virtually all of the focus group participants. They were also important storage devices for multiple types of content, making the prospect of losing one's phone quite upsetting. Emma, a 16-year-old participant who thought they'd lost their phone put it, "I had lots of things in my phone that I didn't really realize, like contacts and like old photos, like screenshots. So, I guess it's just like small things." Laptops, iPads, and Chromebooks were other common means for gaining Internet access, although use of these devices was more frequently associated with doing schoolwork either in school or at home. In a number of cases, focus group participants shared these devices with others, such as family members. For example, Xiu, a 13-year-old participant, reported sharing with "only my family so like it's safe."

Application

The focus group participants primarily connected with the Internet for leisure and education purposes, although occasionally their leisure pursuits involved information gathering that could be associated with civic engagement. Connectivity related to leisure pursuits involved both communicating with others and seeking out entertainment. While most of our participants communicated with family and friends primarily through cell phone texting, they also used Snapchat and Instagram, with some of them curating their Instagram to differentiate public from private audiences of friends and family. WeChat's video call function was also a popular means for Chinese newcomer focus group participants to communicate with family and friends who were still in China. As Xiu put it, "[s]o other than you can talk with them, so you can also see them is more convenient. It's like when you see them and talk to them in real life."

The focus group participants' leisure pursuits involved seeking out entertaining content (such as Vines and memes) on platforms and apps such as Instagram, Amino, Kik, Tumblr, YouTube, Netflix, and Twitter, and gaming sites such as Fortnite. In some cases, participants' entertainment-seeking activities were also forms of community building. Members of our LGBTQ focus group who use Amino, for example, described it as an opportunity to connect with others from around the world with shared interests such as fandoms. Similarly, for some of the Chinese newcomer focus group participants, watching Netflix became a way of gaining cultural capital that then allowed them to participate in face-to-face conversations in school about popular shows. They also used Chinese platforms such as Bilibili in order to gain access to popular culture from their homeland. In certain cases, information seeking on public issues was part of our participants' leisure activities. For example, several followed prominent public figures such as politicians (Donald Trump), tech gurus (Elon Musk), and well-known entertainers (Lin-Manuel Miranda) on Twitter.

Music was another popular online leisure pursuit for our participants, who use platforms and apps such as Spotify, iTunes, BlackPlayer, and QQ (which one Chinese focus group participant, Tommy, age 14, characterized as "a Chinese version of Spotify"). For one of our participants, algorithmically generated recommendations, such as on Spotify, were a generally inaccurate and unwelcome product of a for-profit agenda. Emma noted, "I'll be less likely to listen to [a recommendation] or enjoy it, simply because I've decided in my mind that this might just be because of money."

Email, Google Drive, and Google Docs were platforms that our participants generally only used to connect with educational activities. Google Drive, in particular, was considered by some as stressful because of its association with homework assignments. As Tommy put it, "Every time I use Google Drive, I need to do a lot of school stuff, like assignments and it's pretty stressful." While Skype and Facebook were considered by Tommy to be "kind of old," or as platforms used mainly by older people, both were still used to a limited extent by some participants. For example, one participant used Skype for English lessons, while other participants found they had to use Facebook in order to access school communications, information about volunteer opportunities, and, to a lesser extent, news. On the other hand, several found that access to certain content was blocked while they were in school, which as Annie, age 13, commented, "can sometimes get annoying."

Adoption

Based on a preliminary analysis of the focus group comments, we focus on several adoption issues related to safety, privacy, and what government or corporations might do. A more complete analysis of the focus groups is underway, but our early review reveals a number of relevant insights.

Regarding safety, the focus group participants identified four main sources that negatively affect their online experiences, especially on social media: other people, corporations, malevolent anonymous interactions, and being hacked. The main source of concern is other people—specifically negative, inappropriate, mean, self-serving, harassing, or nasty posts and messages (e.g., use of the "n" word, calling things "so gay," and intentional or ignorant ways of silencing members of marginalized communities). There was a recognition that, as Tommy put it, "These things happen all the time" but also that, as Emma commented, they "feel bad for all of the people involved." Interestingly, the main response to such negative posts is "to ignore them" (Malinda, age 14). Participants also engage in proactive behaviour, for example, with respect to posting of photos. As one trans participant, Josh (age 16), related:

> But like, if they're taking a picture of you without asking you, without saying anything, it's like they could be, like, posting it—they could be, like, taking this to make fun of me. They could be, like, taking—like taking this for, like, some weird, like, malicious intent. Like, it's just creepy. That's weird and it happens a lot with that, like—cosplayers [costume players]—have to, like, basically be like, "Please don't take photos of me without asking because it's creepy."

These comments mirror the results of earlier studies of online behaviour of youth that indicate the importance, and creativity, of self-management. The participants in our groups accepted that there was a likelihood of somewhat nasty behaviour from other people yet demonstrated a confidence in handling and moving past it. Their responses reflect learning from experience to develop the necessary skills. In some cases, participants reported this type of management behaviour but with a sense of resignation that it might not help. As Andrew, a 13-year-old racialized participant, said: "I don't know what happened after that. I don't care about that anymore."

A second source of negativity identified by our participants is the behaviour of corporations, especially in terms of what participants fear is going on behind the scenes. For example, on Instagram, Shan (age 13) related that, "Every time I download something, they would also say, like, 'Oh, we can—can we access your camera?' and all that, and I'm... Yeah, that's kind of creepy. Especially when they don't need the camera. So, I just... Yeah, I would—I would uninstall it if it does that." There is also a sense that some of the corporate offerings made to be attractive in ways that are misleading—for example, Snapchat (and its Snap Map), which Josh described as a "dangerous platform because people get, like, this sense of, like, 'Oh, it's—it's gonna disappear, so I can say whatever'... But ... nothing on the internet is ever gone." When asked who *should not* see their information, participants of one focus group centred attention on data sharing and integration across multiple platforms owned by the big corporations, specifically mentioning Google, Apple, Instagram, and Amazon. Julie (age 15) gave as an example the targeted ads that appear on Instagram after searching on Amazon, noting that the practice "kind of scares me. Because like, then you know for sure that they're kind of collecting data on you" and "Instagram and Amazon, they're like two completely different apps, and seeing them somehow have a relationship, well, it's kind of like, woah." Julie also raised concerns about covert monitoring of activity (e.g., microphone, camera, texts), noting that "sometimes it seems like your phone is listening to you" because you can be talking to someone about a product and then you get an ad for it later on. The same issue came up in another focus group with a similar response from participants; as Annie exclaimed, "So, they could, like, see what I've talked about with other people? ... That feels ... weird, like I'm spied on." George, a 17-year-old participant referred to this as "extreme capitalism," while Luke, a 15-year-old participant, described it as "Big Brother." Participants voiced frustration with the tech companies—that they were neither transparent with their practices nor held accountable for overstepping what was expected.

A third source of negativity, mentioned less than the above two, relates to people with malicious intent outside of one's social circle. Participants expressed concerns about online anonymity because they wanted to make sure they were not talking to, as Cody (age 14) described, a "dangerous person." A fourth concern emanated from experiences of being hacked, which also affected future behaviour: George discussed an experience in which hackers "broke into my account, changed the password, and then started posting, like, a bunch of, like, pornography from my account until the account got deleted. So, that's just why I'm really anxious."

In terms of measures that might address the negativity online, participants believed much of the responsibility had to rest with social media users themselves. For example, Shan commented, "When I think of, like, people posting, like, mean stuff on social media, I don't really think that's the social media's responsibility to fix that." An interesting exchange in one focus group with Chinese newcomers included a list of "do's and don'ts" including "make the right decisions" and "don't talk to strangers" (Janaan, age 13); "don't tell someone your personal information" (Ken, age 13); "be polite, trying to control yourself, not saying bad words or your comments to other people, otherwise they'll fight back to you" (Malinda); and, "don't follow fake accounts" and "don't watch some videos … like violence or pornography" (Andrew).

Participants do not generally read privacy notices or terms of service, which they find too long (as 16-year-old Patrick said, "to force you not to read it"), purposely hard to understand, "convoluted," and difficult to understand ("they can sometimes sneak things in there that just flips everything on its head," said Alex, a 14-year-old demigirl). In two focus groups, participants did note that they were more likely to look at the notices after the Facebook—Cambridge Analytica scandal.

Participants did not believe there was much that the government or corporations could do to mitigate the negativity. Some participants thought the government or corporations should block sites or take down comments that were hateful or racist, but most participants had a more nuanced view, noting the difficulties of making these distinctions and recognizing the potential negative implications for freedom of speech. A number of participants had reported issues to social media sites but were concerned that the sites lacked "context" to evaluate photos or comments and would likely take down reported posts because, as Emma exclaimed, "What's the easy way out? 'Let's just delete the post.'" Annie emphasized that platforms could assist with "security improvements" that reduced the possibility of account hacking. In general, participants seemed to think that corporations were motivated by money and the government by rich people—and that there was not much either could, would, or should do.

Conclusion: Digital Inclusion to Digital Justice

In May 2019, Innovation, Science and Economic Development Canada (ISED) released their *Digital Charter* emphasizing three broad areas of concern—the future of work, the impact of innovation, and trust and privacy. Echoing earlier discourses, youth are positioned in the report as needing to be prepared for the "workplace of the future," through adequate digital skills and literacy, especially in STEM fields. Youth were also mentioned with respect to strengthening PIPEDA rules (e.g., making it easier to delete content and withdraw consent) to give them greater control over their personal information and reputation. A sidebar on "What Young Canadians Said" (ISED, 2019, p. 11) mentions their belief that access is fundamental, especially to improve digital government services and online resources for education. It further mentions that strong digital literacy initiatives in a climate of misinformation and improving privacy, trust, and consent through transparent agreements are needed for a democracy. The *Digital Charter* made no mention of regulating tech companies, nor did it specify what a rights-respecting networked environment with elements of the IMLS Framework would entail. The *Digital Charter* commitment to address online hate appears to be primarily connected with Canada's decision to sign on to the Christchurch Call to Action,[2] which focuses largely on terrorism and radicalization and came about in response to an attack at a mosque in Christchurch, New Zealand. While these are no doubt important equality issues, there is a notable lack of attention to day-to-day acts of discrimination, corporate monitoring, and other forms of negativity that undermine inclusivity in digital spaces.

For young people, the persistent commercialization and datafication—the systematic collection and analysis of massive amounts of data sets—of their communicative practices raise ethical tensions and privacy concerns about whether they can maintain control of their digital identity over the course of their life cycle (Smith & Shade,

2018). Digital inclusion aims to improve quality-of-life and economic well-being (Rhinesmith, 2016), and is a constituent element of digital justice, "concerned with fair and equitable access to technologies and skills; appropriate instructional approaches and design tailored to different groups; and safe, secure and inclusive spaces online" (Pelan & Smythe, 2019, para. 1). Digital justice includes data literacy, which extends core components of digital literacy (an ability to critically understand and create digital media content and tools), to encompass an awareness of datafication processes, design, and policies. Seen through an intersectional lens (Bailey et al., 2019), and reflected in our findings, digital justice highlights how the intersectional social location of youth shapes their online experiences, and how corporate platforms, through infrastructural design, opaque algorithms, and complex and obfuscatory terms of service and privacy policies, can stifle online equality for youth.

Writing during the current global pandemic of COVID-19 palpably highlights the pertinence of digital inclusion as outlined by the IMLS Framework of access, application, and adoption. An affordable and universal Internet is a basic necessity when social distancing measures and shelter-in-place orders shutter schools and businesses. Online learning that relies on platforms and programs that are privacy- and equality-protective offers potential for reducing the negative effects of interruptions in learning. However, any advantages it may offer will only benefit those children and families who possess basic domestic Internet access. For these reasons, as Michael Geist notes in Chapter 10 of this book, policy goals must go beyond consideration of cultural consumption to include the broader objectives of providing universal and affordable access. Moreover, ministries of education and school boards should ensure that all software programs used for education comply with young people's rights, under the UN Convention on the Rights of the Child, to education and privacy, as well as to participate in decisions that platforms make that affect them.

We conclude with several policy suggestions. The first is that platform companies must be held accountable and become more transparent about their data collection and privacy protection practices through producing coherent and well-designed terms of service. Only a few participants in our focus groups read the privacy policies on the social media sites they use. Patrick's response was typical: "No. It's too long ... to force you not to read it." Shan said that she tried to "start reading the privacy … like, conditions" but that, "I don't really … understand anything." Annie stated that she sometimes skimmed through the terms of service for "anything that really … pops out or that seems … bad … but not usually," while George related that platform companies "know that nobody reads the terms."

Our participants were both cynical and resigned about the power of social and other platform companies. Alex expressed distrust with platform companies because "they can sometimes sneak things in there that just flips everything on its head. Like Facebook and that big privacy leak." When participants were asked how they felt about behavioural marketing, Alex stated, "Violated … but it's the price you have to pay." Luke addressed the surveillance capitalism inherent in online media, stating that, "it's really difficult to find an actual, like, good-natured website that's trying to do stuff. They want to make money and so, they're going to pretty much … get into every little bit of your life that they can to generate the most profit. They're going to just … just … they, like, watch you."

Holding the digital industry accountable for children's online safety is the focus of the UK government. In their white paper *Online Harms* they call on tech companies whose business model relies on user-generated content to demonstrate how they fulfill a *duty of care* to "make companies take more responsibility for the safety of their users and tackle harm caused by content or activity on their services" (Secretary of State, 2019, p. 7). A duty of care is also addressed in consultations to update the 30-year-old UN Convention on the Rights of the Child through the UN Committee on the Rights of the Child's General Comment on children's rights in relation to the digital environment (2019). Acknowledging children as agentic users and rights holders in the digital sphere is thus part of the requirement that states "fulfil their fundamental duty of care to children in the digital environment" (Third et al., 2019, p. 401).

The second policy suggestion is to ensure funding for enriched digital literacy programming for schools, parents, and young people to strengthen digital skills, knowledge about the dynamic nature of datafication, and to unpack and discourage discriminatory comments and behaviours. Digital-privacy policy literacy provides knowledge about the political economy of platforms and their privacy rights with respect to meaningful consent under privacy legislation, whether PIPEDA or the GDPR. Citizenship education for school-aged youth is also an essential component of digital literacy. An innovative example that fosters democratic engagement is the pan-Canada Student Vote, led by the registered charity CIVIX, where over 1.1 million students cast ballots in a mock 2019 Canadian federal election (CIVIX, 2019).

And finally, we need to bring the voices of youth into policy-making. With respect to the development of the CRC's General Comment on children's rights in relation to the digital environment, Canada was not among the 28 countries that submitted an initial concept note in 2019, with the exception of the submission by Global Kids Online, of which The eQuality Project is an academic partner. As the initial findings from our focus groups demonstrate, Canadian youth have rich perspectives to offer on how to create a rights-respecting networked environment.

Acknowledgements

The authors thank the Social Sciences and Humanities Research Council of Canada for their funding of The eQuality Project.

Notes

1. This research was conducted by The eQuality Project, a seven-year partnership of scholars, community organizations, educators, policy institutes, policy-makers, and youth, funded by the Social Sciences and Humanities Research Council of Canada, which explores young people's experiences with privacy and equality in networked environments, with a particular focus on youth from marginalized communities (see http://www.equalityproject.ca/our-project/). In this paper, all participants are referred to by pseudonyms and, where applicable, by their self-identification (ex: boy, demi-girl).
2. Christchurch Call to Eliminate Terrorist & Violent Extremist Content Online, May 2019. https://www.christchurchcall.com/.

References

Bailey, J. (2015). A perfect storm: How the online environment, social norms and law constrain girls' online lives. In J. Bailey & V. Steeves (Eds.), *eGirls, eCitizens* (pp. 21–53). University of Ottawa Press. https://press.uottawa.ca/egirls-ecitizens.html

Bailey, J. & Steeves, V. (Eds.). (2015). *eGirls, eCitizens*. University of Ottawa Press. https://press.uottawa.ca/egirls-ecitizens.html

Bailey, J., Steeves, V., Burkell, J., Shade, L. R., Ruparelia, R., & Regan, P. (2019). Getting at equality: Research methods informed by the lessons of intersectionality. *International Journal of Qualitative Methods, 18*, 1–14. https://journals.sagepub.com/doi/full/10.1177/1609406919846753

Blanchfield, M. (2019, May 29). Big data committee wraps up third and final day of hearings on Parliament Hill. *The Globe and Mail.* https://www. theglobeandmail.com/politics/article-mozilla-executive-tells-big-data-committee-he-was-shocked-when-he/

Children's Online Privacy Protection Act of 1998, 15 U.S.C. 6501–6505.

CIVIX. (2019, October 23). *Mock federal election for students also ends in Liberal minority* [Press release]. https://studentvote.ca/canada/canadian-press-mock-federal-election-for-students-also-ends-in-liberal-minority/

Committee on the Rights of the Child [CRC]. *(2019). General comment on children's rights in relation to the digital environment.* UN Human Rights, Office of the High Commissioner, Committee on the Rights of the Child. https://www.ohchr.org/EN/HRBodies/CRC/Pages/ GCChildrensRightsRelationDigitalEnvironment.aspx

House of Commons Standing Committee on Access to Information, Privacy and Ethics [ETHI]. (2019, June). *Report of the Standing Committee on Access to Information, Privacy and Ethics* (Report No. 20, 42nd Parliament, 1st Session). House of Commons of Canada. https://www. ourcommons.ca/DocumentViewer/en/42-1/ETHI/report-20/

Innovation, Science and Economic Development Canada [ISED]. (2019). *Canada's digital charter in action: A plan by Canadians, for Canadians.* Government of Canada. https://www.ic.gc.ca/eic/site/062.nsf/eng/ h_00109.html

Marwick, A. & boyd, d. (2014). Networked privacy: How teenagers negotiate context in social media. *New Media & Society, 16*(7), 1051–1067.

Montgomery, K. C. (2015). Youth and surveillance in the Facebook era: Policy interventions and social implications. *Telecommunications Policy, 39*(9), 771–786.

Ontario Digital Service: Key priorities. (2017, May 29). Government of Ontario. Retrieved March 29, 2019, from https://www.ontario.ca/page/ ontario-digital-service-key-priorities#section-9

Pelan, D., & Smythe, S. (2019, March 6). *Digital literacy and digital justice.* Brookfield Institute for Innovation + Entrepreneurship. https://brook-fieldinstitute.ca/commentary/digital-literacy-and-digital-justice/?mc_cid=3c769f2243&mc_eid=9d606cc7bf

Personal Information Protection and Electronic Documents Act [PIPEDA], S.C., c. 5 (2000).

Public Policy Forum [PPF]. (2018). *Ontario digital inclusion summit: Summary report.* https://ppforum.ca/publications/ontario-digital-inclusion-summit-summary-report/

Rhinesmith, C. (2016). *Digital inclusion and meaningful broadband adoption initiatives.* The Benton Foundation. https://www.benton.org/ inclusion-adoption-report

Secretary of State for Digital, Culture, Media & Sport and the Secretary of State for the Home Department. (2019). *Online harms* [White paper]. HM Government. https://dera.ioe.ac.uk/33220/1/Online_Harms_White_Paper.pdf

Shade, L. R., Porter, N., & Sanchez, W. (2005). "You can see anything on the Internet, you can do anything on the Internet!" Young Canadians talk about the Internet. *Canadian Journal of Communication, 30*(4), 503–526. https://www.cjc-online.ca/index.php/journal/article/view/1635/1776

Smith, K. L., & Shade, L. R. (2018). Children's digital playgrounds as data assemblages: Problematics of privacy, personalization, and promotional culture. *Big Data and Society, 5*(2), 1–12. https://journals.sagepub.com/doi/10.1177/2053951718805214

Steeves, V. (2005). *Young Canadians in a wired world, phase II: Trends and recommendations.* MediaSmarts. http://mediasmarts.ca/publicationreport/young-canadians-wired-world-%E2%80%93-phase-ii-trends-and-recommendations

Steeves, V. (2014). *Young Canadians in a wired world, phase III: Online privacy, online publicity.* MediaSmarts. http://mediasmarts.ca/ycww/online-privacy-online-publicity

Steeves, V. (2015). Privacy, sociality and the failure of regulation: Lessons learned from young Canadians' online experiences. In B. Roessler & D. Mokrosinska (Eds.), *Social dimensions of privacy: Interdisciplinary perspectives* (pp. 244–260). Cambridge University Press.

Steeves, V. (2016). Swimming in the fishbowl: Young people, identity and surveillance in networked spaces. In I. van der Ploeg & J. Pridmore (Eds.), *Digitizing identities* (pp. 125–139). Routledge.

Steeves, V. & Macenaite, M. (2019). Data protection and children's online privacy. In G. G. Fuster, R. Van Brakel, & P. De Hert (Eds.), *Research handbook on privacy and data protection law: Values, norms and global politics* [Book submitted for publication]. Edward Elgar Publishing.

Third, A., Livingstone, S., & Lansdow, G. (2019). Recognizing children's rights in relation to digital technologies: Challenges of voice and evidence, principle and practice. In B. Wagner, M. C. Kettemann, & K. Vieth (Eds.), *Research handbook on human rights and digital technology* (pp. 376–410). Elgar Online.

Zuboff, S. (2019). *The age of surveillance capitalism: The fight for a human future at the new frontier of power.* PublicAffairs.

Zuboff, S. (2019, May 28). Written testimony submitted to the International Grand Committee on Big Data, Privacy, and Democracy. https://www.ourcommons.ca/Content/Committee/421/ETHI/Brief/BR10573725/br-external/ZuboffShoshana-e.pdf

PART II

BUILDING DEMOCRATIC INSTITUTIONS IN A DIGITAL CONTEXT

CHAPTER 4

Government in the Connected Era

Kent Aitken

Abstract

Digital government is not just about putting government documents and services online; rather, it requires a public sector that understands and exists fully in a digital world, which includes understanding the reasonable limits of digital approaches and the relative merits of the analog world. The digital era has created unprecedented speed and reach for citizens accessing government services to voice their opinion about the policies behind those services. It has created ways for citizens to directly change or circumvent government programs. And, perhaps most importantly, the digital age has revealed many previously invisible voices and perspectives. This chapter will explore how Canadian governments are evolving, what digital government means for citizens, and what questions remain unanswered.

A s Canadians change in response to new possibilities and pressures of a digital world, so must Canada's public institutions. At its core, the role of government is to keep citizens safe and provide for the common good through the development of policy and the provision of programs and services. The digital age raises questions on how government fulfills these responsibilities and what responsibilities it should have in the first place.

While "digital" has a precise meaning—data expressed through a series of ones and zeros, which would be closer to the term "digitization"—it carries a set of particular meanings in a government context. In this chapter we explore this through four lenses:

1. Digital government: the modernization of government and in particular government services to citizens through the use and understanding of digital technologies and approaches.
2. Policy for the digital world: creating and revising government policies, laws, and regulations to adapt to new technologies, digitally driven trends, and impacts on citizens—that is, where technology is the subject of the issue at hand.
3. Digital democracy: using knowledge, approaches, and tools of the digital era to connect government and citizens, which could include digitally enabled collaborative or consultative policy development, the broader public-discourse environment, or direct democracy features like referenda or e-voting.
4. The state in a digital era: the digital era not only creates ways for citizens to interact differently with government, but also with each other in ways that, in many cases, circumvent the state altogether. As commerce, community, and culture increasingly transcend borders and jurisdictional authority, it challenges the authority of the state as provider for the common good.

Two caveats to start: first, these four lenses are non-exclusive. A "digital" government capable of understanding and implementing modern digital practices is more likely to be able to recommend smart and effective policy interventions, navigate digital democracy models, and understand foundational cultural shifts that could impact the role of the state. Likewise, a government that provides simple, effective services and creates meaningful opportunities for citizens to influence policy may see less people losing trust and circumventing the state. For example, tax delinquency goes down in jurisdictions with higher rates of democratic participation and when citizens feel that their government is genuinely addressing their concerns (Feld & Frey, 2002; Frey et al., 2004; Torgler, 2005).

Second, these lenses are not even necessarily digital (New Brunswick's digital strategy makes a point of noting, "This is not a technology plan") (Government of New Brunswick, n.d., para. 3). One hallmark of "digital government" is human-centred design and research, followed by continuous testing and improvement. In many cases the research involves field study, interviews, and focus groups: all long-standing and usually analog approaches. Referenda could be either analog or digital; digital approaches may just lower the cost and make frequent referenda a viable option.

There is one theme common to each thread. The societal discourse about each has moved from a sense of early skepticism based on the unknown to concern based precisely on what we do know. The proposal for Sidewalk Labs in Toronto was the target of criticism about data governance for "smart cities." Political dis- and misinformation are frequent concerns in public discourse. The once-revered Silicon Valley companies that government was told to emulate are now the subject of disillusionment and fear in the wake of data leaks and an abdication of responsibility for how people use their technology. At the Connected Canada conference, participants consistently expressed the need for equity and inclusion as fundamental principles for Canada's discourse about changing technology (Dubois & Martin-Bariteau, 2018).

Ultimately, this concern is a good thing, reflecting increasing understanding and maturity in how we're viewing the impact of a hyper-connected world on the relationship between citizens and their government. The question, however, is how effectively our public institutions pursue possible benefits while navigating costs and risks.

This chapter aims to provide a framework for understanding the relationship between public sector institutions and digital era concepts, such as those explored throughout this book, and to put forth a central argument: we are reaching a point in the connected era where both the benefits and costs to society are coming into sharper focus, replacing early overenthusiasm on one side and fear and skepticism on the other. With the role of stewardship for the public good, governments have a vested interest in this maturation, the research that reveals it, and the gaps in understanding that remain.

Digital Government

In 2017, Hillary Hartley was appointed Ontario's first chief digital officer (Hartley, 2018), while the Government of Canada launched the Canadian Digital Service. In 2018, the federal government released a set of digital standards (Government of Canada, 2019) while the Government of New Brunswick released a 5-year digital strategy (Government of New Brunswick, 2018). In 2019, Nova Scotia followed Ontario's lead and appointed a chief digital officer (The Chronicle Herald, 2019) while Ontario introduced the *Simpler, Faster, Better Services Act* to "set a new bar for digital services" (Ministry of Government and Consumer Services, 2019). Meanwhile, Quebec launched its digital transformation strategy (Lachance, 2019).

This barely scratches the surface of initiatives and investments under the banner of digital government, all of which have the potential for having real and meaningful impacts on the lives of Canadians. Yet, there remains work to be done to establish evidence of impact. Amanda Clarke (2017) noted an absence of evidence for the success of government digital units designed to reform service design, while Ines Mergel (2018) concluded the same for digital co-production (i.e., third-party actors creating value by adding to government digital infrastructure, such as open source code or open data). Paul Waller and Vishanth Weerakkody (2016) mince fewer words with their paper titled "Digital Government: Overcoming the Systemic Failure of Transformation." A common post-mortem theme across high-profile and high-value digital projects (such as transformation of the government email system, a unified Canada. ca, and the federal pay system) was that the level of complexity was greater than organizations were prepared for (Aitken, 2018).

In the meantime, the need for transformation is real. The United States Digital Services's Haley Van Dyck explained it like this in 2016:

> The [US] federal government is the largest institution in the world. It spends over 86 billion dollars a year—86 billion—on federal IT projects. For context: that is more than the entire venture capital industry spends annually—on everything. Now, the problem here is that we the taxpayers are not getting what we pay for, because 94 percent of federal IT projects are over budget or behind schedule … 40 percent of those never end up seeing the light of day. They are completely scrapped or abandoned.

The United States is not alone in that experience, and so governments are investing in digital. "Digital government" is a broad and amorphous term used to describe the current period of modernization for government with a focus on the changing role of technology. The ideological history behind the term helps frame the connection to citizens' lives and what the differences are now, and the standard in the literature is Karen Layne and Jungwoo Lee's four-stage model (2001).

In this model, early e-government efforts (late 1990s, early 2000s) were about *cataloguing*: listing government resources and services online and how they could be accessed (which was rarely online itself). Then we moved into *transaction*, which was about creating online options (e.g., updating accounts, using email channels for inquiries, and submitting forms online). The third stage was *vertical integration*, centred on sharing data and connecting similar functions—initial forays into piecemeal user-centred simplicity. The fourth stage is described by Layne and Lee as *horizontal integration*, which other authors have variously renamed *transformation* or *contextualization*. At this stage, government is reorganizing its own structures to make policies—and the visible front-office services that connect people to them—coherent and seamless to people. An example would be connecting two data systems so that people don't have to update their address to multiple departments. The integration phases reflect the growing realization, from data and experience, that simply digitizing paper processes is an incredibly limited lens.

Going digital, as opposed to "digitizing," has a more holistic, life-cycle model. Here's a hypothetical case:

1. A form is available online;
2. People's interactions with the form create a data stream about how it's working in real life;
3. This leads to user research and testing, which might be online or in person;
4. The form is subsequently redesigned, with small changes and tests occurring over time;
5. The research and data highlight problems with the underlying policy, so the policy people work with the service designers to rewrite the policy;
6. A revised policy is also tested in beta with real users;

7. To support changes over time and to support policy-service partnerships, governance strategy shifts to become more iterative, collaborative, and delivery-oriented.

Ultimately, the organization redesigns itself to support delivery in this way. In what now seems prescient for a 2001 book, Jane E. Fountain was one of the first to use the term "digital government" instead of "E-government": "The government then turned to the task of building digital government, in part through the strategy of creating virtual agencies. The virtual agency, following the web portal model used in the economy, is organized by client. … A [virtual state] is a government that is organized increasingly in terms of virtual agencies, cross-agency and public-private networks whose structure and capacity depend on the Internet and web" (p. 4). The inclusion of the words "organized by client" foreshadows the modern mantra of "user-centred design" in digital services units and the "Users First" stickers adorning the laptops of government technologists.

One of the results of this shift to digital is that it is data-rich: we know more about the world and the people in it, in a more granular and personal way. Which brings us to a theme that is prevalent across the four lenses of this chapter and is crucial for understanding government's roles in a changing Canada: with maturity comes complexity. It's easy to make bad web or mobile services that still work for some people. Digital maturity, however, includes effective data streams on who is using these services and where people are struggling or abandoning tasks altogether. It includes in-depth research into people's needs that reveal the work required to optimize the uptake of services across demographic and cultural lines, if the equity emphasized by the Connected Canada conference participants is indeed the goal (Dubois & Martin-Bariteau, 2018).

A digitally mature organization is characterized by a commitment to outcomes, fuelled by direct engagement with users and systematic review of the data about how services are being used. In the public sector context, mechanisms for public accountability can create pressure for improvements. For example, if a digital service is systematically hard to access for some Canadians more than others because hard-to-understand language or other issues of accessibility, the data would be there to make the issue known.

This leads us to the evolution referenced in this chapter's introduction. Appealing to another early e-government model, Keng Siau and Yuan Long (2005) described the evolution beyond *transaction* into the *transformation* stage, analogous to our *integration* or *maturity* stage, and pointed to why the change required now is different and more challenging than in times past. The first two stages were simply changes in technology, automating different processes to provide information online, and then interaction. The work left to be done to truly organize government services around citizens' needs are not *technology* leaps, but rather *cultural* and *political* shifts. Meaning that what worked to get governments through the first phases of modernization won't work for the next ones.

To compound this, the next phase of digital government reflects an increasing recognition of governments' limits in realizing this vision. No matter how effective and optimized government can make a service interaction, there are still people on the other side of the equation. Some have visual or physical disabilities (temporary or permanent), differing language backgrounds, limited access to smart-phones or computers, and varying levels of trust and comfort in inter-acting with government or via the Internet (e.g., sending personal financial information online). Ipsos put 23.5 percent of Canadians in the "low" and "very-low" digital participation categories (e.g., only 5 percent of people in the "very low" category choose to use government services online all or most of the time, as compared to 37 percent of the "high" category) (Ipsos Public Affairs, 2016).

Canada's reassuring figure that more than 90 percent of the country has access to broadband actually drops to around 60 percent to 65 percent when we look at the lowest quartile for income, or the highest quartile for age (Statistics Canada, 2012; this is in line with additional and more recent Statista [2019] findings). Increasingly, government's efforts toward digital services start to blend into digi-tal policy questions, where programs for Internet access and digital skills start becoming part of the equation, such as Ontario's digital inclusion initiative: "In a digitally inclusive Ontario, all people can access and benefit from digital technologies in their lives—regardless of skill, ability, location or socio-economic situation. Closing digital divides and achieving digital inclusion is an obligation of people-centred organizations as we become more digitized and design with our users in mind" (Government of Ontario, 2018, p. 15).

Where other works paint a portrait of plausible futures for digital government in Canada (e.g., Olivia Neal's chapter on digi-tal transformation in Benay, 2018), this section centred instead on the relationship between citizens and digital government. I argue that increased attention on access and ability issues is the natural expansion of the principle of user-centred design, leading to another, deeper layer of government redesign to support the goals of digital government. The advantage of attention on the wider digital access and digital ability spectrum across Canada is twofold: (1) it will help fill the skills gaps among public servants, which likewise hamper digital government initiatives, and (2) it will equally support many governments' stated digital policy goals that rely on digitally literate and innovative public, private, social, and academic sectors.

Policy for the Digital World

Governments hear calls to take action on emerging technologies, whether it's regulating use, relaxing regulations, or supporting research and development. There are calls to involve citizens in policy development and decision-making using digital technology, and to make government operations open and transparent to citizens (Canadian Open Government Civil Society Network, 2016). In the case of a cross-cutting technology like artificial intelligence (AI), this may happen all at once across government accountabilities. For instance, at the federal level alone, one department introduced a program to accelerate AI research (Innovation, Science and Economic Development [ISED], 2018), another introduced research and guide-lines on its use by government (TBS, 2019) and took steps to brace the labour market for impacts (Employment and Social Development Canada, 2019) as academics and observers warned of job loss or changes to skills required (Organisation for Economic Co-operation and Development, 2016; Bakhshi et al., 2017; Frey & Osborne, 2013). In parallel, the government created a standing advisory committee on AI, recognizing that the field and its impact on society will con-tinuously change (ISED, 2019).

And that's just for one area of technology, albeit one that serves as a foundation to widespread change across the digital landscape. A 2018 article by Iain Klugman and the former head of the federal public service, Kevin Lynch, is a representative overview of the public discourse around the digital challenges facing governments:

> It wasn't so long ago that the fourth industrial revolution—
> marked by breakthroughs in areas such as robotics, artificial

intelligence, quantum computing, the Internet of Things and nanotechnology—heralded the promise of a new paradigm, a rewired, freer, more open society.

In the past year that narrative has been subsumed by one best described as disturbing, even sinister.

Fake news. Robots that will put humans out of work, or worse, take over. Chronic gender and race issues at tech firms large and small. Enormous pools of capital and influence controlled by a handful of ever-larger technology firms. Data misused and privacy breached, capped by the recent revelations surrounding Cambridge Analytica and Facebook. (paras. 1–3)

Our world is rife with powerful technologies that emerge quickly. They have their conveniences and benefits but soon reveal their downsides and frightening plausible futures. This is not new, though: if this is the "fourth industrial revolution," then that means society has already weathered three. What is different this time?

The most common explanation is the pace of change for the development and adoption of technology. Mark Saner makes the case that the window between technological emergence and widespread use has become too short for governments to react—that they go from an information deficit where there isn't sufficient understanding to a power deficit where companies or people are too invested in a technology's benefit for government to intervene (2018). Vincent Mosco, reflecting on his 2005 book chronicling media technology over the century (from telegraph through to telephone, radio, and television), described how the government reaction to the current media landscape represents a discontinuity. He posited that FAMGA—Facebook, Apple, Microsoft, Google, and Amazon—has too much power over public discourse for government to meaningfully intervene now: "This is the first time in history we've largely set aside the public utility debate" (Mosco, 2004; Aitken, 2018). The 2001 *United States v. Microsoft Corp.* antitrust case, about whether it was an unfair monopoly to bundle Internet Explorer with Windows, now seem quaint in comparison.

The information deficit is not an easy one to overcome. Sixty percent of Canadians believe that "law and government policies are not keeping pace with the changes in technology" (Ipsos Canada, 2018a). A former congressional staffer reflected on the work the US Congress did on Internet regulation a few years ago, noting that between the 80 members of Congress and their staff working on this file, only a handful had a technology background: "I didn't feel like I had people or expertise to make informed decisions. To be frank, I was [going home after work and] asking my friend at Google for advice. That's not okay! Decent government in the twenty-first century requires this expertise in-house … every issue is going to be a tech issue" (quoted in Aitken, 2018, p. 57).

In lockstep, we are gaining a better understanding of the impacts of technology, and many Canadians are wary. "There is some very real technology fatigue and some people (especially older Canadians) are struggling to keep up with the pace of change," writes Ipsos Canada President Mike Colledge (Ipsos Canada, 2018a, p. 3). While 81 percent of Canadians think technology will have a very positive or somewhat positive impact on large businesses, only 64 percent think the same for small businesses. And the outlook is bleaker for new immigrants (41 percent), Indigenous Peoples (35 percent), older Canadians (30 percent), and low-income Canadians (29 percent) (Ipsos Canada, 2018b). This mirrors the reality of the digital government lens, where challenges in access and use for government services tend to be concentrated among already marginalized populations (Public Policy Forum, 2018).

Digital Democracy

In the last few years, the Government of Canada has run an unprecedented number of public engagement exercises, ranging from how to roll out an innovation fund to the process for legalizing cannabis (Government of Canada, 2020), to whether peach tree borer pheromones are an acceptable pesticide to deter moths by throwing off their mating (Government of Canada, 2018). This enthusiasm builds on a long foundation of analog engagement through such means as roundtables, focus groups, and Canada Post. Since 1986, every proposed change of a federal regulation has to be announced in the *Canada Gazette*—the official "newspaper" of the Government of Canada—and opened for comment from stakeholders. In parallel, for years, government analysts produced green papers and white papers about policy analyses to circulate to interested communities.

The digital age changes this environment in a few ways. Mass communications technologies lend themselves to scale and reach and can lower the cost of public engagement. At the same time, citizens, led by civic organizations, called for increased engagement, and the existence of the Internet removed any excuse to not have this. Accordingly, we saw a steep rise in online public engagement processes while learning the drawbacks and limitations.

The early days of the Internet were also characterized by lofty visions for its potential to reshape democracy, empower citizens, and create a national—or worldwide—civic dialogue about the future we all wanted. *New York Times* bestsellers proclaimed that mass collaboration would "change everything" (Tapscott, 2008). In today's world of bitcoin-enabled ransomware and AI-enabled deepfakes of videos that make it hard to distinguish the actual person from a computerized manipulation of them, we are more likely to hear the musing that "Maybe the Internet Isn't a Fantastic Tool for Democracy After All" (Read, 2016).

This period follows the typical pattern of overenthusiasm for technological advances, and governments experimented with online engagement past the point of diminishing marginal returns. Over time, practitioners learned that raw input and mass volumes of comments were often less useful for government and less satisfying for citizens than smaller-scale in-depth dialogue (Gregory, 2017). People and organizations, both malicious and well meaning, began flooding such processes with input to give a sense of a public consensus, often using automated bots. Governments learned that the idea of "conversation" doesn't scale well; most online discussion forums cap out at approximately 250 participants, and the largest-scale online engagement platform, pol.is, can reach over 10,000 people by focusing people's attention on binary preference votes (Horton, 2018). Planners paid attention as the federal government's electoral reform engagement was marked by widespread criticism. So, it's perhaps not surprising that when the federal government launched a nationwide dialogue on "Canada's energy future," they chose a demographically representative group of Canadians to deliberate at length and simply report back to the country (Simon Fraser University, 2017). Other programs solicit input at scale through the more established means of syndicated public opinion research.

While government increasingly exists and operates in a digital space, so too do citizens. Through social media, blogs, and discussion forums, Canadians have a plethora of options to engage in civic discourse. In 2017 when the Government of Canada invited comments on Canada's tax policy for small businesses (Department of Finance, 2017), the #cdnpoli community on Twitter crowdsourced and collaborated on data and analysis, which eventually made its way into op-eds and formal responses. In the world of government citizen engagement, it is easy to forget "that communities and individuals have power of their own that is not conferred on them by the decision-maker" (McCallum, 2015).

Two patterns from previous sections repeat. One, we see the deeper pattern around issues of inclusion. Although the Internet was touted as the ultimate leveller of the playing field, where intelligence and ideas would command authority rather than position, we can often find sexism, racism, hate speech, bullying, and abuse driving people from public discourse.

Two, we see the broader pattern of maturity leading to dampened enthusiasm in comparison to the once lofty vision for digital democracy. But this dampened enthusiasm ultimately can lead to more productive uses of technology, in which digital means are truly the best way to connect citizens and their governments.

The State in a Digital Era

"I predict the Internet will soon go spectacularly supernova and in 1996 catastrophically collapse," Robert Metcalfe wrote in a column in 1995, two years before he blended that piece of paper into a smoothie and consumed it at the World Wide Web Conference to literally eat his words (Strohmeyer, 2008, para. 16).

In the early days of the now quarter-century-old Internet, people frequently viewed the online world as something that was fleeting, incomplete, and elsewhere. Academics asked questions like "can the Internet be used to mobilize social movements?," and one social media leader warned that "you have to realize that what you do online has impacts in the real world" (quoted in Aitken, 2018, p. 13). Culturally, we're moving away from these mental patterns and the "the idea of the virtual … has since receded into the background" (Hui, 2016). Steffen Christensen, an expert in AI and foresight at Policy Horizons Canada, says that "the Internet is no longer a place. It is us. It *is* the world. We live in it" (quoted in Aitken, 2018, p. 13).

Making deliberate choices between digital and analogue methods is a sign of maturity for the era of the Internet, where we no longer go digital because it's interesting or because we can, but instead pick what best serves our needs and goals. At the edges of this definition are the existential questions for government. If that which is digital is real, and people can access real services, products, communities, and security, then the logic of citizenship and jurisdiction bounded by physical lines starts to erode.

When Lincoln Dahlberg (2011) constructs a range of models for digital democracy, some bear a resemblance to that initial optimism and others, to the dark side that proponents may have overlooked. He describes the ability for people to be individually empowered in seeking political information and engaging in political life (he calls these people *liberal consumers*) and describes the ability to dialogue with others toward consensus (he calls this *deliberative*—the once-presumed end state). However, the Internet also creates additional options for mobilization against the state for both better and worse (these actors he terms *counter-publics*), and for a fourth model to exist, whereby people self-organize not to interact with the state but to circumvent it entirely (these he calls *autonomous Marxists*).

This self-organization has become mainstream in our lives via peer-to-peer accommodations platforms like HomeAway and Airbnb,[1] digital file-sharing platforms starting with Napster, and online marketplaces like Craigslist and Kijiji. Statistics Canada (2017) reported that from November 2015 to October 2016 an estimated 9.5 percent of people (2.7 million) aged 18 and older living in Canada participated in the sharing economy by using peer-to-peer ride services or private accommodation services, spending $1.31 billion. This is a subsection of what the Canada Revenue Agency terms the "underground economy" of about $45.6 billion (2018). This, depending on your ideology, does contain downsides: it creates a tax gap of $8.7 billion (Canada Revenue Agency, 2018) less for spending on public infrastructure and services. Similarly, though people might have saved money on weekend trips by using peer-to-peer accommodations instead of hotels, we now are seeing that these markets are "having rather large impacts on our housing markets" and driving up rental and house prices and hurting younger people and first-time homebuyers (Wachsmuth & Weisler, 2018). A co-author of that research seems to align his thinking with Saner's on the opportunity gap for governments intervening on emerging trends: "'Airbnb, HomeAway and other companies in the sector enjoyed a period of several years where policy-makers weren't really paying attention,' [Wachsmuth] said. 'I think that period is over now'" (quoted in Cardoso & Lundy, 2018, para. 38).

But in many ways, the underground and peer-to-peer economy also means a boundaryless space defined by interests and markets as much as geographic jurisdictions. The transaction pattern and enabling technology are much the same whether you're renting a room from a neighbour or interacting with international corporations, communities across the globe, or malicious actors operating for personal profit or political mischief. Governments have a much more difficult time defining and enforcing their responsibilities without borders to create delineation. On the most benign end of the spectrum, it's renting out rooms. At the most virtuous, it's government working with civil society to map non-government, community services that newcomers to Canada can draw on via Ajah's SectorLandscape tool (Ajah, 2020). At the worst, the Internet can equally be used as a tool for political misinformation, bullying, identity theft, phishing, ransom, and immigration and human trafficking scams. The question is, to what extent are governments responsible for protecting citizens from their own decisions to work outside the system?

Governments have to increasingly get used to actors and actions that are beyond their jurisdiction and beyond their control—but that have real and tangible impacts on Canadian citizens and soil, and moving at the speed of information of 300,000 km/s.

Conclusion: The Future of Government in a Connected World

In this chapter, we have explored four lenses through which to look at government's role in a digital era:

1. As a service provider going through modernization to meet rising expectations, captured by the term *digital government*;
2. As a governance body adapting to increasingly rapid changes that do (or should) impact *policy for the digital world*;
3. As an aggregator of the public interest where democratic relationships are increasingly conducted online—a *digital democracy*;
4. As an entity threated by changing cultural and geopolitical forces that many say threaten the relevance of *the State in a digital era*.

Through each lens, we have seen how the promise of the Internet era has been challenged by setbacks, unforeseen negative consequences, rising expectations, and (if nothing else) a challenge in establishing an evidence base for the impacts on society. The need for timely and responsive research to support those governing or observing the changing world from a public good perspective has never been greater, and can only increase from here.

The research agenda presented throughout this book is, in many ways, also the research agenda required to respond to the trends described throughout this chapter, particularly through the lens of *policy for the digital world.*

There is a need to establish, in lockstep, a firmer understanding of the impacts and success factors for different approaches to digital government, as per the gaps described by Amanda Clarke (2017), Ines Mergel (in Mergel, Kattel, Lember, and McBride [2018]), and Paul Waller and Vishanth Weerakkody (2016). This work would benefit from a closer ongoing relationship between governments and the academic community, and more proactive engagement from governments on research interests. Specifically, governments should identify forward-looking priorities and use existing granting mechanisms to support the academic community in building theoretical and evidence bases for emerging questions. The government policy community should also increasingly consider governance and the digital sphere as fields requiring analytical rigour, engaging with the available literature and building program-to-expert relationships with Canada's leading scholars.

While many authors have explored the intersections of trust, digital government, and digital democracy (Mahmood et al., 2014; Mahmood, 2018; Tolbert & Mossberger, 2006), firm conclusions have been few and far between. Digital government discourse lacks solid foundations, as Clarke describes in Chapter 5 of this volume on digital government and data governance.

More important than the research agenda, however, is the structure that supports governments and academics working together to identify and adjust research programming to support emerging understandings and promising initial findings. The Connected Canada conference and subsequent works are one model for collaborative issue exploration and agenda setting; developing additional avenues will be crucial to Canada's maturation as a connected country.

Note

1. It's odd the extent to which Airbnb has captured the attention of people writing about digital disruption, given that HomeAway has been doing the exact same thing, albeit for a more niche market, for over 20 years.

References

Aitken, K. (2018, September). *Governance in the digital age.* Public Policy Forum. https://ppforum.ca/publications/governance-in-the-digital-age/

Ajah (2020). *Sector Landscape.* http://landscape.ajah.ca/?limit=100&source=&page=1&search=&name=&sort=&city=&province=&date_from=0&date_to=0&instance_slug=

Bakhshi, H., Downing, J. M., Osborne, M. A., & Schneider, P. (2017). *The future of skills: Employment in 2030.* Pearson.

Benay, A. (2018). *Government digital: The quest to regain public trust.* Dundurn.

Canada Revenue Agency. (2018). *Underground economy strategy 2018–2021.* Government of Canada. Retrieved August 1, 2019, from https://www.canada.ca/en/revenue-agency/programs/about-canada-revenue-agency-cra/corporate-reports-information/underground-economy-strategy-2018-2021.html

Canadian Open Government Civil Society Network. (2016). *About The Canadian Open Government Civil Society Network.* https://www.open-govdialogue.ca/about.html

Cardoso, T., & Lundy, M. (2019, June 20). Airbnb likely removed 31,000 homes from Canada's rental market, study finds. *The Globe and Mail.* https://www.theglobeandmail.com/canada/article-airbnb-likely-removed-31000-homes-from-canadas-rental-market-study/

Clarke, A. (2017). Digital government units: Origins, orthodoxy and critical considerations for public management theory and practice. http://dx.doi.org/10.2139/ssrn.3001188

Dahlberg, L. (2011). Re-constructing digital democracy: An outline of four "positions." *New Media & Society, 13*(6), 855–872.

Department of Finance. (2017). *Tax Planning Using Private Corporations.* Retrieved June 26, 2020 from https://www.canada.ca/en/department-finance/programs/consultations/2017/tax-planning-using-private-corporations.html

Dubois, E., & Martin-Bariteau, F. (2018). *Canadians in a digital context: A research agenda for a connected Canada.* http://dx.doi.org/10.2139/ssrn.3301352

Employment and Social Development Canada. (2019, February 14). *Government of Canada takes action to ensure Canadian workers are prepared for the jobs of tomorrow* [Press release]. https://www.canada.ca/

en/employment-social-development/news/2019/02/government-of-
canada-takes-action-to-ensure-canadian-workers-are-prepared-for-
the-jobs-of-tomorrow.html

Feld, L. P., & Frey, B. S. (2002). Trust breeds trust: How taxpayers are treated. *Economics of Governance, 3*(2), 87–99.

Fountain, J. E. (2001). *Building the virtual state: Information technology and institutional change.* Brookings Institution Press.

Frey, B. S., Benz, M., & Stutzer, A. (2004). Introducing procedural utility: Not only what, but also how matters. *Journal of Institutional and Theoretical Economics (JITE), 160*(3), 377–401.

Frey, C. B., & Osborne, M. (2013, September 17). *The future of employment: How susceptible are jobs to computerisation?* [Working paper]. Oxford Martin Programme on Technology and Employment.

Government of Canada. (2018). *Consultation on (Z, Z)-3,13-octadecadien-1-yl acetate and its associated end-use products, proposed re-evaluation decision PRVD2018-07.* Retrieved on December 19, 2019, from https://www.canada.ca/en/health-canada/services/consumer-product-safety/pesticides-pest-management/public/consultations/proposed-re-evaluation-decisions/2018/octadecadien.html

Government of Canada. (2020). *Consulting with Canadians.* Retrieved June 26, 2020 from https://www.canada.ca/en/government/system/consultations/consultingcanadians.html

Government of Canada. (2019). *Government of Canada Digital Standards.* https://www.canada.ca/en/government/system/digital-government/government-canada-digital-standards.html

Government of New Brunswick. (n.d.). *Digital New Brunswick.* https://www2.gnb.ca/content/gnb/en/corporate/promo/dnb.html

Government of New Brunswick. (2018, April 27). *Digital strategy envisions redesigned government services* [News release]. https://www2.gnb.ca/content/gnb/en/news/news_release.2018.04.0449.html

Government of Ontario. (2018, March 20). *Start with users. Deliver together.* Retrieved January 20, 2020, from https://www.ontario.ca/document/start-users-deliver-together/sparking-new-vision

Gregory, R. S. (2017). The troubling logic of inclusivity in environmental consultations. *Science, Technology, & Human Values, 42*(1), 144–165.

Hartley, H. (2018, April 23). *One year in: A retrospective.* Medium. https://medium.com/ontariodigital/one-year-in-a-retrospective-30600f7f3efc

Horton, C. (2018, August 21). *The simple but ingenious system Taiwan uses to crowdsource its laws.* MIT Technology Review. https://www.technologyreview.com/2018/08/21/240284/the-simple-but-ingenious-system-taiwan-uses-to-crowdsource-its-laws/

Hui, Y. (2016). *On the existence of digital objects.* University of Minnesota Press.

Innovation, Science and Economic Development Canada [ISED]. (2018, February 15). *Government of Canada's new innovation program expected to create tens of thousands of middle-class jobs* [Press release]. https://www.canada.ca/en/innovation-science-economic-development/news/2018/02/government_of_canadasnewinnovationprogramexpectedtocreatetensoft.html

Innovation, Science and Economic Development Canada [ISED]. (2019, May 14). *Government of Canada creates advisory council on artificial intelligence* [Press release]. https://www.newswire.ca/news-releases/government-of-canada-creates-advisory-council-on-artificial-intelligence-838598005.html

Ipsos Canada. (2018a). *Tech for Good: A Canadian Perspective* [Survey]. https://canadianinnovationspace.ca/wp-content/uploads/2018/05/IpsosCanadaNext_TrueNorth_May22.pdf

Ipsos Canada. (2018b). *CanadaNext.* https://www.ipsos.com/en-ca/knowledge/society/CanadaNext-2018

Ipsos Public Affairs. (2016). *Public perspectives: Participation in the digital economy 2.0.* https://www.ipsos.com/sites/default/files/publication/2015-12/7086-report-2.0.pdf

Lachance, N. (2019, June 3). *Le gouvernement entame une vaste transformation numérique.* Le Journal du Québec. https://www.journaldequebec.com/2019/06/03/le-gouvernement-entame-un-vaste-tournant-numerique

Layne, K., & Lee, J. (2001). Developing fully functional e-government: A four-stage model. *Government Information Quarterly, 18*(2), 122–136.

Klugman, I., & Lynch, K. (2018, April 27). It's time for technology to deliver on its promise to make lives better. *The Globe and Mail.* https://www.theglobeandmail.com/business/commentary/article-its-time-for-technology-to-deliver-on-its-promise-to-make-lives

Mahmood, M. (2018). *Does digital transformation of government lead to enhanced citizens' trust and confidence in government?* Springer.

Mahmood, M., Osmani, M., & Sivarajah, U. (2014). *The role of trust in e-government adoption: A systematic literature review.* Brunel University London.

McCallum, S. R. (2015, March 12). *Re-imagining the IAP2 spectrum.* Medium. https://medium.com/@RedheadSteph/re-imagining-the-iap2-spectrum-9d24afdc1b2e

Mergel, I., Kattel, R., Lember, V., & McBride, K. (2018). Citizen-oriented digital transformation in the public sector. *Proceedings of the 19th Annual International Conference on Digital Government Research: Governance in the Data Age.* Association for Computing Machinery. https://dl.acm.org/doi/10.1145/3209281.3209294

Ministry of Government and Consumer Services. (2019, April 30). *Ontario delivers simpler, faster, better services for Ontarians with new digital plan* [Press release]. https://news.ontario.ca/mgs/en/2019/04/

ontario-delivers-simpler-faster-better-services-for-ontarians-with-new-digital-plan.html

Mosco, V. (2005). *The digital sublime: Myth, power, and cyberspace*. MIT Press.

Organisation for Economic Co-operation and Development. (2016). *Automation and independent work in a digital economy: Policy brief on the future of work*. https://www.oecd.org/employment/Policy%20brief%20-%20Automation%20and%20Independent%20Work%20in%20a%20Digital%20Economy.pdf

Public Policy Forum. (2018). *Ontario digital inclusion summit: Summary report*. https://ppforum.ca/wp-content/uploads/2018/05/PPF-Report-Ontario-Digital-Inclusion-Summit-English-May-2018.pdf

Read, M. (2016, November 27). Maybe the Internet isn't a fantastic tool for democracy after all. *New York Magazine—Intelligencer*. http://nymag.com/intelligencer/2016/11/maybe-the-internet-isnt-a-tool-for-democracy-after-all.html

Saner, M. (2018, April 16). *The trouble with emerging technologies (Solutions to the Collingridge dilemma)* [PDF slides]. Carleton University. https://carleton.ca/rgi/wp-content/uploads/CC2018_Trouble-With-Emerging-Technologies_Saner.pdf

Siau, K., & Long, Y. (2005). Synthesizing e-government stage models—a meta-synthesis based on meta-ethnography approach. *Industrial Management & Data Systems, 105*(4), 443–458.

Simon Fraser University, Morris J. Worsk Centre for Dialogue. (2017, July 27). *The citizen dialogues on Canada's energy future*. https://www.sfu.ca/dialogue/news-and-events/archives/2017/the-citizen-dialogues-on-canadas-energy-future0.html

Statista. (2019). *Internet usage penetration in Canada from 2013 to 2019, by age*. https://www.statista.com/statistics/373955/canada-online-penetration-age/

Statistics Canada. (2012). *Canadian Internet Use Survey, 2012*. https://www150.statcan.gc.ca/n1/daily-quotidien/131126/dq131126d-eng.htm

Statistics Canada. (2017). *The sharing economy in Canada*. https://www150.statcan.gc.ca/n1/daily-quotidien/170228/dq170228b-eng.htm

Strohmeyer, R. (2008, December 31). *The 7 worst tech predictions of all time*. PC World. https://www.pcworld.com/article/155984/worst_tech_predictions.html

Tapscott, D., & Williams, A. D. (2008). *Wikinomics: How mass collaboration changes everything*. Penguin.

The Chronicle Herald. (2019, May 30). *Nova Scotia shuffles deputy ministers, replaces top health bureaucrat*. https://www.thechronicleherald.ca/news/local/nova-scotia-shuffles-deputy-ministers-replaces-top-health-bureaucrat-316885/

Tolbert, C. J., & Mossberger, K. (2006). The effects of e-government on trust and confidence in government. *Public Administration Review, 66*(3), 354–369.

Torgler, B. (2005). Tax morale and direct democracy. *European Journal of Political Economy, 21*(2), 525–531.

Treasury Board of Canada Secretariat [TBS]. (2019). *Ensuring responsible use of artificial intelligence to improve government services for Canadians* [News release]. https://www.canada.ca/en/treasury-board-secretariat/news/2019/03/ensuring-responsible-use-of-artificial-intelligence-to-improve-government-services-for-canadians.html

United States v. Microsoft Corporation, 253 F.3d 34 (D.C. Cir 2001).

Van Dyck, H. (2016). *How a start-up in the White House is changing business as usual.* https://www.ted.com/talks/haley_van_dyck_how_a_start_up_in_the_white_house_is_changing_business_as_usual

Wachsmuth, D., & Weisler, A. (2018). Airbnb and the rent gap: Gentrification through the sharing economy. *Environment and Planning A: Economy and Space, 50*(6), 1147–1170.

Waller, P., & Weerakkody, V. (2016). *Digital government: Overcoming the systemic failure of transformation.* Working Paper 2, Brunel University London. http://dx.doi.org/10.2139/ssrn.2803233

CHAPTER 5

Data Governance: The Next Frontier of Digital Government Research and Practice

Amanda Clarke

Abstract

Picking up on a global orthodoxy calling for digital government transformation, governments across Canada are now introducing ambitious service reforms and broader changes to the organization and culture of public service institutions. These reforms are primarily justified on the grounds that they are necessary if governments wish to meet the expectations of citizens accustomed to the innovative digital service offerings of the private sector. Yet with digital transformation agendas come notable changes to the ways that public sector data is collected, applied, and shared across the state and among private firms. These data governance reforms may prove unacceptable to citizens should they lead to privacy breaches, betray principles of equity, transparency and procedural fairness, and loosen democratic controls over public spaces and services. This chapter presents three cases that illustrate the data governance dilemmas accompanying contemporary digital government reforms. The chapter next outlines a research and policy agenda that will illuminate and help resolve these dilemmas moving forward, with a view to ensuring that digital era public management reforms bolster, rather than erode, Canadians' already precarious levels of trust in government.

For the past decade, digital government research and practice have focused on the institutional and cultural reforms required to build more data-driven, user-focused, open, and entrepreneurial public sector institutions. This new orthodoxy has become widely accepted as the only means by which government can meet citizens' expectations for services—an imperative framed as essential to preserving the state's legitimacy in the digital age.

Inspired by this call to action, governments are investing in new types of data collection, sharing, and use. These efforts bring to light a series of complex data governance challenges that have, to date, largely been overlooked in the quest for digital government transformation. These challenges relate less to the managerial and institutional reform questions that occupied early digital government work and instead speak to complex ethical questions on the principles and values that should inform data collection, use, and sharing in the public sector and within the ecosystem of private actors implicated in public service delivery.

This chapter begins by outlining the digital government orthodoxy that has captured the attention of governments in Canada and globally in the past decade. Next, three recent examples of digital government reforms are explored in order to underscore the data governance dilemmas that accompany the new digital government orthodoxy. The chapter concludes with three recommendations to guide a new policy and research agenda on data governance, in order to inspire immediate and widespread attention to this overlooked but critical challenge to democratic governance in Canada.

Digital Era Public Management Reform: The Existing Research Landscape

Since the mid-2000s, governments and academics have advanced a remarkably consistent vision of digital era public management reform (Clarke, 2017; Dunleavy et al., 2006; Mergel, 2017; Mergel et al., 2019; O'Reilly, 2011). This common orthodoxy asserts that in order for civil service institutions to be resilient, effective, and relevant in a digital context, they must initiate radical reforms to their institutional structures, their cultures, and their policy and legal regimes. This orthodoxy can be summarized by its six central tenets, which dictate that digital era governments should:

1. Be horizontal and "joined up" such that policies, programs, and services are conceived and managed through so-called platform models that cut across or dissolve departmental and functional silos;
2. Enable greater discretion and entrepreneurialism throughout the civil service by streamlining and reducing hierarchical oversight and approval processes, and challenging a status quo-oriented/risk-averse managerial culture;
3. Invest in digital skills (e.g., design, user research, data science, and product management) within the civil service, and better integrate those with these skills into all policy and program design and management, as well as at the highest levels of bureaucratic decision-making;
4. Be open—defined broadly and in some cases nebulously, and covering a range of activities, including the release of government data (open data); citizen consultation and stakeholder engagement; a transparent and informal culture of government communications (especially via social media); and a willingness to engage private actors in public service delivery;
5. Treat data as a high-value public asset, enabling sophisticated data-driven decision-making across all government functions;
6. Adopt the tenets of design thinking, especially through iterative, agile service design practices that prioritize user experience as a primary input in the development of policies, programs, and services.

These prescriptions are not strictly new.[1] However, they are now invoked with a greater sense of urgency. In some cases, these reforms are justified on the grounds that they will generate much-needed cost savings and administrative efficiencies. But most commonly, digital government reforms are framed as essential given advances in the private sector's online service offerings. Here, the argument goes that, as citizens access information and as they complete transactions online with relative ease in their private lives, they become ever more disenchanted with government, whose services are presumed to be clunkier, slower, and less digital friendly than those on offer from the Amazons and Googles of the world. Absent the reforms listed above, governments are, as the orthodoxy goes, doomed to lose citizen trust and, in turn, the democratic licence to govern.

This preoccupation with citizens' service expectations is reflected in a definition, now widely adopted, of "digital" offered by the former UK Government Digital Service leader, Tom Loosemore. Writing in 2016 on Twitter, he defined "digital" as the act of "applying the culture, practices, processes and technologies of the Internet-era to respond to people's *raised expectations*" (Loosemore, 2016, emphasis added). Loosemore's perspective was reflected in a 2019 study that probed the views of digital government experts, both from within and outside of the public sector, on the drivers of digital government reforms. These experts agreed that because "citizens, businesses, and politicians experience the technological change in their environment, life, and work, [they] expect public administrations to adapt accordingly and to provide similar technology in their public service delivery" (Mergel et al., 2019, p. 2). Echoing this view, Canada's first Minister of Digital Government explained in 2018 that "we can't be a Blockbuster government serving a Netflix citizenry" (Brison, 2018, para. 23).

With this orthodoxy so firmly settled, the bulk of the existing research on digital government has focused not on how governments should be reimagined for a digital age—on the target and goals of reform—but rather on the means by which governments can adapt to become more horizontal, entrepreneurial, data-driven, and user-focused. This research emphasizes in particular the barriers that prevent these digital era reforms from being implemented and laments the bureaucratic risk aversion, dated legal and policy instruments, and skills gaps that prevent governments from modernizing into competent, digital-ready organizations that satisfy the expectations of their digital citizenry (Clarke, 2019; Longley & Zimmerman, 2011; Margetts & Dunleavy, 2013).

Until recently, this focus on barriers and the various means by which they might be tackled was inevitable, at least as far as empirical studies of digital government went. Few governments were actually implementing the reforms that the digital government orthodoxy calls for, so these reforms and their effects on governance could not be studied in action. However, in the past few years, a number of governments have made notable investments in digital era reforms, such that the digital government orthodoxy now at work is to scale, or at least at more advanced stages of implementation. In Canada, we see this in the creation of digital government units at the federal level, and provincially in Ontario and Nova Scotia. We also see this orthodoxy at play in new pieces of legislation, as in Ontario's recently introduced *Simpler, Faster, Better Services Act* (2019), and in the introduction of new senior leadership roles across a range of Canadian governments, such as deputy minister-level chief digital officers and ministers of digital government. Aspects of the new digital government orthodoxy are also driving interest in so-called smart city initiatives at the municipal level across Canada, and underpinned the recently concluded federal Smart Cities Challenge.[2]

These initiatives open up an important new avenue of research for digital government scholars and policy-makers. It is now possible not simply to probe the reasons the digital government orthodoxy has not been implemented, but rather to investigate the effects these reforms have on public sector governance when they are put to work. Early investigations in this space raise a crucial and until now largely overlooked question: Have we been too quick and uncritical in adopting the new digital government orthodoxy as a superior model of public management, one that should be aggressively pursued to meet citizen expectations? The next section responds to this question, focusing on data governance dilemmas as just one set of challenges that accompanies the new digital government orthodoxy when it is put into practice.

Data Governance: An Overlooked but Crucial Issue for Digital Governments

Three recent Canadian cases illustrate the data governance challenges that can arise when the new digital government orthodoxy is implemented. These cases are already inspiring, and should further spur, a research agenda that unpacks, critiques, and adds greater nuance to the digital government orthodoxy that has become widely accepted as gospel in the literature and in practice to date.

Case 1. Public Data Pulls from Private Actors: Statistics Canada and Canadians' Financial Data

In 2018, Statistics Canada requested the collection of detailed personal financial information of over 500,000 Canadians from the country's largest banks. The request was permitted under both the *Statistics Act* (1985) and the *Personal Information Protection and*

Electronic Documents Act (PIPEDA, 2000), given the data's collection could be justified on the grounds that such data supports government administration. Moreover, internationally, many jurisdictions see their financial institutions share such data with their governments in order to support government policy work. However, the initiative was quickly cancelled in response to mass public outrage following its announcement.

Citizens expressed concerns about privacy infringements, but also a broader set of data governance questions, including those covering how such data would be used by the government, and specifically whether it could be applied to target and punish citizens by, for instance, being shared with police in criminal investigations, or if such data were used to identify fraudulent government benefits or tax claims. Adding to these concerns, critics questioned whether Statistics Canada had sufficiently robust cybersecurity measures in place to protect the personal financial data of citizens that it sought to collect. Most fundamentally, the case illustrates the potential mismatch between pre–digital era laws governing public use of data—in this case, laws allowing Statistics Canada to ask private firms to share their documents and information for use in public administration—and the realities of the scope and scale of data and the sophisticated data analytic techniques that are now available to private and public firms (Scassa, 2018a).

Case 2. Governments Sharing Data with Governments: "Tell Us Once" Digital Service Reforms

So-called tell us once service reforms dictate that when citizens submit information to government it should be shared across different departments so that it need not be resubmitted by citizens at subsequent interactions. This approach is now being pursued globally as a best practice in digital era service design, including in Canada between different orders of Canadian government through the recently developed Canadian Digital Exchange Platform (D'Andrea, 2018; Treasury Board Secretariat [TBS], 2018a).

The "tell us once" model is justified on the grounds that it supports horizontal, "joined up" government and service design which better meets the needs of users, who are presumed to be little interested in repeatedly entering information into time-consuming government forms. At the same time, "tell us once" initiatives raise a range of controversial data governance questions for Canadian governments.

At present, outside certain exemptions, the *Privacy Act* (1985) does not allow personal information collected by government to be disclosed to other actors (even within the same government) without consent, unless such disclosure is compatible with the purpose for which the information was collected or the information will be used in a way that is consistent with that purpose.

To navigate this legislative constraint, early forays into "tell us once" approaches that facilitate data sharing rely on an opt-in, consent-based model to support such data exchange. Yet, as Teresa Scassa explores in further detail in Chapter 9, and as already noted in the case of Statistics Canada's efforts to collect banking data, existing models of consent and the broader legislative regime protecting privacy rights in Canada are widely viewed as ineffective and ill-equipped for the dynamics of digital era data collection and use. Reflecting this perspective in the context of "tell us once" initiatives challenging departmental silos, a representative of the Office of the Privacy Commissioner explained in a 2016 speech that "while silos come crashing down in the name of modernization, the pillars of privacy protection that once accompanied them are not being replaced by anything nearly as modern" (Kosseim, 2016, para. 9).

Beyond these privacy concerns, the "tell us once" initiative also raises questions about which government actors will have access to citizen data and for what purposes; how such data can be applied to decisions about, for example, an individual's eligibility for particular services or benefits; and for what purposes linked data could be used to "nudge" certain behaviours among citizens.

Case 3. Private Data Governance as Governance Writ Large: The Case of Sidewalk Toronto

In 2017 Waterfront Toronto, a joint federal-provincial-municipal public corporation, issued a request for proposals for a "smart city" development within Toronto's Quayside District. Sidewalk Labs, a sibling company to Google within the Alphabet corporate family, was selected to submit a proposal for the development. Sidewalk Labs' proposal for the Toronto development was released in June 2019 (Sidewalk Toronto, 2019).

As with smart city initiatives globally, Sidewalk Toronto draws on the logic of the new digital government orthodoxy, promising more efficient, effective, and user-friendly local services through data-driven decision-making, data exchange between and among public and private actors, digital user feedback mechanisms, and bottom-up entrepreneurial innovation.

At the same time, the development has been challenged for potentially breaching basic standards of democratic accountability, a critique that has recently been launched at smart cities internationally (Green, 2019; Tieman, 2017; Wylie, 2017).

Most commonly, media and other public commentators seize on the privacy breaches that ubiquitous sensor technologies and video monitoring may usher in (van Zoonen, 2016). But the Sidewalk Toronto case also puts on the table more fundamental questions about the role that private firms should play in the governance of public services and spaces (Scassa, 2018b; Wylie, 2019).

This is not an entirely new concern. There is a long-standing literature and public discourse targeting the risks inherent in public service privatization (Christensen & Lægreid, 2002; VanDerWerff, 1998) and the use of public-private partnerships for land development (Krawchenko & Stoney, 2011). The digital government literature in particular is already preoccupied with the risks of private sector involvement in digital public service design and delivery (see Dunleavy et al., 2006; Johnson & Robinson, 2014), as evident in tech firms' provision of cloud computing capacity to governments, and in the role of banks in supporting online identity verification for government services (a practice adopted by the Government of Canada and others). However, the Sidewalk Toronto case vividly illustrates how private governance of public services and spaces can become more fraught with risks when it also involves vast data collection and data-driven decision-making. Do citizens want such data to be collected, and how would they want them applied to decisions around the design and management of their communities? Should such data be shared with the public, with other private firms, or with government, and under what conditions and for what purposes?

Most importantly, how should we go about answering these questions? Do we need new, private governance mechanisms to address these challenges, or are our governments equipped to provide sufficient oversight to design and manage the data governance arrangements necessitated by smart cities?

The Sidewalk Toronto case underscores how data governance can slide into governance in general. When public services and spaces are digitized, they produce and are subsequently shaped by vast troves of data. In these circumstances, the data steward (the actor or actors that control and manage those data) become de facto or de jure depending on the arrangement, the dominant governance actor wielding policy, oversight, and regulatory controls.

It is far from certain that in the case of digital government reforms involving private actors, the state is occupying a role as either the data steward itself or as an overseeing body that has the upper hand over private actors taking on this data stewardship role on their behalf. Where governments do not occupy either of these two roles, it is unclear how any data governance arrangement involving public spaces, services, or goods is democratically accountable.

Next Steps: A Research and Policy Agenda to Improve Data Governance and Digital Government in Canada

The data governance dilemmas discussed in this chapter should not necessarily lead the scholarly or practitioner community to discard wholesale the digital government orthodoxy that has emerged as the gold standard globally for contemporary public management. Rather, these data governance dilemmas should instead inspire a new research and policy agenda that refines this orthodoxy by balancing its goals of innovation, efficiency gains, and service improvements with sufficient attention to core democratic principles of equity, representation, and accountability. This work should be guided by three objectives.

Foster Greater Government-Researcher Engagement

In some respects, governments are further ahead of the public management and administration research community in awakening to the data governance challenges that accompany digital government reforms. Estonia, widely considered a global digital government leader, is regularly applauded for the security and privacy measures that shape how data are collected, shared, and used by government agencies. Likewise, the European Union's *General Data Protection Regulation* (GDPR) of 2016 sets comparatively robust standards for data minimization and consent. In Canada, the federal government has received international attention for recently developed frameworks on the responsible use of artificial intelligence in government (TBS, 2018b). We also see an acute appreciation for the data governance issues at play in digital reforms among senior executives on the digital file in Canada, as evident in testimony provided by government officials in 2019 to a parliamentary study of privacy and digital government services (ETHI, 2019b).

Moreover, Canadian governments are investing to varying degrees in the digital skillsets and data literacy of their existing staff, acknowledging that they will be ill situated to tackle data governance challenges without this expertise on hand. For example, the Canada School of Public Service launched a new Digital Academy in 2018, and certain governments are working with the non-profit Code for Canada to recruit tech talent on short-term contracts.

These government-led efforts can only be improved by greater contributions and scrutiny from the research community. At a basic level, academic partnerships may be one way of addressing the digital skills and data expertise shortage in government in the short term.

More importantly, the research community needs to scrutinize the policy and legislative changes that are accompanying digital reforms. That said, in some jurisdictions, these changes are emerging at such a large scale and such a rapid pace that deep engagement from researchers becomes incredibly taxing, and in certain cases, simply unrealistic. For instance, Ontario's new *Simpler, Faster, Better Services Act* (2019) contemplates changes to a wide range of policies and legislative regimes, covering procurement, privacy, communications, and data sharing. The act was passed in the spring of 2019, and at the time of writing, three discussion papers soliciting feedback were to be released in the fall of the same year. The data strategy implementing its directives was set to be launched by the end of 2019. The speed with which this potentially massive set of reforms will be designed and implemented demands enormous, and arguably unrealistic, turnaround times for researchers hoping to contribute to the consultations.

In considering researchers' roles in this external oversight, it is important to note that data governance reforms emerging across Canadian governments are still often primarily rationalized on the grounds that they will lead to more efficient and user-friendly services, echoing the language of current digital government orthodoxy. This leaves open the question of whether and how these objectives will be balanced in practice with concerns such as equity, representation, and accountability—concerns which may add time and costs to digital reforms or may justify halting them altogether. In these cases, it is essential that the research community illuminate the democratic principles that may be traded away in the name of digital service "innovations" and expose cases of "ethics washing" at play in data governance regimes.

In addition, researchers should ensure that the scope of data governance regimes introduced by governments is not focused on the narrow sub-issue of privacy alone, which to date has tended to be the dominant if not sole focus of governments claiming to be protecting citizens' digital rights amid new approaches to data collection and use. For example, documents discussing "tell us once" service reforms only mention privacy as a counterweight concern that will temper the initiative (see TBS, 2018a). And notably, the parliamentary study discussed in this chapter is titled *"Privacy* of Digital Government Services" (ETHI, 2019b, emphasis added), a focus that at times led committee members to ask witnesses to artificially and awkwardly limit their testimony on data governance and digital services solely to this one sub-issue.[3] Privacy protections absolutely deserve significant attention when designing data governance regimes but addressing privacy concerns alone is insufficient.

Finally, the research community should play an auditing function in evaluating the data governance arrangements that governments are already adopting, in particular in cases where these arrangements are not explicit either in their design or in their publicization, and where they involve private actors as mediators between citizens and state services. For instance, Canadians now use a host of privately run mobile apps and digital tools that support public service delivery (e.g., transit apps and tax filing software such as TurboTax). Researchers need to probe how data generated from these privately delivered services are managed and shared (or not) with private and government actors, and whether these services use and share data in ways that marginalize or benefit certain populations over others (Clarke, 2018, 2019; Scassa, 2015).

Uncover Canadians' Views on Data Governance and Digital Government Services

Remarkably—given the frequency with which this claim is made—there appears to be no concrete data to support the idea that citizens are disenchanted with their governments because the services they offer are viewed as below par compared to those on offer from Amazon and Google. To be sure, despite rising slightly in 2019, Canadians' reported levels of trust in government remain low (Edelman, 2019). However, studies on citizen trust are typically unable to unpack distinctions between the public's views of government in general and the civil service specifically. And even if low trust scores do reflect citizens' views of the civil service specifically—versus, say, Parliament, parties, or their local representatives—there is no evidence to suggest that poor public service experiences necessarily drive this disillusionment. Moreover, other studies, such as the one reported on by Petit-Vouriot and Morden in Chapter 2, suggest that Canadians are in general satisfied with their democracy (although again, such findings do not necessarily speak to citizens' views on public service quality per se, but rather the quality of elected representatives, political processes, etc.).

Observational studies connecting service experience and trust in government have at best identified a correlation between these variables; it remains unclear if trust in government can be improved by raising the quality of the public services a government offers (Bouckaert & van de Walle, 2003; Lægreid & Christensen, 2005). Moreover, studies on the trust-service relationship have not yet unpacked how the data governance arrangements underpinning a digital service innovation affect citizen trust in the state.

This last point is important to underscore since, as noted initially, the digital government orthodoxy has to date primarily been justified by the claim that governments will become redundant and that we will face a crisis of confidence in the state if government does not "meet citizen expectations." At present, we know very little about what these expectations are. We have no evidence to suggest that citizens want or expect their public services to look like those of private technology firms, and we may in fact find that citizens are ever less enthused by this proposition in the wake of the Facebook-Cambridge Analytica scandal and given daily reports of mass data breaches and controversial data mining conducted by firms in the private sector (Nair, 2019).

In fact, the little evidence we do have on citizen views of digital reforms suggests that Canadians do not unconditionally prioritize speedy, seamless service delivery when it comes to the online services they receive. For example, a 2018 study of citizens' views of smart cities found that, with some variation across demographics, Canadians are worried about how their data is collected, sold, and used to shape their behaviours in their cities and that they are unhappy with the current models of consent they are offered by governments and private firms (Bannerman & Orasch, 2019). Similarly, polling from Ipsos and the World Economic Forum suggests that Canadians have greater trust in the state than in the private sector to handle their data (Colledge, 2019). Another poll from the Canadian Marketing Association found that just over three quarters of Canadians (76 percent) are comfortable with personal data being shared when this comes with a benefit (e.g., an improved service) and when the data is properly secured (Canadian Marketing Association, 2018). Focusing again on privacy concerns at play in "tell us once" initiatives specifically, 2018 public opinion research conducted by the Government of Canada found that 58 percent of Canadians are very or somewhat comfortable with their personal information being shared across federal services, and between the federal and provincial and territorial governments. Here again, though, the research found that citizens' support for data sharing was conditional on their being given the option to opt in or out of these arrangements, and that they would want to know what information was being shared, with whom, for what purpose, and that the information would be secure (Phoenix Strategy Perspectives, 2018).

These findings only uncover the tip of the iceberg. In certain respects they raise more questions than answers when it comes to understanding what citizens value and expect regarding the use of their personal information, and data more generally, in the design and delivery of government services. For instance, existing research rarely asks citizens to factor in concrete trade-offs between data policy and service reforms when probing views on data governance, nor do studies sufficiently evaluate whether respondents understand the risks and benefits that certain data governance reforms would usher in.

In addition, we are sorely lacking in data that identifies how citizen views on data governance questions vary across demographics, and especially among traditionally marginalized populations (but see Bannerman & Orasch, 2019; Colledge, 2019). This is a particularly important avenue of enquiry given the role that data collection and surveillance have historically played and continue to play in the racial targeting (Lum & Isaac, 2016) and colonial oppression of Indigenous people (Kukutai & Taylor, 2016; Rainie et al., 2019).

Last, we lack data evaluating citizens' views on various solutions to public data governance dilemmas. For instance, much attention has been paid of late to data trusts and to oversight models that allow citizens to audit who accesses their data across government (the model adopted in Estonia, for instance). Yet it remains unclear if these sorts of governance models will alleviate citizen concerns over governments' and private actors' collection and use of data.

In sum, without more varied and nuanced data describing public expectations and concerns on public data governance, governments and researchers driving ambitious data governance reforms in the name of service improvements are largely acting blindly on a set of assumptions that may lead to policy choices that betray rather than meet citizen expectations, especially in cases where citizens actually expect their governments to act in accordance with the democratic compact—respecting principles of procedural fairness, equity, and transparency—and not that they strictly deliver fast and easy-to-use services.

Engage a Broad, Multidisciplinary Group of Researchers

The field of critical data studies and the literature on smart cities in particular have spent considerable time and effort to dig into the challenges of data governance facing today's public institutions (Cardullo & Kitchin, 2018; Lauriault & McGuire, 2008). There are few connections between this research and that produced by academics focused on digital government and public administration reform. There is equally room for fruitful collaboration between public policy and administration scholars, legal academics, philosophers, and computer and data scientists; each of these disciplines will likely hold part of the answer to the ethical dilemmas that data governance raises for today's governments.

Researchers across all of these fields will strengthen their analyses by taking a longer historical view of the issues they are tackling. The pre-digital literature on co-production, horizontal governance, public management reform, and public service privatization are rich with insights that are relevant to current debates on data governance. In fact, many of the dilemmas on the table today were entirely predictable had researchers and practitioners crafting and advocating for the new digital government orthodoxy taken heed of the lessons offered by these fields of study (Ansell & Gash, 2007; Brandsen & Pestoff, 2006; Christensen & Lægreid, 2002; Needham, 2008; Peters, 1998; Phillips & Howard, 2012). In particular, research on the failures of mass privatization under the New Public Management reforms of the 1980s and on the historical barriers to effective and democratically accountable cross-government collaboration have much to offer those grappling with the challenges of digital era data governance (Clarke, 2018).

Conclusion

A "Made in Canada" approach to digital government must be steeped in the values and democratic principles held by Canadians. These values and principles—and not simply the desire for fast, friction-free online transactions—invariably drive citizen expectations for government services. Accounting for these values may mean that Canadian digital government moves more carefully, with services remaining in some instances slower or clunkier than what we see in the private sector or in other government jurisdictions that are less concerned with or obliged to respect these principles. The upside: Canadians' faith in the democratic accountability of their state will remain intact (or at least not be further degraded). On this front, Canadian academics and policy-makers should become far less concerned with global rankings of digital government innovation. Citizens may be entirely comfortable seeing their government fall behind China, Denmark, India, and Singapore if lagged digital adoption also comes with robust protections for things like procedural fairness, privacy, and transparency.

Yet, at present, the digital government orthodoxy dominating research and practice leave little space to acknowledge the value that lagged adoption may play in securing sustainable, democratically legitimate digital government reform. To be sure, further research may reveal that Canadians "want it all"—services that rival those of Amazon alongside robust democratic controls, transparent process, and privacy protections.[4] In this case, having identified these potentially competing expectations, the task for governments and their observers becomes one of public education about the trade-offs inherent in various data governance and digital government arrangements, in order to support more informed public debate on these questions. But before any of this work can begin, we need far more research to understand how data governance is currently unfolding in Canada and, most importantly, how Canadians want it to unfold. This chapter's provocations aim to kickstart this essential new research and policy agenda.

Acknowledgements

The author would like to acknowledge the financial support of Carleton University's Faculty of Public Affairs Research Excellence Chair program, and the Social Sciences and Humanities Research Council (grant no. 430-2015-00501).

Notes

1. Calls for "joined up" government (Bakvis & Juillet, 2004; Peters, 1998), public sector innovation (Bason, 2010; Borins, 2001; Osborne & Gaebler, 1992), investment in technocratic expertise (Aucoin & Bakvis, 2005; Wellstead, 2019), transparency (Yu & Robinson, 2012), evidence-based policy-making and engagement with service users (Axworthy & Burch, 2010; Pressman et al., 1973) are well established, and form part of a longer history of public management reforms that have since at least the 1970s explicitly endeavoured to upend the practices of twentieth-century industrial models of public sector bureaucracy (Clarke, 2019).

2. For more information on the Smart Cities Challenge, see: https://www.infrastructure.gc.ca/cities-villes/index-eng.html.

3. At one point in the committee proceedings, Member of Parliament and committee member Charlie Angus said,

    > Well, I have my government phone here and I get messages all the time telling me that I have to do such-and-such function right away, and I try to do the function and then it says that I'm not allowed to do it, because it won't recognize my phone. That's all interesting, but it's not what our committee is here to discuss. We are the privacy, ethics and accountability committee; we're not the government operations committee. There are many cool things and many neat things we could do. We could try saying that we're doing better government services, and if we believe that we can turn it all around, I think that's great. But our committee's job is to protect citizen rights, end of story. (ETHI, 2019a, paras. 152–153)

4. See David Eaves's testimony to the House of Commons Standing Committee on Access to Information, Privacy and Ethics (ETHI, 2019a).

References

Ansell, C., & Gash, A. (2007). Collaborative governance in theory and practice. *Journal of Public Administration Research and Theory, 18*(4), 543–571.

Aucoin, P., & Bakvis, H. (2005). Public service reform and policy capacity: Recruiting and retaining the best and the brightest. In M. Painter & J. Pierre (Eds.), *Challenges to state policy capacity: Global trends and comparative perspectives* (pp. 185–204). Palgrave Macmillan.

Axworthy, T. S., & Burch, J. (2010). *Closing the implementation gap: Improving capacity, accountability, performance and human resource quality in the Canadian and Ontario public service.* Queen's University. http://www.queensu.ca/csd/sites/webpublish.queensu.ca.csdwww/files/files/publications/wps/Closing_Gap_Main.pdf

Bakvis, H., & Juillet, L. (2004). *The horizontal challenge: Line departments, central agencies and leadership.* Canada School of Public Service.

Bannerman, S., & Orasch, A. K. (2019). *Privacy and smart cities: A Canadian survey.* McMaster University. https://smartcityprivacy.ca/wp-content/uploads/2019/01/Bannerman-Orasch-Privacy-and-Smart-Cities-A-Canadian-Survey-v1-2019.pdf

Bason, C. (2010). *Leading public sector innovation: Co-creating for a better society.* Policy Press.

Borins, S. (2001). Innovation, success and failure in public management research: Some methodological reflections. *Public Management Review, 3*(1), 3–17.

Bouckaert, G., & van de Walle, S. (2003). Comparing measures of citizen trust and user satisfaction as indicators of "good governance": Difficulties in linking trust and satisfaction indicators. *International Review of Administrative Sciences, 69*(3), 329–343.

Brandsen, T., & Pestoff, V. (2006). Co-production, the third sector and the delivery of public services. *Public Management Review, 8*(4), 493–501.

Brison, S. (2018, March 11). *Democratic government. Is there an app for that?* [Speech]. TEDxMoncton, Moncton, New Brunswick. Retrieved June 27, 2019, from https://www.canada.ca/en/treasury-board-secretariat/news/2018/02/speaking_notes_forthehonourablescottbrisonpresidentofthetreasury.html

Canada, House of Commons, Standing Committee on Access to Information, Privacy and Ethics [ETHI]. (2019a, February 7). [Evidence]. Meeting no. 135. 42nd Parliament, 1st Session. https://www.ourcommons.ca/DocumentViewer/en/42-1/ETHI/meeting-135/evidence

Canada, House of Commons, Standing Committee on Access to Information, Privacy and Ethics [ETHI]. (2019b, June). [Privacy and digital government services]. Committee report no. 19. 42nd Parliament, 1st Session. https://www.ourcommons.ca/DocumentViewer/en/42-1/ETHI/report-19/

Canadian Marketing Association. (2018, May 24). *A majority of Canadians are OK with sharing their personal data* [Press release]. Retrieved June 28, 2019, from https://www.the-cma.org/resource/newsroom/2018/majority-of-canadians-are-ok-with-sharing-their-personal-data

Cardullo, P., & Kitchin, R. (2018). Smart urbanism and smart citizenship: The neoliberal logic of "citizen-focused" smart cities in Europe. *Environment and Planning C: Politics and Space, 37*(5), 813–830.

Christensen, T., & Lægreid, P. (2002). New public management: Puzzles of democracy and the influence of citizens. *Journal of Political Philosophy, 10*(3), 267–295.

Clarke, A. (2017). Digital government units: Origins, orthodoxy and critical considerations for public management theory and practice. https://papers.ssrn.com/sol3/papers.cfm?abstract_id=3001188

Clarke, A. (2018). The evolving role of non-state actors in digital era government. https://papers.ssrn.com/sol3/papers.cfm?abstract_id=3268084

Clarke, A. (2019). *Opening the government of Canada: The federal bureaucracy in the digital age*. UBC Press.

Colledge, M. (2019, April). Do Canadians Know What Is Happening with Their Personal Information and Who Do They Trust? Ipsos Public Affairs. Presentation delivered at Carleton University, Ottawa.

D'Andrea, T. [@TDAndrea23]. (2018, March 16). *Our Digital Exchange Platform (DXP) will provide the foundation for OneGC, allowing systems to easily share information with provinces, territories...* [Tweet]. Twitter. Retrieved June 28, 2019, from https://twitter.com/tdandrea23/status/9747176090 13739520?lang=en

Dunleavy, P., Margetts, H., Bastow, S., & Tinkler, J. (2006). *Digital era governance: IT corporations, the state, and e-government*. Oxford University Press.

Edelman. (2019). *2019 Edelman trust barometer*. https://www.edelman.com/sites/g/files/aatuss191/files/2019-02/2019_Edelman_Trust_Barometer_Executive_Summary.pdf

Green, B. (2019). *The smart enough city: Putting technology in its place to reclaim our urban future*. The MIT Press.

Johnson, P., & Robinson, P. (2014). Civic Hackathons: Innovation, Procurement, or Civic Engagement?: Civic Hackathon: Procurement or Civic Engagement? *Review of Policy Research, 31*(4), 349–57.

Kosseim, P. (2016, December 5). *Promoting transparency and protecting privacy: What better government and public trust mean in a digital era* [Address]. Preparing for the Future of Data-Rich Environments in Canada

Conference, Ottawa, Canada. https://www.priv.gc.ca/en/opc-news/speeches/2016/sp-d_20161205_pk/

Krawchenko, T., & Stoney, C. (2011). Public-private partnerships and the public interest: A case study of Ottawa's Lansdowne Park development. *Canadian Journal of Non-profit and Social Economy Research, 2*(2), 74–90.

Kukutai, T., & Taylor, J. (Eds.). (2016). *Indigenous data sovereignty: Toward an agenda*. Australian National University Press. http://www.oapen.org/download?type=document&docid=624262

Lægreid, P., & Christensen, T. (2005). Trust in government: The relative importance of service satisfaction, political factors, and demography. *Public Performance & Management Review, 28*(4), 679–690.

Lauriault, T. P., & McGuire, H. (2008, February). *Data access in Canada: CivicAccess.ca*. Technology Innovation Management Review. http://timreview.ca/article/120

Longley, C., & Zimmerman, D. (2011). Practitioner response to "beyond smokestacks and silos: Open-source, web-enabled coordination in organizations and networks." *Public Administration Review, 71*(5), 697–699.

Loosemore, T. [@tomskitomski] (2016, May 10). *Digital: Applying the culture, practices, processes & technologies of the Internet-era to respond to people's raised expectations* [Tweet]. Twitter. https://twitter.com/tomskitomski/status/729974444794494976

Lum, K., & Isaac, W. (2016). To predict and serve? *Significance, 13*(5), 14–19.

Margetts, H., & Dunleavy, P. (2013). The second wave of digital-era governance: A quasi-paradigm for government on the Web. *Philosophical Transactions of the Royal Society A: Mathematical, Physical and Engineering Sciences, 371*, 20120382. https://royalsocietypublishing.org/doi/10.1098/rsta.2012.0382

Mergel, I. (2017). *Digital service teams: Challenges and recommendations for government*. IBM Center for The Business of Government. http://www.businessofgovernment.org/report/digital-service-teams-challenges-and-recommendations-government

Mergel, I., Edelmann, N., & Haug, N. (2019). Defining digital transformation: Results from expert interviews. *Government Information Quarterly, 36*(4), 101–385.

Nair, S. (2019, April 8). *Trust in tech is wavering and companies must act*. Edelman. Retrieved July 31, 2019, from https://www.edelman.com/research/2019-trust-tech-wavering-companies-must-act

Needham, C. (2008). Realising the potential of co-production: Negotiating improvements in public services. *Social Policy and Society, 7*(2), 221–231.

O'Reilly, T. (2011). Government as a platform. *Innovations, 6*, 13–40.

Osborne, D., & Gaebler, T. (1992). *Reinventing government: How the entrepreneurial spirit is transforming the public sector.* Plume.

Personal Information Protection and Electronic Documents Act [PIPEDA], S.C. 2000, c. 5.

Peters, B. G. (1998). Managing horizontal government: The politics of coordination. *Public Administration, 76*(2), 295–311.

Phillips, S. D., & Howard, C. (2012). Moving away from hierarchy: Do horizontality, partnerships and distributed governance really signify the end of accountability? In H. Bakvis & M. D. Jarvis (Eds.), *From new public management to new political governance: Essays in honour of Peter C. Aucoin* (pp. 314–341). McGill-Queen's University Press.

Phoenix Strategy Perspectives. (2018). *Service delivery and privacy public opinion research.* http://epe.lac-bac.gc.ca/100/200/301/pwgsc-tpsgc/por-ef/treasury_board/2018/092-17-e/summary/summary-eng.html

Pressman, J. L., Wildavsky, A. B., & Oakland Project. (1973). *Implementation: How great expectations in Washington are dashed in Oakland: Or, why it's amazing that federal programs work at all, this being a saga of the economic development administration as told by two sympathetic observers who seek to build morals on a foundation of ruined hopes.* University of California Press.

Privacy Act, R.S.C., 1985, c. P-21.

Rainie, S. C., Kukutai, T., Walter, M., Figueroa-Rodriguez, O. L., Walker, J., & Axelsson, P. (2019). Issues in open data—Indigenous data sovereignty. In T. Davies, S. Walker, M. Rubinstein, & F. Perini (Eds.), *The state of open data: Histories and horizons.* https://www.stateofopendata.od4d.net/chapters/issues/indigenous-data.html

Regulation (EU) 2016/679 of the European Parliament and of the Council of 27 April 2016 on the protection of natural persons with regard to the processing of personal data and on the free movement of such data, and repealing Directive 95/46/EC (General Data Protection Regulation) [GDPR], O.J., L. 119, 4.5.2016, p. 1–88.

Scassa, T. (2015). Public transit data through an intellectual property lens: Lessons about open data. *Fordham Urban Law Journal, 41*(5), 1759–1810.

Scassa, T. (2018a, October 31). Statistics Canada faces backlash over collection of personal financial information (or: Teaching an old law new tricks). Retrieved June 28, 2019, from https://www.teresascassa.ca/index.php?option=com_k2&view=item&id=291:statistics-canada-faces-backlash-over-collection-of-personal-financial-information-or-teaching-an-old-law-new-tricks&Itemid=80

Scassa, T. (2018b, November 25). *Some thoughts on smart cities and data governance.* Retrieved June 28, 2019, from https://www.teresascassa.ca/index.php?option=com_k2&view=item&id=293:some-thoughts-on-smart-cities-and-data-governance&Itemid=80

Sidewalk Toronto. (2019). Documents. Retrieved June 28, 2019, from https://www.sidewalktoronto.ca/documents/

Simpler, Faster, Better Services Act, 2019, S.O. 2019, c. 7, Sched. 56.

Statistics Act, R.S.C., c. S-19 (1985).

Treasury Board Secretariat [TBS]. (2018a). *Digital operations strategic plan: 2018–2022.* Retrieved June 28, 2019, from https://www.canada.ca/en/government/system/digital-government/digital-operations-strategic-plan-2018-2022.html

Treasury Board Secretariat [TBS]. (2018b, November 22). *Responsible use of artificial intelligence (AI).* Retrieved June 28, 2019, from https://www.canada.ca/en/government/system/digital-government/modern-emerging-technologies/responsible-use-ai.html

Tieman, R. (2017, October 26). *Barcelona: Smart city revolution in progress.* Financial Times. Retrieved October 26, 2018, from https://www.ft.com/content/6d2fe2a8-722c-11e7-93ff-99f383b09ff9

VanDerWerff, J. A. (1998). Privatization and citizen empowerment. *Journal of Public Administration Research & Theory, 8*(2), 276.

van Zoonen, L. (2016). Privacy concerns in smart cities. *Government Information Quarterly, 33*(3), 472–480.

Wellstead, A. M. (2019). From Fellegi to Fonberg: Canada's policy capacity Groundhog Day? *Canadian Public Administration, 62*(1), 166–172

Wylie, B. (2017, December 5). Smart communities need smart governance. *The Globe and Mail.* https://www.theglobeandmail.com/opinion/smart-communities-need-smart-governance/article37218398/

Wylie, B. (2019, April 20). *Sidewalk Toronto: Violating democracy, entrenching the status quo, making markets of the commons.* Medium. Retrieved June 28, 2019, from https://medium.com/@biancawylie/sidewalk-toronto-violating-democracy-entrenching-the-status-quo-making-markets-of-the-commons-8a71404d4809

Yu, H., & Robinson, D. G. (2012). The new ambiguity of "open government." *UCLA Law Review Discourse, 59,* 178–208.

CHAPTER 6

The Conversation Canada: Not-for-Profit Journalism in a Time of Commercial Media Decline

Mary Lynn Young and Alfred Hermida

Abstract

This chapter tackles two pressing gaps in the journalism studies literature on the business of news in Canada: analysis of digital born journalism organizations and early implications of not-for-profit journalism. We use a case study approach to assess the launch and growth of The Conversation Canada, a national journalism organization that launched in 2017, and is one of eight affiliates of the global not-for-profit Conversation network of journalism sites. This case study is timely as Canada is seeing a growth in digital-born journalism organizations, which are often seen as innovators and saviours compared to legacy media. At the same time, not-for-profit and publicly funded journalism organizations are increasingly considered an antidote to commercial journalism decline. We find The Conversation Canada contributing to journalism and innovating in its reach to traditional and non-elite audiences, its experimentation with not-for-profit democratic organizational models, and its access to non-traditional revenue sources in the form of university membership fees and competitive research funding.

This chapter tackles two pressing gaps in the journalism studies literature on the business of news in Canada: analysis of digital-born journalism organizations and early implications of not-for-profit journalism (Nielsen, 2019). We use a case study approach to assess the launch and growth of The Conversation Canada,[1] one of eight affiliates of the global not-for-profit The Conversation network of journalism sites. The journalism model of The Conversation is novel as it pairs academics and experienced journalist editors to create evidence-based explanatory journalism and commentary, distributing it for free to anyone to republish under a Creative Commons licence. We focus on a single case study of The Conversation Canada in its first few years of operation for three reasons.

First, Canada is seeing a growth in digital-born journalism organizations with approximately 70 journalism start-ups launching since 2000 (Hermida & Young, 2019a). Second, start-ups are often seen as saviours, "better able to embrace … innovation" than legacy journalism organizations (Deuze, 2017, p. 10). And third, not-for-profit and publicly funded journalism organizations are increasingly being seen as an antidote to a decline in commercial journalism (Pickard, 2017).

We also have unique access to the organization. We co-founded The Conversation Canada in 2017. We are current directors on the board of the not-for-profit organization that operates the site, the Academic Journalism Society. As a result, we approach this topic as both participant-observers and "reflective practitioners" (Iacono et al., 2009, p. 39). We find this stance an appropriate way to examine fast-changing and emergent industries such as the contemporary context for journalism (Iacono et al., 2009). In order to mitigate bias, we have built on an unpublished study of not-for-profit journalism start-ups by Taylor Owen (2017), and research on local news outlets by April Lindgren (2019). We also integrate other national comparison data to assess The Conversation Canada in its early development stage, as well as to locate it within larger changes in the journalism landscape (Hermida & Young, 2019b). Our goal in being transparent is to support knowledge generation and capacity building in this space. We do not work for, consult, or receive any revenue from our participation in The Conversation Canada or any related organization that would benefit from this article.

Similar to other media systems that have been well studied (Cagé, 2016; Deuze, 2017; Edge, 2016; Nielsen, 2019), the media system in Canada is seeing decline in some commercial journalism organizations, job loss in legacy media, and growth in digital-born journalism organizations, along with evidence of a shifting regulatory and policy climate toward government funding of the media (Edge, 2016; Owen, 2017; Public Policy Forum [PPF], 2017, 2018). The economic context is considered so dire for commercial journalism that the Canadian government has created a financial subsidy package for journalism organizations, beyond existing forms of financial support for the media sector and despite long-standing opposition to this policy approach. This funding includes more than $600 million to support journalism in the form of tax credits for labour and reader subscriptions, as well as an extension of the definition of charity to include journalism organizations. The Conversation Canada, along with some of the other digital-born journalism start-ups, as well as players in legacy media, stand to benefit from some of these policy changes.

We approach innovation and change in the journalism sector drawing from other studies that have examined a wide array of practices and forms as representative of "innovation" in journalism. These include: increases in creation and dissemination of online news (Boczkowski, 2009); newer forms of journalism (Zeller & Hermida, 2015); new business models (Nielsen, 2016); and newer roles, identities, and genres, along with shifting boundary work, in relation to who is a professional journalist and what they could and should do in relation to multiple and participatory publics (Lewis, 2012). Digital media and journalism organizations (such as The Conversation Canada) are also increasingly a vehicle through which citizens engage within a globally networked and "contested" public sphere (Wahl-Jorgensen et al., 2017, p. 743). According to Wahl-Jorgensen et al., "We are now living in a society whose discussion about itself no longer takes place primarily in and through conventional mainstream news media, such as newspapers, television, and radio, but is increasingly diverse, variegated, and fragmented through social media, blogs, and other platforms" (p. 743).

In this vein, we find evidence of innovation in the model of The Conversation Canada in three ways. First, The Conversation Canada has been able to increase global and non-elite dissemination of its journalism (through dissemination by global actors as well as peripheral journalism actors) in what has been considered a parochial national journalism landscape (Gasher, 2007; Hermida & Young, 2019b). Second, it has been able to experiment with not-for-profit democratic organizational models, which is an addition to the Canadian commercial journalism landscape. And third, its governance structure, along with its relationship to the higher education sector, has supported access to non-traditional seed capital and revenue sources in the form of university membership fees and competitive research funding. (Other digital-born journalism organizations in Canada have also been successful in the research funding space.) Long-term funding, however, remains a key goal, highlighting the challenges faced by early stage digital-born journalism organizations in similar media markets. This evidence of The Conversation Canada's impact is relevant to citizenship in a digital context, as it suggests that, at least in the digital-born journalism space in Canada, digital technologies are expanding the nature of identities vis-à-vis their analogue legacy media peers, as well as potentially offering research-driven journalism as a remedy to mis- and disinformation concerns in a contested digital ecosystem.

Not-for-Profit Journalism Models

Two emergent areas of investigation from journalism studies and the business of journalism are relevant to our research. They address questions that include: (1) whether not-for-profit and foundation-funded journalism models can and are living up to their potential to affect change, innovate in, and (by extension) "repair" or "reform" journalism (Benson, 2017; Cagé, 2016; Coates Nee, 2014; Graves & Konieczna, 2015); and (2) whether and how digital-born journalism start-ups and journalism organizations, specifically not-for-profit ones, are financially viable (Bruno & Nielson, 2012; Cagé, 2016; Deuze, 2017; Naldi & Picard, 2012; Nielsen, 2019).

A number of scholars have approached the first question from a variety of perspectives. One of the most provocative approaches that addresses largely commercial media systems, such as Canada's, is Julia Cagé's 2016 book *Saving the Media*. Cagé locates many of the problems of twentieth-century journalism in capitalism and in media ownership by the wealthy or by publicly traded companies. She argues that, as a result, the only way to save journalism is by shifting from a largely commercial governance model to a novel and hybrid not-for-profit democratic governance and revenue model that incorporates crowd funding.

At the same time, scholars have tried to assess whether not-for-profits and foundation-funded journalism organizations are part of a conscious effort to address, by repair or reform, some of the challenges and losses associated with twentieth century for-profit journalism models, drawing from economics (Cagé, 2016), from field studies (Benson, 2017; Graves & Konieczna, 2015), and from social responsibility theory (Coates Nee, 2014). For example, in their study of news sharing at US fact-checking organizations and investigative not-for-profits, Lucas Graves and Magda Konieczna (2015) find examples of field repair in which actors are uncoupling historic cultural and economic capital orientations as they "seek to legitimize new approaches and new ways of thinking about their work, as necessary to protect the autonomy and integrity of the field as a whole" (p. 1979).

The notion of whether not-for-profit news can save journalism has been addressed by other scholars largely through an examination of various funding models and their efficacy. Rodney Benson (2017) examined three types of news organizations—board membership, (US) foundation, and not-for-profit—to see if they are capable of reforming the field in an article titled: "Can foundations solve the journalism crisis?" The study surfaced concerns about funding bias, "media capture," and short-term funding cycles oriented around seed capital that prevented these organizations from reaching their potential. As a result, he argues that not-for-profit and philanthropic journalism "supplements and increasingly cooperates" with legacy journalism norms, practices, and models (2017, p. 4). He also argues that, similar to other studies, such journalism is more focused on repairing the current system than reforming it (2017, p. 4). For Benson, reform would require "fundamental changes in foundation operations and budgeting (e.g., more long-term, non-project-based, no-strings-attached funding), greater recourse to small donor 'crowd-funding' linked to more dispersed, democratic ownership power (Cagé, 2016), and more effective development of modes of distribution that reach beyond elite and partisan silos" (2017, p. 16).

Other studies have focused on the impact of various financial models, largely in the US or largely in a commercial context (or both), and their impact on success. In one of the few studies of not-for-profit journalism organization financing, Coates Nee (2014) interviewed ten US journalism leaders about the relationship between government funding and financial sustainability. Specifically, she was interested in whether increased government funding of news organizations is needed to respond to the industry's financial crisis. She found that access to diverse revenue streams is difficult, and relying on phi-lanthropy is "tenuous" (Coates Nee, 2014, p. 338). She also found an aversion to government funding. She noted, however, that a number of the organizations she studied use space at public universities and benefit from partnerships with other not-for-profits that may receive government subsidies. She concludes that, despite tax uncertain-ties for not-for-profits and the precedence for government loans to media in other national contexts, "Funding of independent commu-nity news startups will continue to be left to the marketplace, the benevolence of philanthropists, and the hope for voluntary public support" (p. 339).

Growing Digital Born Start-up Landscape in Canada

For this chapter, we completed an initial analysis of the digital-born journalism landscape and found that more than 70 media organiza-tions (both for-profit and not-for-profit) have launched in Canada since 2000 (Hermida & Young, 2019a). This research builds on Owen's unpublished 2017 study of not-for-profit and philanthropic journalism organizations, which found 14 distinct organizations in this space in Canada, including foundations. April Lindgren's (2019) research on local news found that 51 new local news outlets have opened in Canada since 2008, some due to mergers and launches of affiliates within existing organizations. Her study counts new outlets as part of existing chains; our count focuses on wholly new entities. Our research advances the literature on the business of journalism in Canada, as previous studies of the Canadian media landscape have tended to focus on commercial and publicly held companies, such as Canwest Global and regional newspaper groups (Edge, 2001, 2016), and market-level analyses of media competition and concentration (Edge, 2016; Winseck, 2010).

The more than 70 start-ups (compared to the United States, which has more than 230 members in the Institute for Nonprofit News) identified in total include a range of commercial, not-for-profit,[2] and charitable organizations, which are the three main vehicles (business corporation, not-for-profit organization, and registered charity) available for journalism organizations in Canada according to tax regulations (Manwaring & Valentine, 2010). Prominent commercial examples include Vancouver-based *National Observer*, which is owned and operated by the privately held

Observer Media Group, and The Tyee, launched in 2003. Foundation-funded outlets include *Hakai Magazine,* which is operated by the Tula Foundation. Not-for-profits include early digital-born entrants, such as Rabble.ca (founded in 2001) and funded through a mix of advertising and reader donations, as well as university-affiliated think tanks, such as the Centre for International Governance Innovation (CIGI).

Included in this list is The Conversation Canada, an independent not-for-profit which launched in June 2017, with five journalist-editors in two newsrooms located at the University of Toronto and University of British Columbia. It is affiliated with the Melbourne-based The Conversation Media Group, which runs operations in Australia and New Zealand. There are six other independent organizations in the The Conversation's network (Africa, France, Indonesia, Spain, the United Kingdom, and the United States). The Conversation network started in Australia, in 2011. A French-language site, La Conversation Canada, was launched in December 2018, with the newsroom based in Montréal. For the purposes of this chapter, we focus on the English-language site as we do not address the Francophone media environment in Canada.

To start with a brief background on the development of The Conversation Canada: we approached The Conversation Australia founder Andrew Jaspan toward the end of 2014 about the possibility of piloting a Canadian version. We received a small competitive federal research grant to start to explore its viability (see also Young & Hermida, 2017, in which we wrote about the launch process). We applied successfully for a larger competitive research grant (almost $200,000) in 2016 to pilot the site, and to develop the financial and organizational infrastructures for launch. In 2017, the not-for-profit society was incorporated with four founding board members. The board hired Scott White, a veteran journalist with an extensive leadership career in legacy media—largely with Canadian Press, the national wire service—as founding editor. The funding model (similar to the rest of The Conversation network of sites), included a combination of university membership fees (17 university members at launch and 27 by year two, out of the country's 94 universities, as identified by Universities Canada), foundation contributions, and government research funds.

As an affiliate of the global network, The Conversation Canada has a licence agreement with the Australia-based The Conversation Media Group. This agreement enabled the organization to offset significant technology infrastructure and start-up costs by accessing the existing network content management system, data analytics, and technology infrastructure for an annual fee. The agreement outlined costs for operational technology that were less than the percentage costs allocated by other digital-born journalism not-for-profits for which information is available. For example, Rabble.ca lists technology and server fees as 21 percent of overall operational costs in its 2016 reporting period, whereas the fees for The Conversation Canada have averaged less than 10 percent (between 7.5 percent and 9 percent) of operational costs.

Two years after launching in June 2019, The Conversation Canada was reaching approximately 1.5 million page views monthly, and a total of 31 million page views over 24 months of operation. These page views are both direct to the website and through the republishing of The Conversation articles on third-party publications in Canada and globally. In terms of on-site traffic, The Conversation Canada website had a total of 8 million unique visitors since launch in 2017, with 3 million in the first year and 5 million in the second. Republishers include a combination of legacy and non-traditional, non-elite outlets. The legacy journalism organizations include the *National Post*, *Maclean's*, *The Washington Post*, CNN, and the *Daily Mail*. Canadian outlets tend to access The Conversation content through the organization's relationship with Canadian Press, which shares its stories on the news wire. Among the non-traditional and non-elite outlets are Sci Fi Generation, IFLScience, Raw Story, and The Weather Network (Canada), which is the largest republisher in terms of reach. Overall, articles have found a significant reach outside of Canada, with the United States accounting for one third of page views. While page views are a widely used measure in the media industry, we are cognizant of their limitations, noting how they can be biased by automated bots and a small number of users who may be responsible for a number of page views.

These figures compare favourably with the average monthly page views, using data publicly reported by the organizations themselves, of two of the largest and most successful national digital-born journalism organizations since 2000. Rabble.ca, launched in 2001, reported 1.3 million unique users and more than 4 million page views in its 2018 annual report, with 87 percent of its readers from Canada and 14 percent [*sic*] from the States (Rabble.ca, 2018). The Observer Media Group, which launched its national site, *National Observer*, in

2015, had 500,000 average monthly page views (National Observer, n.d.). Other digital-born players are largely regional operations. The Tyee, one of the early digital-born journalism entrants in 2003, reports 500,000 to 1 million page views a month and between 300,000 and 400,000 unique visitors per month (The Tyee, n.d.). In the context of the larger media environment, the 2017 Public Policy Forum report on the state of the news media in Canada makes the point that the reach of digital-born organizations is still developing compared to their paid subscription-based commercial competitors such as *The Globe and Mail*, which had 7.4 million monthly unique visitors in 2019 (*The Globe and Mail*, 2019).

Beyond Elite Journalism Organizations

In terms of its early funding, The Conversation Canada is comparable with other digital-born organizations—not-for-profit and commercial—where there are figures available. Similar to the rest of The Conversation's network, the organization launched with almost $1.5 million in start-up funds over three years, and a funding model that combined university membership fees, government research funds, and philanthropy. Launch funding for The Conversation Canada compares favourably to examples of start-up funding for US journalism. Naldi and Picard (2012, p. 72) describe the not-for-profit MinnPost, which launched with more than US$1 million in foundation funding and grants, as "one of the most well-funded start-ups" in the United States.

A closer comparison to The Conversation Canada's not-for-profit structure in Canada is Rabble.ca, which launched in 2001 with $200,000 in funding—$120,000 of its start-up funds originating from one foundation (Kuitenbrouwer, 2001). Rabble.ca's 2018 annual report online indicates that its operating budget for 2018 was $350,408. The bulk of its funding originated from sustaining partners (largely labour organizations) at 49.8 percent and individual donations at 34.79 percent. Special events accounted for 0.01 percent, grants and sponsorship for 14.11 percent, and advertising for 0.57 percent (Rabble.ca, 2018). As a comparison for this level of funding, though not a digital-born venture, *The Walrus* magazine has been one of the most sustainably funded journalism charitable organizations in Canada in the not-for-profit space, with a $5 million endowment.

Similar to the findings of Deuze's 2017 global study of start-ups, The Conversation Canada's main funding sources were non-journalistic (as stated above, a combination of the higher education sector, government research funding, and a small amount from foundations). Its range of sources is distinct compared to those listed in the data from the Institute for Nonprofit News in the United States, which identifies four main revenue streams of its members: foundations (43 percent), individuals (39 percent), earned sources such as ads and events (12 percent), and other charitable sources (6 percent) (McLellan & Holcomb, 2020).

The Conversation Canada was perceived as an attractive opportunity to the higher education sector because of The Conversation Canada's growing commitment to knowledge mobilization and exchange, and its interest in gaining a competitive advantage globally, while filling a news gap for research-based commentary and analysis. This attractiveness was evident by the uptake of university membership growth, with 12 of the 15 U15 university members signing up by the end of The Conversation Canada's second year in operation (14 by the end of year three). The U15, according to its website, is a "collective of some of Canada's most research-intensive universities" (U15 Group, n.d., para. 1). Other evidence includes the launch of its French-language site in late 2018. In part as a result of the membership growth, The Conversation Canada had adequate capital for the first three years, which is considered a milestone in start-ups as the literature suggests that many fail during that time (Usher and Kammer (2019). In addition, it was digitally born and part of a global network with high-cost technology infrastructures already in place that limited the need for significant seed capital related to technology development.

An additional factor in its early success was the ability to defray other costs normally associated with starting up a new journalistic enterprise. For example, one of the most prominent recent US start-ups, The Correspondent, secured US$1.8 million in runway funds to support the development and fundraising for the English-language version of its Dutch counterpart, De Correspondent (Pfauth, 2018). At The Correspondent, 50 percent of its pre-launch budget covered management and legal and technology costs associated with starting a digital-born journalism organization. In the case of The Conversation Canada, these costs were non-existent or decreased because of support from the University of British Columbia. Additionally, as tenured professors at the University of British Columbia, we did not have to draw on any organizational funds for time spent on developing and launching The Conversation Canada.

The Public Policy Forum, the main federal journalism organization doing research on digital journalism and policy, recognized The Conversation Canada in its 2018 report on the state of the industry for its ability to "highlight the opportunity to tap into post-secondary institutions and recent graduates as part of strengthening the media system" (PPF, 2018, p. 12). The report goes on to suggest that part of its success—as well as the impact of other journalism organizations operating out of universities—is that foundations are able to give tax-free funds to universities as registered charities. At the same time, there has been some critique. Some prominent journalists and journalism educators have questioned whether the *Conversation* model fits within a traditional definition of journalism. Some of these questions relate to the independence of the organization from its university funders and whether its content could be considered as university communications (PPF, 2017).

Conclusion: Looking Ahead

To summarize, two years after launch, The Conversation Canada had accumulated significant financial resources in a nascent and underfunded digital media ecosystem (PPF, 2017). It has generated year-over-year growth in audience reach, accessing a significant proportion of its audience outside of Canada largely due to its republication strategy. Its strategic audience development has been supported by decline in the wider journalism sector and demand for free high-quality journalism content, against a background of continued concerns about mis- and disinformation in the media. The Conversation Canada is still a work in progress, and our conclusions are therefore early findings and assessments of a start-up's development in its first 24 months of operation. With this caveat, however, we find The Conversation Canada one of a growing number of not-for-profit start-ups in Canada that shows signs of innovation in journalism. As other studies of start-ups in this space have shown, long-term sustainable funding needs to remain a key focus and concern moving forward. The business model is largely based on an annual membership renewal model, which has sustainability challenges embedded in it.

The business model also has similarities to the conditions identified by Lucia Naldi and Robert Picard for a not-for-profit to have the "highest level of initial success" (p. 90) and "highest probability of survival" (2012, p. 91). Considering these conditions, The Conversation Canada met its initial objectives, maintained a flexible business plan that allowed room for adaptation, and "had a small but steady flow of capital from outside sources" (Naldi & Picard, 2012, p. 91). The successful not-for-profit identified by Naldi and Picard further outpaced one of its commercial competitors in that, they found, it along with another start-up studied had, "the greatest potential for long-term growth" (p. 91).

As co-founders, we had a number of experimental questions and commitments going into this project alongside initial goals of economic survival and sustainability, including: capacity building in journalism innovation and academic explanatory journalism within the national journalism ecosystem; experimentation with democratic not-for-profit governance models for journalism organizations; and commitments to an inclusive and equitable labour context. Looking forward, our research examines whether the model of The Conversation advances journalism epistemology through scholarly research (Hermida & Young, 2019b), and whether it can participate in repair and reform in the journalism ecosystem in Canada, and more broadly, within conversations about the emerging role of journalism in a networked and increasingly contested space for citizenship in a digital context.

Acknowledgements

This research was supported by the Social Sciences and Humanities Research Council of Canada and by The Conversation Media Group. The authors would like to sincerely thank the reviewers and book editors for their valuable comments.

Notes

1. See: https://theconversation.com/ca.
2. The Canada Revenue Agency defines a non-profit organization as a "club, society, or association that's organized and operated solely for social welfare, civic improvement, pleasure or recreation, [or] any other purpose except profit" (Canada Revenue Agency, 2019). The benefit of a not-for-profit structure includes greater flexibility in allowable purposes

for incorporation with less onerous regulatory filing requirements compared to a registered charity. A charity in Canada, for example, must meet objective requirements that include a focus on a few domains of charitable activities defined as "relief of poverty," "advancement of education," religion, or other purposes beneficial to the whole community (Kitching, 2006, p. 2), in addition to public financial filings. Manwaring and Valentine (2010) suggest that not-for-profit status is appropriate for organizations that among other things can "rely on member fees … to accomplish social goals" (p. 402).

References

Benson, R. (2017). Can foundations solve the journalism crisis? *Journalism, 19*(8), 1059–1077.

Boczkowski, P. J. (2009). Rethinking hard and soft news production: From common ground to divergent paths. *Journal of Communication, 59*(1), 98–116.

Bruno, N., & Nielsen, R. K. (2012) *Survival and success: Journalistic online start-ups in western Europe.* University of Oxford, Reuters Institute for the Study of Journalism. https://reutersinstitute.politics.ox.ac.uk/sites/default/files/2017-12/Survival%20is%20Success%20Journalistic%20Online%20Start-Ups%20in%20Western%20Europe.pdf

Cagé, J. (2016). *Saving the media.* Harvard University Press.

Canada Revenue Agency (Modified 2019, June 3) *Non-profit organizations.* https://www.canada.ca/en/revenue-agency/services/tax/non-profit-organizations.html

Coates Nee, R. (2014). Social responsibility theory and the digital nonprofits: Should the government aid online news startups? *Journalism, 15*(3), 326–343.

Deuze, M. (2017). Considering a possible future for digital journalism. *Mediterranean Journal of Communication, 8*(1), 9–18.

Edge, M. (2001). *Pacific Press: The unauthorized story of Vancouver's newspaper monopoly.* New Star Books

Edge, M. (2016). *The news we deserve: The transformation of Canada's media landscape.* New Star Books.

Gasher, M. (2007). The view from here: A news-flow study of the on-line editions of Canada's national newspapers. *Journalism Studies, 8*(2), 299–319.

Graves, L., & Konieczna, M. (2015). Sharing the news: Journalistic collaboration as field repair. *International Journal of Communication, 9,* 1966–1984.

Hermida, A., & Young, M. L. (2019a, September 12–13). *Transition or transformation? The precarity of responses to journalism market failure*

[Paper presentation]. Future of Journalism Conference: Innovations, Transitions and Transformations, Cardiff University, Cardiff, United Kingdom.

Hermida, A., & Young, M. L. (2019b). From peripheral to integral? A digital-born journalism not for profit in a time of crises. *Media and Communication*, 7(4), 92–102.

Iacono, J., Brown, A., & Holtham, C. (2009). Research methods—A case example of participant observation. *Electronic Journal of Business Research Methods*, 7(1), 39–46.

Kitching, A. (2006, February 28). *Charitable purpose, advocacy and the Income Tax Act*. Parliamentary Information and Research Service Canada, 2–3.

Kuitenbrouwer, P. (2001, April 19). Rabble-rouser: Publisher Judy Rebick's new online magazine offers a forum for leftist thinkers and those descending on Quebec this week. *National Post*.

Lewis, S. C. (2012). The tension between professional control and open participation: Journalism and its boundaries. *Information, Communication & Society*, 15(6), 836–866.

Lindgren, A. (2019). *Local news map database*. Local News Research Project. http://localnewsresearchproject.ca/wp-content/uploads/2019/06/LocalNewsMapDataasofJune12019.pdf

Manwaring, S., & Valentine, A. (2010, October 26). What's the law: Canadian structural options for social enterprise. *The Philanthropist*, 23(3), 399–404.

McLellan, M., & Holcomb, J. (2020). *INN Index 2019: The state of nonprofit news*. Institute for Nonprofit News. https://inn.org/innindex/

Naldi, L., & Picard, R. (2012). "Let's start an online news site": Opportunities, resources, strategy, and formational myopia in startups. *Journal of Media Business Studies*, 9(4), 69–97.

National Observer. (n.d.). *Advertise on National Observer!* https://www.nationalobserver.com/advertise-national-observer

Nielsen, R. K. (2016). The business of news. In T. Witschge, C. W. Anderson, D. Domingo, & A. Hermida (Eds.), *SAGE handbook of digital journalism* (pp. 51–67). Sage Publications.

Nielsen, R. K. (2019). Economic contexts of journalism. In K. Wahl-Jorgensen & T. Hanitzsch (Eds.), *The handbook of journalism studies* (2nd ed., pp. 324–340). Routledge.

Owen, T. (2017). Analysis of Nonprofit Journalism in Canada. [Unpublished.]

Pfauth, E. (2018, May 14). *The Correspondent raises $1.8M in runway funding and teams up with Blue State Digital*. Medium. https://medium.com/de-correspondent/runway-funding-blue-state-digital-b5df3c1736d9

Pickard, V. (2017, April 27). *Can charity save journalism from market failure?* The Conversation. http://theconversation.com/can-charity-save-journalism-from-market-failure-75833

Public Policy Forum [PPF]. (2017, January). *The shattered mirror: News, democracy and trust in the digital age*. Public Policy Forum. https://shattered-mirror.ca/wp-content/uploads/theShatteredMirror.pdf

Public Policy Forum [PPF]. (2018, September 25). *What the Saskatchewan Roughriders can teach Canadian journalism*. Public Policy Forum. https://ppforum.ca/wp-content/uploads/2018/09/WhatTheSaskatchewanRoughridersCanTeachCanadianJournalism-PPF-SEPT2018.pdf

Rabble.ca. (2018). Annual Report. http://www.rabble.ca/sites/default/files/2018_annualReport_webVersion_May16.pdf

The Globe and Mail. (2019). Media kit. https://globelink.ca/wp-content/uploads/2019/03/Globe-Digital-MediaKit-2019.pdf

The Tyee. (n.d.). The Tyee ad kit. https://thetyee.ca/About/TyeeAdKit.pdf

U15 Group of Canadian Research Universities. (n.d.) *About us*. http://u15.ca/about-us

Usher, N. & Kammer, A. (2019). News Startups. In H. Örnebring (Ed.), *Oxford Encyclopedia of Journalism Studies*. Oxford: Oxford University Press.

Wahl-Jorgensen, K., Bennett, L., & Taylor, G. (2017). The normalization of surveillance and the invisibility of digital citizenship: Media debates after the Snowden revelations. *International Journal of Communication, 11*, 740–762.

Winseck, D. (2010). Financialization and the "crisis of the media": The rise and fall of (some) media conglomerates in Canada. *Canadian Journal of Communication, 35*(3), 365–393.

Young, M. L., & Hermida, A. (2017, June 25). *It's time to start The Conversation in Canada*. The Conversation. https://theconversation.com/its-time-to-start-the-conversation-in-canada-79877

Zeller, F., & Hermida, A. (2015). When tradition meets immediacy and interaction. The integration of social media in journalists' everyday practices. *Sur le journalisme, About journalism, Sobre jornalismo, 4*(1), 106–119.

CHAPTER 7

Influencing the Internet: Lobbyists and Interest Groups' Impact on Digital Rights in Canada

Megan Beretta

Abstract

This chapter provides a summary of empirical research investigating the relationships and perceptions of Members of Parliament, public policy professionals, and lobbyists engaged with technology files in Canada, and their understanding of digital rights. Findings from 16 qualitative elite interviews with professionals indicate various levels of trust between these actors, and various levels of understanding of technological business models and technology issues. The chapter examines the potential impacts of the political communication dynamics between actors on the digital rights agenda in Canada. It also examines the future of digital rights in Canada and the impacts of the public policy environment on the digital rights agenda by drawing on more recent public policy announcements in Canada, such as the release of the *Digital Charter* in 2019 and the subsequent federal election.

The Internet is an inseparable part of Canadian society with a 90 percent adult usage rate (CIRA, 2018). Internet-enabled tools, such as mobile phones, search engines, computers, software, and wearable technology, are the digital technology essential to modern life. Designating the Internet as a basic service was the Canadian government's first active declaration of digital rights, which the Canadian Radio-television and Telecommunications Commission did in 2016 (Kupfer, 2016). Digital rights are human rights because they exist in the digital era and are an emerging concept in the human rights and technology fields (Hutt, 2015). However, there may be wider interpretations to rights that are emerging as extensions of known human rights as technology evolves, such as privacy, data protection, and sovereignty; discrimination in AI and machine learning; and Internet freedom and access (Gladstone, 2018).

Digital rights are becoming more urgent as Canadians experience harassment online, as the digital divide between rural and urban communities grows, and as Canadians participate in civic life and discussion all over the Internet (CIRA, 2018). Finding ways to appropriately regulate the Internet and manage the challenges it presents—not all of which are new, but many of which are larger in scale—is one of the great challenges of this medium. Understanding who influences that process is an important factor in better understanding the stakes. Digital rights are inherently linked to understanding citizenship in a digital context, as the civic experience is tied to laws, the rights citizens and residents have, and the practices that complement or violations that contradict those rights. In everything from privacy, services (see Amanda Clarke, Chapter 5, for more on digital government, data, and services), regulation of technology firms, and the role of AI in society, a government's relationship with digital rights can impact the civic experience and people's relationship with the state. The responsibilities that digital rights create could fundamentally change the types of technology built and further impact citizenship in a digital context because these rights could influence the mediated interaction between the citizen and civic society.

At the same time, the relationship between governments and technology firms in Canada and around the world has been tested as technology has integrated into every area of life. As governments and corporations have navigated their relationship, they have failed to prevent widespread scandals involving citizens and democratic processes. In Canada, the Minister of Democratic Institutions launched the Canada Declaration on Electoral Integrity Online (Government of Canada, 2019), with social media companies and search engines for the 2019 election (Sharp, 2017). Facebook moved data servers to escape regulation in Europe (Hern, 2018), and was called before Canadian parliamentary committees to explain the data-sharing and election targeting scandal with Cambridge Analytica (House of Commons Standing Committee on Access to Information, Privacy and Ethics [ETHI], 2018). The company Uber has spread its app-based services across Canada over the last few years while violating many municipal government's regulations. Cities like Toronto were unable to shut down Uber's operations but instead wrote regulations accommodating Uber's business model (Canadian Press, 2015). The roles of technology firms and their influence on citizenship has also been highly debated in the case of Toronto's proposed smart city development, Sidewalk Labs (a subsidiary of Alphabet, alongside Google)—how their technology, integrated into infrastructure, can impact digital and physical citizenship. Critics have questioned how the government agreed to the project given the lack of regulations and new issues around data governance and surveillance that it introduces into the city (Shieber, 2019). These and other events have generated debate about digital rights. Digital rights broadly describe the extension and respect of human rights in digital realms (Mathiesen, 2014). While governments struggle to decipher the technological, economic, political, and value-laden decisions that come with regulating technology firms, issues around digital rights have emerged in these real-world contexts, further complicating discussion of regulation.

There are also high levels of skepticism about the role of lobbying in Canadian politics; consequently, Canada's lobbying system is transparent and strictly regulated (Office of the Commissioner of Lobbying of Canada [OCL], 2018). There has been less critique, however, about the role of technology firms in the public policy process in Canada. Over the last few years, firms such as Google, Twitter, and Facebook have hired former political staff and candidates, high-level civil servants, and consulting firms to staff their lobbying teams (Pilieci, 2018). There is a clear growth in the technology industry's government relations practice in Canada, all while technology scandals are mounting concerns to the point that governments can no longer ignore the impact of unregulated digital technology on Canadians' lives (Ingram & Volz, 2018). These two dynamics—the growth of technology industry engagement in public policy through lobbying, and the importance and risks of technology in Canadians' lives—are worth examining together.

In this chapter, I focus on factors influencing the discussion of digital rights among politicians, public policy actors, and lobbyists in Canada. I rely on findings from sixteen interviews conducted in the spring of 2018, as part of my MSc thesis (Beretta , 2018) and build from that study with new information related to the 2019 federal election. I conclude with a discussion of the policy proposals around digital rights which have been released in 2019.

Lobbying in Context

Registering lobbyists was a controversial concept introduced in a wide package of public sector reforms by Brian Mulroney's government in 1985, which achieved royal assent three years later (Rush, 1994). Since then, the new *Lobbying Act* of 2006 came into effect. This act is based on the principle that since "free and open access to government is an important matter of public interest" and lobbying is a legitimate activity, it is desirable for public office holders and the public to know who is engaged in lobbying. It is also desirable that paid lobbyists should not impede open access to government (OCL, 2015). The Lobbying Registry (OCL, 2020) is a public database that reveals who is being paid to lobby and on what subjects, as well as the connections between parent and subsidiary organizations and coalitions.

The Lobbying Registry is limited in transparency and effectiveness through its structure. High penalties for the offence of misregistering encourages lobbyists to be careful, often causing firms to over register their communications and lobbyists on a file (Rush, 1994). This dynamic weakens the chain of investigation if the Office of the Commissioner for Lobbying were to suspect any malfeasance. The registry system also does not capture the entirety of the government relations industry. Many consultant firms offer a variety of services which fall outside the scope of the registry, including polling, monitoring and attending committees, offering strategic advice, and hosting events. Though only one service is registered, there may not be a measurable difference in purchasing direct representation or purchasing strategic advice, as they both provide a critical advantage in the policy process (Rush, 1994). Despite critiques, this registry is still viewed favourably worldwide as a comprehensive and well-implemented system (Furnas, 2014; Organization for Economic Cooperation and Development [OECD], 2014). However, open data still only capture what the system asks of it, and that leaves something to be desired for transparency and accountability that are even more comprehensive.

Literature and Existing Research Agenda

There has been very little work that examines lobbying or technology firms or has a consistent understanding of interest groups in the policy process in Canada, which leaves comparative politics and grounding in political communication theories as assets for theoretical grounding for this study. In the 1960s, Lester Milbrath first identified lobbying as a communication process. Where Milbraih (1960) and subsequent authors fall short, based on their own descriptions and analysis, is in failing to examine the impact of communication flow on policy. In further research on lobbying, the nuance and power of political communication has been inadequately studied as a domain.

I frame lobbying as a political communication issue because lobbying is a communication process that can influence the selection of issues for political attention by signalling issue salience and using persuasion to primarily move the dial on issue attention (De Bruckyer, 2014). In a context such as Canada's, agenda setting as a function of lobbying is a much more convincing account of the main purpose of lobbying given that individual legislators' votes on bills are not as vital to the legislative system, and there are few benefits that lobbyists can provide to decision makers outside of information. This is directly related to Canada's pluralistic policy process because information tools are used to shape and legitimize public ideas over instrumental forces like taxes or legislation in democracies where negotiation and compromise are more vital to the process (Deschamps, 2017).

In pluralist understandings of democracy, the politics of interest groups plays an important role in political dynamics. The participation of specialist policy communities, which operate outside the public's view and provide specialist information to the policy development process, is a normal part of Canadian public policy development (Smith, 2014). Lobbyists are part of interest groups and are portrayed particularly badly in the media, suffering a crisis of illegitimacy as they are depicted receiving undeserved favours from the government (Montpetit, 2010). Technology firms hold a distinct role as an interest group due to their emergence as not just part of telecommunications infrastructure and consumer products, but as playing a role in every facet of society.

Recently, authors have started publishing work describing the power of technology firms. Rasmus Kleis Nielsen sees the development of platform power in addition to hard and soft power and describes five dynamics within its development as a realm of power: "the power to set standards; power to make and break connections; power of automated action at scale; power of secrecy; and power that operates across domains" (2018). This account of platform power convincingly describes the dynamics present in this study, particularly the power to set standards and decide on measures that can affect entire industries and social dynamics that operate on top of the platforms. Furthermore, the implications of this allow discussion of the problematic dynamics that emerge when technology firms lobby the government: there is powerlessness on the side of government when it has an institutional and individual dependency on the service these firms provide.

These complex political and policy dynamics are important to further investigate, given the immense role digital technology plays in society and the challenges it has already presented in the realm of policy. A better understanding of who is influencing this field of policy and how it interacts with Canada's unique lobbying and government relations environment can contribute to thinking critically about technology policy. The specific research questions that guided the interviews were:

1. How does lobbying activity inform and shape the way that government policy actors understand technology and digital rights in Canada?
2. What are the implications of these interactions on citizens' digital rights in Canada?

These questions are answered with empirical research and an analysis of emerging policy in the context of these questions.

Methods

The research that underlies this chapter was designed to investigate individuals from multiple groups that are active in policy development: consultant and in-house lobbyists, Members of Parliament (MPs) on technology committees, and public policy actors and advocates (hereafter, public policy professionals). The recruitment efforts required significant persistence and creativity for these three groups of elite participants (Esselment & Marland, 2018). I interviewed six current and former MPs, six registered lobbyists[1] and four public policy professionals.[2] To recruit participants, I crafted a list of every MP who served on a committee related to science and technology since the first session of the 41st Parliament of September 2013 or since the creation of the committee or department (approximately 150 MPs). The committees and ministries were: Public Services and Procurement; Infrastructure and Communities; Industry, Science and Technology; Access to Information, Privacy and Ethics; Canadian Heritage; Treasury Board Secretariat; and Innovation, Science and Economic Development. I contacted sitting MPs via email, and I researched online those who were no longer in Parliament and contacted them where available. As a result, I contacted 82 current or former MPs, and through a mixture of personal connections, emails, phone calls, and attending their committees, I was able to interview six of them. In the half-hour interviews, I spoke to participants about three main subject areas related to the research questions: (1) how they perceive their roles and experience with lobbying; (2) their knowledge about technology and level of comfort with issues of technology; and (3) their understanding and perceptions of digital rights. These themes facilitated discussion around lobbying and digital rights, while allowing an understanding of each participant's level of experience and expertise on the topic.

Notably, the MPs were the most difficult to recruit; it was much easier to recruit lobbyists and public policy professionals. The variance in response and participation rates are not unexpected: MPs are notoriously difficult to interview, given their schedules and commitments, and may be wary of junior researchers with whom they are unfamiliar. Personal referrals and attending committees were more effective than cold contacting for recruiting. Many lobbyists were reluctant to participate because of client confidentiality, whereas public policy professionals were more enthusiastic to share their experiences. Elite interviews present challenges for validity, given the power imbalance between participant and researcher, and because of the challenges of recruiting these participants (Esselment & Marland, 2018). Due to their elite status, I was limited to interviewing whoever responded to my requests, which means it is likely those whom I interviewed are more invested in the field of technology and rights than an average committee member. This potential bias of the information is vital to consider when evaluating the data. However, it also reflects the reality that they are the ones invested in shaping this field, and their biased opinion may be most important to analyze.

Research Findings

The findings of the study are characterized by conflicting accounts of the state of technology lobbying; the evidence demonstrates the differing positions of the participants. All participants are anonymous, and all have been given labels matched with a random number under 10, where LB represents lobbyists, PP represents public policy professionals, and MP represents Members of Parliament. Here, specific quotes complement the summarized data across interviews. These themes are just a sample of those investigated.

How Information Is Exchanged

> Sometimes it's by their request where they want us to come and sort of help fill in the gaps. Sometimes it is our request saying, "You guys are going to screw this up, please make sure that we're not abandoned in this process and can make sure we help you get it right."—PP6

Lobbyists and public policy professionals both describe their role and the need for their role as, providing education, and this information dynamic was acknowledged by most of the actors. The MPs mostly feel like they have excellent support from the Library of Parliament's research team, who provide non-partisan research support for information gathering. MPs demonstrated their own skills in independent information seeking, such as using travel time to read up on the technology industry or employing research assistants. Several described talking to public interest organizations, mentioned talking to academics, and discussed learning from committee testimony from experts and witnesses.

Trust

> In a new policy area, you want to
> establish trust with government, so
> relationship building is key. —LB5

The participants indicated different trust dynamics. Public policy professionals held little trust in the intentions and motivations of technology companies and felt skeptical about the processes that should allow their voices to be heard in Parliament. MPs had mixed levels of trust: some did not mention any issues with the information they were being provided by interest groups; others pointed out technology firms were biased, so they cross-checked information with other sources, such as public policy organizations. One MP was critical of the current government's trust in technology firms, which they identified as misleading the government. When discussing the ethics and legal dimensions, three lobbyists mentioned that lobbying is a highly regulated field, one saying it was a benefit for the ethical and legal lines to be very clear. Other lobbyists stated that lobbying could be restrictive, hindering information through the registry and restricting opportunities to speak with MPs.

Perceptions of Digital Rights

The original question of the research was about emerging digital rights, and it was met with confusion and needed clarification. After being prompted with suggestions such as the right to be forgotten, data protection, and rights concerning algorithms, many participants then discussed rights in which they had interest, some of which were hot-button subjects of the day. MPs mostly mentioned AI ethics, and ethics around autonomous vehicles, save for two MPs who were more aware and politically active on the issue of digital rights.

It is noteworthy that "digital rights," as a term, is not top of mind for participants such as lobbyists and MPs. The public policy participants were all well informed and ready to discuss the topic because their work mostly centres on digital rights. One public policy participant highlighted that they and Google would both agree on some digital rights as vital, but their motivations differed: the participant for users' rights, and Google for corporate benefits. Only two participants framed companies' interest in human rights as an altruistic pursuit, including the "Tech for Good"[3] movement, where technology firms pursue civic-impact or charitable technology projects. Two MPs felt that digital rights were not particularly present in the conversation because they served no immediate political purpose. Thoughts were mixed on how government thinks about how technology may impact human rights, and whether technology has a negative effect on society and human rights. One MP felt that some colleagues in Parliament were unaware of these issues, and the colleagues would ask questions that demonstrated a lack of awareness of the state of technology.

Digital Rights in the Future

> I think it really is an opportunity, because you have to be thoughtful and careful about it, and it's probably not a discussion that should be left simply to technology companies and the government, quite frankly. It probably has to involve a lot of people.
> —LB5

According to participants, there needs to be a societal discussion around digital rights and the power of technology firms within the public sector. Some discussed the need for enforcement, as regulation and laws are often flaunted or just ignored by technology firms due to disagreements over jurisdiction. Some participants discussed the typical government dichotomy of the urgent overtaking the important, and that digital rights are not on the agenda. Although most identified it indirectly, a few participants mentioned that there could be impacts on citizenship and democracy. Two public policy professionals discussed funding as a method to improve non-partisan education and awareness, and to build expertise in civil society. One public policy professional called for the government to see digital rights as normal rights, like those offline, and saw the digital aspect as obfuscating the obligations of decision makers. Overall, there was a lack of direction for the way forward on digital rights, except for the acknowledgement that a public conversation will be necessary to address values and ethics on this industry and its regulation.

Discussion

This data demonstrates that there is a high level of conflict in accounts about the environment around technology lobbying and little direction on a way forward for digital rights in Canada. Through the lobbying process, public policy professionals and lobbyists provide expertise in technology, which is considered and used by decision makers in public policy making.

Several MPs discussed bias in the information that lobbyists provide. However, a public policy professional said that they felt that companies were "pretty straight" with them, whereas another public policy group was discredited by a committee member; a reputation that spread to the Canadian telecommunications regulator. These very different expressions demonstrate a competitive environment with different levels of trust between members. Trust as a relationship of risk management, however, is only truly executed on action (Blöbaum, 2016). Trust, or a lack thereof, was demonstrated among the participants when some chose to consult additional sources after receiving information or invited those sources to private meetings. Trust in information, then, will have impacts on digital rights: setting public policy will be the moment where decision makers take risks associated with trusting interest groups and their information.

Another participant brought up the small size of the Canadian market providing no incentive for large technology firms to comply with government regulatory or enforcement measures. Participants identified a lack of solutions for enforcing any regulation that was developed. This demonstrates the risks of platform power. It also demonstrates that the power may not lie just with certain companies, but in the way that they do business relying on user consent for their information and data (Culpepper & Thelen, 2018). Though platform companies, particularly, are monopolies, that is not the only risk factor to the rights of their community, rather as one lobbyist noted, "It's not just about size, but it's about the responsibility that you carry with the size of a company." This speaks directly to the concerns, noted previously, of a growing platform power that is resonating with this community, especially given that interviewees from each participant group identified it as their main concern.

The second research question probed the implications of the above dynamics on citizens' digital rights in Canada. The clear answer that emerged from the uncertainty in the data is that there is not yet a clear government agenda on digital rights, and decision makers are just in the process of understanding the importance of digital rights as they begin to make decisions on technology policy. While interest groups vie for attention, no significant resources are being allocated institutionally to these issues; much of the work is being done by individually motivated MPs and committees.

Outside of the public policy professionals who were experts on digital rights, there were very few statements from participants that recognized the risks to citizenship and democracy. Those public policy participants did not feel that they were competitive enough with technology firms in terms of the extent to which they could lobby or engage in government relations to advocate. However, decision makers were aware of the public policy advocates' policy positions and trusted them as educators and witnesses on committees, which indicates the advocates are being heard and included, at least by committee members. However, when final directions and decisions are often set by the Cabinet, that trust may be less impactful.

The implications identified speak to the problematic dynamics that emerge in the issue of technology firms lobbying the government: there is a powerlessness on the side of government when there is institutional and individual dependency on the service these firms provide. MPs in the committee who saw Facebook executives testify spoke of their own use of the social networking site and how important it had become to their work as politicians (ETHI, 2018). One lobbyist stated that lobbying for technology procurement business is not a good business to be in as a lobbyist, as you assume great risk of public scrutiny in trying to procure the best possible product for government needs. This is an interesting reflection of this dynamic and brings the conversation back to the idea of infrastructural power that Sabeel Rahman et al. (2018) describe as similar to a public utility and the platform power, described by Kleis Neilson (2018), that is more powerful than governments. It is possible that this conflict, and the now inextricable relationship that all people have with the Internet, not to mention the electoral motivations of governments, will necessitate a new approach to policy processes, consultation, procurement, and regulation.

In 2018, I recommended (Beretta) that there should be a Canada-wide project about digital rights, where neutral voices are mixed with key players, which would strengthen the impact of these messages to resonate, not just as opinions but as necessities. The participants in this study, from all groups, felt strongly that public discussion on digital rights was necessary to deal with these complex issues, which are not just technical, but ethical and value-laden. With loaded stakes, power must shift to the people and their representatives to create a collective understanding of interests so that power cannot be exerted in ignorance. Public conversation and debate on digital and societal values, and thus digital rights, is necessary.

The *Digital Charter* and Public Policy Ahead

Two years after this data was collected and this analysis made, is there a further public agenda for digital rights? The Liberal government's *Digital Charter* was announced in May 2019, following the international meeting at which Canada committed to the Christchurch Call to Action (ISED, 2019) and consultations with the public and industry. The Liberal government, along with six appointed digital engagement leaders, held 30 roundtables with 580 participants, and there were around 2,000 comments on their consultation website and other platforms. It is not a significant enough sample of the population in Canada to consult on this type of declaration of potentially new rights, and certainly major regulations, that will affect everyone. From the consultation documents and report, we do not know who participated in the consultations, who was invited to take part, or how they were engaged. It is unclear whether digital rights experts, human rights organizations, or privacy experts took part in the process leading to the development of the *Digital Charter*. Further, there is no discussion of human rights within the report, nor does the *Digital Charter* promise digital rights or any bold legislation that will hold companies to account. Finally, framing the *Digital Charter* as key to digital innovation, the marketplace, and the economy fails to take into account a rights agenda.

The economic frame is difficult to reconcile with a digital rights agenda because it fails to identify the connections between the problematic business models of technology firms, which are identified as challenges to democracy in the present chapter. Without mentions to regulation, new legislation, or rights (Birch, 2019), the *Digital Charter* so far has no legal value and is taking a risk-averse, economic-centric approach familiar to this Liberal government's tenure. The *Digital Charter* came without any significant implementation agenda at the end of a mandate with no push to implement it before the end of the

Parliament. The only reference to implementation in the documen-
tation around the *Digital Charter* has been a strengthened Privacy
Commissioner and "other key enforcement bodies" (ISED, 2019).

The government seems to want to set an agenda with the *Digital
Charter*; however, the government is perhaps not yet sure of its interests. Without any plans for implementation or larger debate during
the 2019 federal election, the digital rights agenda that the Liberal
government is attempting to set does not seem to be truly a part of
an agenda in Canadian politics. For digital rights to be about people's
needs, from a human rights framework perspective, it appears there
needs to be a greater pluralistic policy process and greater public
engagement. However, it is possible that announcing a vague *Digital
Charter* gives the government a better opportunity to improve its
policy positions and arguments, in preparation for an upcoming
negotiation process. Lobbyists and public policy groups now have
an opportunity to craft their positions suited to at least one party,
and possibly others who may follow the Liberals' more thematic
promises. This positioning may also help prepare public servants to
work on policy so they are prepared for the upcoming challenges the
technology industry poses to public policy. Finally, civil society can
start conversations on digital rights with this opportunity, directing
citizens' engagement toward policy.

Conclusion

There are significant implications of this research: There is no
consensus around the trustworthiness of the information around
technology, there is a lack of understanding of the business models
of digital technology, and platform power is growing in a market
where there are few incentives for companies to comply with local
regulation. This research also coincides with the Liberal government
winning the 2019 federal election and implementing their proposed
Digital Charter. There continues to be an opportunity for public
policy-makers, MPs, and lobbyists to set an agenda on the actions
and implementations of the digital rights agenda that the Liberal
government is putting forward. This research has shown that Canada
should act now to address the challenges identified and to ensure
that there is a dynamic discussion of digital rights involving diverse
actors. These policy recommendations capture the evidence in this
research (see Clarke, Chapter 5, for more policy recommendations

related to data governance). The federal government and partners should implement the following measures:

1. Foster an active discussion and review of the *Digital Charter* in Parliament and engage in cross-party discussion of what items should be prioritized to implement during this Parliament;
2. Perform public opinion research that can provide data as to what Canadians expect and need from citizenship in a digital context, which can inform the progression of digital rights in Canada;
3. Host extensive consultation sessions on citizenship in a digital context and digital rights with representative groups, which includes education about these issues, so that a wider audience who may not have pre-existing literacy on the issue can still take part and have their voices included;
4. Implement digital literacy education for MPs, and senior public servants;
5. Fund a digital research institute that would provide multi-partisan or non-partisan expert research from multidisciplinary technology researchers, one that is trustworthy for decision makers and the Canadian public.

Finally, there should be further research into the digital rights space, and the contributions of different policy actors should be closely followed during any further negotiations on a digital charter or rights agenda. Following the change to privacy legislation in Canada—who is included in the conversation, who it benefits, and who suffers—will be important to understanding the public policy environment. Further, studying more deeply the public service's actions, in which public servants may work with or support technology companies, will indicate how they involve, partner with, and rely on these companies to self-regulate and co-operate. It is essential to better understand where expertise lies in the government, and whether there are enough decision makers who understand the nuance of technology issues and have the power to impact it, because it will impact the process and development of balanced and necessary public policy.

Acknowledgements

Thank you to Victoria Nash, Oxford Internet Institute, who supervised this research. Funding to travel to Canada for interviews was provided by St. Hugh's College, University of Oxford.

Notes

1. I used a publicly available lobbying registry to identify lobbyists registered to technology companies and contacted active lobbyists through their firms' websites. As I worked at a small lobbying firm in 2016, I used personal contacts and snowball sampling for recruitment. While lobbyists were easier to contact than MPs, they were reticent to participate for client confidentiality concerns. I contacted 18 lobbyists and interviewed six of them.
2. I recruited public policy professionals by researching organizations working on digital human rights in Canada. After learning that most organizations would be attending the global RightsCon 2018 conference in Toronto, I acquired a ticket to do my research. I recruited ten participants attending the conference by contacting eight organizations and interviewed four people.
3. For an example of the "Tech for Good" corporate movement, see: https://canadianinnovationspace.ca/tech-for-good/.

References

Beretta, M. (2018). *Influencing the Internet: Lobbyists and interest groups' impact on digital rights in Canada* [Unpublished manuscript]. University of Oxford, Oxford Internet Institute.

Birch, K. (2019, May 24). Five reasons Canada's Digital Charter will be a bust before it gets going. *The Globe and Mail.* https://www.theglobeandmail.com/business/commentary/article-five-reasons-canadas-digital-charter-will-be-a-bust-before-it-even/

Blöbaum, B. (2016). *Trust and communication in a digitized world: Models and concepts of trust research.* Springer International Publishing.

Canada, House of Commons, Standing Committee on Access to Information, Privacy and Ethics [ETHI]. (2018, April 19). [Evidence]. Meeting no. 100. 42nd Parliament, 1st Session. http://www.ourcommons.ca/Committees/en/ETHI/StudyActivity?studyActivityId=10044891

Canadian Internet Registration Authority [CIRA]. (2018). *Canada's Internet factbook 2018.* https://cira.ca/factbook/canada%E2%80%99s-internet-factbook-2018#section-1

Canadian Press. (2015, December 14). *John Tory: It's impractical for Toronto to try to shut down Uber.* HuffPost. Retrieved December 24, 2016, from https://www.huffingtonpost.ca/2015/12/14/john-tory-says-it-would-be-impractical-for-toronto-to-try-to-shut-down-uber_n_8805490.html

Culpepper, P. & Thelen, K. (2018). *It's hard to unplug from the Matrix: Consumers and the politics of platform power* [Manuscript in preparation]. Blavatnik School of Government, University of Oxford.

De Bruycker, I. (2014, September 4). How interest groups develop their lobbying strategies: The logic of endogeneity [Conference paper]. ECPR General Conference, 2014, Glasgow, Scotland. https://ecpr.eu/Filestore/PaperProposal/81ba85d3-2d34-4636-8bb9-c79f664861a3.pdf

Deschamps, B. R. D. (2017). *Policy agenda setting and Twitter—Three cases from Canada* [Doctoral dissertation, University of Regina]. oURspace. https://ourspace.uregina.ca/bitstream/handle/10294/7752/Deschamps_Bruno-Ryan_200324651_PHD_PPOL_Spring2017.pdf?sequence=1&isAllowed=y

Esselment, A. & Marland, A. (2018). Tips and tactics for interviewing Canadian political elites in the digital media age. In A. Marland, T. Giasson, & A. Lawlor (Eds.), *Political elites in Canada: Power and influence in instantaneous times* (pp. 29–50). UBC Press.

Furnas, A. (2014, May 5). *Transparency case study: Lobbying disclosure in Canada.* Sunlight Foundation. https://sunlightfoundation.com/2014/05/05/transparency-case-study-lobbying-disclosure-in-canada/

Gladstone, N. (2018, May 1). *Digital rights 102: Highlighting the issues affecting Canadians.* Access Now. https://www.accessnow.org/digital-rights-102-highlighting-the-issues-affecting-canadians/

Government of Canada. (2019, May 27). *Canada declaration on electoral integrity online.* https://www.canada.ca/en/democratic-institutions/services/protecting-democracy/declaration-electoral-integrity.html

Hern, A. (2018, April 19). Facebook moves 1.5B users out of reach of new European privacy law. *The Guardian.* https://www.theguardian.com/technology/2018/apr/19/facebook-moves-15bn-users-out-of-reach-of-new-european-privacy-law

Hutt, R. (2015, November 13). *What are your digital rights?* World Economic Forum. https://www.weforum.org/agenda/2015/11/what-are-your-digital-rights-explainer/

Innovation, Science and Economic Development Canada [ISED]. (2019, October 23). *Canada's digital charter: A plan by Canadians, for Canadians.* Government of Canada. Retrieved October 23, 2019, from https://www.ic.gc.ca/eic/site/062.nsf/eng/h_00109.html

Ingram, D., & Volz, D. (2018, February 17). *Facebook faces big challenge to prevent future U.S. election meddling.* Thomson Reuters. https://www.reuters.com/article/us-usa-trump-russia-prevention/facebook-faces-big-challenge-to-prevent-future-u-s-election-meddling-idUSKCN1G102D

Kleis Nielsen, R. (2018, March 29). *The power of platforms* [SlideShare]. Slideshare.net. https://www.slideshare.net/RasmusKleisNielsen/the-power-of-platforms-inaugural-lecture-by-rasmus-kleis-nielsen-u-of-oxford?

Kupfer, M. (2016, December 21). *CRTC declares broadband Internet access a basic service*. CBC. Retrieved December 22, 2016, from https://www.cbc.ca/news/politics/crtc-internet-essential-service-1.3906664

Lobbying Act, R.S.C. 1985, c. 44 (4th Supp.).

Mathiesen, K. (2014). Human rights for the digital age. *Journal of Mass Media Ethics, 29*(1), 2–18. https://doi.org/10.1080/08900523.2014.863124

Milbrath, L. W. (1960). Lobbying as a communication process. *Oxford Journals, 24*(1), 32–53.

Montpetit, É. (2010). The deliberative and adversarial attitudes of interest groups. In J. C. Courtney and D. E. Smith (Eds.) *The Oxford Handbook of Canadian Politics* (pp. 1–21). Oxford University Press.

Office of the Commissioner of Lobbying of Canada [OCL]. (2015, December 1). *The lobbyists' code of conduct*. Retrieved June 19, 2018, from https://lobbycanada.gc.ca/eic/site/012.nsf/eng/h_00013.html

Office of the Commissioner of Lobbying of Canada [OCL]. (2018). *12-month lobbying activity search*. Retrieved July 31, 2018, from https://lobby-canada.gc.ca/app/secure/ocl/lrs/do/clntSmmrySrch

Office of the Commissioner of Lobbying of Canada [OCL]. (Modified 2020, May 15). *Registry of lobbyists*. https://lobbycanada.gc.ca/app/secure/ocl/lrs/do/guest

Organization for Economic Cooperation and Development [OECD]. (2014). *Lobbyists, governments and public trust, volume 3: Implementing the OECD principles for transparency and integrity in lobbying*. OECD Publishing.

Pilieci, V. (2018, May 6). Web of familiar faces connects government with online giants. *The Ottawa Citizen*. https://ottawacitizen.com/news/national/prior-relationships-between-lobbyists-and-senior-federal-staffers-raises-ethical-questions

Rush, M. (1994, December). Registering the lobbyists: Lessons from Canada. *Political Studies, 42*(4), 630–645.

Sabeel Rahman, K., Minow, M., Manning, J., Novak, B., Boyd, W., Pasquale, F., & Lebovitz Earlier, A. (2018). The new utilities: Private power, social infrastructure, and the revival of the public utility concept. *Cardozo Law Review, 39*(5), 1621–1692.

Sharp, A. (2017, September 14). *Facebook to launch election integrity effort in Canada*. Thomson Reuters. https://uk.reuters.com/article/us-facebook-canada-election/facebook-to-launch-election-integrity-effort-in-canada-idUKKCN1BP2ZT

Shieber, J. (2019, October 31). *Sidewalk Labs (Alphabet's grand experiment in smart cities) will move forward with Toronto project*. Tech Crunch. https://techcrunch.com/2019/10/31/sidewalk-labs-alphabets-grand-experiment-in-smart-cities-will-move-forward-in-toronto/

Smith, M. (2014). The role of social movements and interest groups. In K. Kozolanka (Ed.), *Publicity and the Canadian state* (pp. 262–279). University of Toronto Press.

PART III

RETHINKING LEGAL FRAMEWORKS FOR THE DIGITAL CONTEXT

CHAPTER 8

Consumers First, Digital Citizenry Second: Through the Gateway of Standard-Form Contracts

Marina Pavlović

Abstract

The combined effect of the digital and global economy has funda-mentally changed the very concept of a consumer, the consumer's place in the digital society, and the relationship between consumers and other actors, such as governments. By using goods and services, consumers still play the role of passive actors in the market economy. However, in today's society, not only does our consumption behaviour make us consumers, but virtually all aspects of our daily lives and social interactions are made possible by, and conditional upon, being consumers first. To be producers, creators, learners, critical thinkers, and citizens, we must be consumers first, by clicking on or signing lengthy standard-form contracts before getting access to goods and services (including government services). Standard-form contracts have become the dominant regulatory mechanism of con-sumer relationships and, by extension, digital civic participation. This article frames the relationship between consumers and citizens within the growing dependency on standard-form contracts. It identi-fies the ineffectiveness in the current legal rules governing standard-form contracts and provides a related policy research agenda needed to limit the expansive private ordering of standard-form contracts.

The digital and global economy has fundamentally changed the very concept of a consumer, the consumer's place in society, and the relationship between the consumer and other actors, such as governments. By buying goods and using services, consumers still play the role of passive actors in the market economy. However, in today's society, with the increased digitization of goods and services, not only does traditional consumption behaviour make us consumers, but virtually all aspects of our daily lives and social interactions are made possible by, and conditional on, being consumers first. Indeed, citizens must consume digital products in order to fulfill other social, economic, and cultural roles.

Before we acquire a digital good or service that enables us to be producers, farmers, creators, learners, critical thinkers, or citizens, we must click on or sign lengthy terms and conditions—standard-form contracts—imposing the provider's terms of service. Standard-form contracts lead to increased *private ordering* in the digital context—that is, service providers building their own rules and enforcement mechanisms in lieu of, or parallel to, state's rules and enforcement mechanisms.

Standard-form contracts have now become the dominant regulatory mechanism of consumer relationships. Migrated from the commercial space, those standard-form contracts have also become important regulatory mechanisms of digital civic participation, as governments are now using such contracts for service delivery.

This chapter frames the relationship between consumers and citizens within the context of our growing dependency on standard-form contracts that effectively make us consumers first. It identifies the ineffectiveness in the current legal rules governing standard-form contracts and provides a related policy research agenda needed to limit the expansive private ordering of standard-form contracts.

The Paradigm of Consumers First

Up until the rise of the Internet and digital technology, consumers were, as Daniel Defoe noted in 1726, "the last article" (p. 5) or "utmost end" (p. 389) in a trade chain. As buyers and consumers of goods and services, consumers were exclusively situated within the marketplace. They were passive actors in that they were the end consumers of the products and services (Trentmann, 2016). Starting in the 1970s, consumer protection policies and legislation that were introduced in

Canada (and elsewhere) were deeply rooted in this classic paradigm of consumers as passive actors in the marketplace, articulated some 250 years prior. As weaker parties in the marketplace, consumers needed "protecting," hence, for example, a suite of policies were introduced on product safety and warranties (Ramsay, 1985). The same paradigm also underpins, to this day, competition policies, which focus on consumer welfare, defined purely in economic terms of price and market choice (Werden, 2011). While the consumer movement worldwide was built on strong social, political, and (arguably) ideological values (Ramsay, 1993), the remit of consumer activism and government-issued consumer policies was predominantly focused on consumption. There was very little, if any, intersection between the role of individuals as consumers, the goods and services they acquired and used, and their "civic experience" and role as citizens (Dubois and Martin-Bariteau, 2020). Even in socially driven actions, such as consumer boycotts of goods, "Political [activities were] difficult to distinguish from other aspects of consumption activities" (Jacobsen, 2017, p. 183).

As we lead more connected lives, either by choice or by immutable force, in the digital and increasingly global economy the paradigm of consumers as passive actors has fundamentally shifted. Individuals, as consumers, have been propelled from their passive role at the very end of a market transaction to the very beginning of virtually all social interactions, and not just within what has been the purview of market transactions, but also within what has been the purview of other social interactions, including citizenry.

As Margaret Scammell noted, "The act of consumption is becoming increasingly suffused with citizenship characteristics and considerations. ... It is no longer possible to cut the deck neatly between citizenship and civic duty, on one side, and consumption and self-interest, on the other" (2000, p. 352). While the notion of citizen-consumer blurs the line between political and consumptive, in such a relationship, consumerism is subordinate to citizenship, even though citizenship is increasingly expressed through consumption behaviour (Scammell, 2000, p. 352; Cho et al., 2015).

I argue, however, that this shift goes beyond the blurring of the lines. The shift is so fundamental that almost all relationships become subordinate to, and are viewed through, the lens of individuals as consumers, where many aspects of our lives can only be realized by first consuming a digital good or a service. Our purchasing behaviour still makes us consumers, fulfilling the traditional role of passive actors in the marketplace. More importantly, however, virtually all aspects of our daily lives and social interactions are made possible by, and conditional on, being consumers first. When they purchase farm equipment, farmers are being consumers first. When they read digital books, stream documentaries, or submit assignments through learning management systems, students are being consumers first. When we use our phones, the Internet, messaging apps, or social media to communicate with friends and family, we are all being consumers first (see, e.g., Shade et al., in Chapter 3). Political discourse and civic participation at municipal, provincial, federal, or global levels are increasingly happening through digital tools (Dubois & Martin-Bariteau, 2020). When we read the news, follow government announcements on social media, or share our views on issues that matter, we are all consumers first before we can be engaged citizenry.

Standard-Form Contracts as Dominant Regulatory Mechanisms

Standard-form contracts have migrated from the commercial environment into every aspect of our lives. For example, we are required to agree to terms of services before we use social media platforms, create an email account, apply for government services, and so on. In effect, only by first consuming a digital product can we fulfil other social, economic, and cultural roles. The main tool governing this consumptive role is a non-negotiable standard-form agreement (also called contract of adhesion or boilerplate), which is presented on a take-it-or-leave-it basis. As consumers first, we have become "contract takers" (Cohen, 1988, p. 1125). We are presented with a binary choice: either accept the contract terms as they are presented and get access to the services, or decline the contract and effectively be left behind.

Standard-form contracts have been a business reality for almost two centuries (Rakoff, 1983). They are an efficient mechanism to standardize frequent transactions and significantly reduce, if not eliminate, transaction costs. In the commercial environment, where these contracts originated, the parties have the commercial acumen to understand the consequences of the terms of a standard-from contract, to assess, and, if necessary, absorb any future legal or business risk arising from it (Pavlović, 2016, pp. 406–409).

Freedom of contract and party autonomy are foundational principles of contract law and by extension, private law. The state does not interfere in the private contractual bargain between parties, unless the contract itself is fundamentally flawed. For example, if the parties lack legal capacity to contract, the contract is unconscionable, illegal, or against public policy objectives. Historically, each of these exceptions has been interpreted narrowly, and over the decades their scope has gotten even narrower. These exceptions define the outer boundaries of the contractual relationships. Such a broad scope of what is permissible, the theory goes, is essential for the markets to function and the state has little interest (or capacity) to police how these individual and private relationships are ordered. In other words, what is within these rather expansive boundaries is permissible behaviour. What is out of the boundaries is not permissible. As a result, the courts rarely interfere with or alter the contractual bargain. In the industrial society, there are few, if any, challenges to this type of private ordering. Private ordering generally affects only the commercial parties and it affects their mutual relationship. It does not affect third parties or ordinary people, and it does not pose significant challenges to society as a whole (Trebilcock, 1995).

The initial migration of standard-form contracts from the purely commercial sphere into the consumer environment was reserved for odd transactions such as tickets, standardized waivers of liability for dangerous sports, rent-a-car agreements, or major financial transactions. Canadian courts have generally enforced these contracts, pending sufficient notice to consumers (*Tilden Rent-A-Car v. Clendenning*, 1978; *Trigg v. MI Movers International Transport Services*, 1991).

The true scope of the intrusion of these contracts into the daily lives of individuals happened at the confluence of digitization and the ever-growing role of the Internet. Standard-form contracts became an integral and unavoidable gate through which we pass, as consumers first, into the realm of digital services and our collective digital lives. In the digital environment, as Ian Kerr put it, these contracts have become "the rule[,] and [the businesses,] the rulers." (Kerr, 2005, p. 191). Rakoff's observation from the last quarter of the Twentieth century captures the significance of the rule-making power of these contracts: "The use of form documents, if legally enforceable, imparts to firms ... a freedom from legal restraint and an ability to control relationships across a market" (1983, p. 1229). The current reality where virtually all aspects of our lives are subject to standard-form contracts leads to a significant expansion of private ordering beyond what Rakoff originally contemplated and has significant implications, not just for consumer rights proper but also, and perhaps more importantly, for civic participation and human rights more broadly.

On their own, boilerplate standard-form contracts are arguably not what is problematic. It is the way in which they have effectively become the main rule-making instrument in the digital environment and have expanded the role of private ordering into all realms of digital life. Unilaterally defined contracts implement an online private ordering which allows private actors to effectively work around states' laws. This migration of standard-form contracts, from the commercial environment to consumer space and numerous social spaces, raises many challenges and questions about the appropriate limits of private ordering in the digital society.

First, the commercial environment in which these contracts have developed is markedly different from the current environment in which we are consumers first. There is a fundamental informational and bargaining asymmetry between the contracting parties—businesses, on the one hand, decide unilaterally on the terms with complete information about services and risks, and consumers (or citizens), on the other, can only accept the terms not fully aware of all the risks. This asymmetry is at the core of why the boilerplate contracts are currently being used to push the boundaries of private ordering.

Second, people do not have a real ability to opt out of these contracts. While for certain services, there may be an alternative service that arguably does not come with the same restrictions, often there is no practical alternative, or the alternative comes with a very similar standard-form contract (Pavlović, 2016, p. 423). More fundamentally, it is not about whether there are alternatives; it is about the lack of choice and the lack of any control that people have over the terms of these relationships (see Shade et al., in Chapter 3). The rapid shift toward digitization of everything means that every aspect of our lives and social activities—from work to entertainment to civic participation—is now governed by these contracts. This concern is further amplified in relationships where people do not have any choice—such as government services or a growing number of formal or informal public-private partnerships that are taking over what once was a realm of public services (for example, the increasing use of Google Classroom in delivering K–12 education).

Third, the way these contracts are structured—from their length, to their readability, to their need for instantaneous acceptance, makes it impossible for consumers to realistically understand the rights and obligations under the contract, assess the risks, and make a truly informed choice (Bakos, 2014; Ben-Shahar & Schneider, 2014; Shade et al., in Chapter 3).

And, lastly, if there is a serious problem with the goods, services, or the provider's practices, due to restrictive contractual terms (such as arbitration clauses, forum selection clauses, or class action waivers) that limit consumer's access to domestic courts, it is virtually impossible for an individual to obtain a recourse, which renders any rights that one may have under the contract (or even under a legislative or regulatory mechanism) effectively meaningless. In addition, even if consumers had unobstructed access to domestic courts, the perennial problem of consumer complaints has been that the cost of pursuing a claim is much higher (by multiple amounts) than the value of the claim (Best, 1981). The value of consumer claims is often in the range of several hundred dollars (or, at a higher end, several thousand dollars), while the cost of the legal process, including legal representations, is often in the tens of thousands of dollars. The high cost of pursuing the claim acts as a significant barrier to seeking enforcement of one's rights or challenging unfair practices. While collective recourse, such as class action, may provide an avenue for resolving problems that affect the collective user base or the underlying unfair practices, meaningful dispute resolution is increasingly being contracted out in standard-form contracts through arbitration clauses, forum selection clauses, and class action waivers (Pavlović, 2016; Enman-Beech, 2020). The contracting out of meaningful access to a judicial process (as a necessary vehicle toward access to substantive justice) makes the standard-form agreements virtually impenetrable since it eliminates an accountability mechanism to challenge the service providers' practices.

Limitations of the Current Regulation of Standard-Form Contracts

Despite a normative view that the enforcement of (electronic) standard-form contracts poses challenges and risks in the consumer context (Radin, 2013; Ben-Shahar, 2007), Canadian courts, over the last two decades, have prioritized commercial certainty and party autonomy over the social reality of standard-form contracts and their regulatory role by routinely enforcing consumer electronic standard-form contracts. What follows is a brief summary of the most important Canadian cases on electronic contracts insofar as they exemplify the courts' approach to regulating the contracts from the perspective of consumers as passive market (and social) actors.

Rudder v. Microsoft (1999) was the first Canadian case involving electronic standard-form contracts and exemplifies this approach, which has been subsequently carried through in a number of consumer cases involving boilerplate contracts. In what is now an oft-cited paragraph, Justice Winkler prioritized party autonomy and commercial certainty over the collective interests of consumers, which were perhaps not as apparent then as they are today. The following quote from Justice Winkler also exemplifies the classic paradigm of consumers as having no other role other than being market participants:

> Neither the form of this contract nor its manner of presentation to potential members are so aberrant as to lead to such an anomalous result. To give effect to the plaintiffs' argument [to not enforce the forum selection clause] would, rather than advancing the goal of "commercial certainty" ... move this type of electronic transaction into the realm of commercial absurdity. It would lead to chaos in the marketplace, render ineffectual electronic commerce and undermine the integrity of any agreement entered through this medium. On the present facts, the Membership Agreement must be afforded the sanctity that must be given to any agreement in writing. (*Rudder v. Microsoft*, 1999, para. 16)

When the case was decided, in 1999, electronic commerce and electronic consumer contracts were nascent, and it may have been difficult to imagine how pervasive these contracts and digital services over the Internet would become in the daily lives of individuals. By focusing on party autonomy and commercial certainty, the court set an almost irreversible course for electronic standard-form contracts, whose negative consequences are strongly felt even today.

In *Kanitz v. Rogers Cable* (2002) and *Dell Computer v. Union des consommateurs* (2007), the courts have further entrenched the view that these contracts are about freedom of choice and party autonomy, and, as such, should be given the same effect as freely negotiated contracts in the commercial environment. Such a narrow approach is particularly challenging for contemporary circumstances, in which standard-form contracts are regulating a much wider swath of social relationships. By routinely enforcing standard-form contracts, the courts are effectively giving private actors much more power than to regulate pure market relations.

In contrast, the Supreme Court of Canada's decision *in Douez v. Facebook* (2017) represents a significant shift toward both understanding the regulatory role of standard-form contracts and their implication to both economic and social relationships. The majority of the Supreme Court (which included two decisions, one by Justice Karakatsanis for the majority and a concurring opinion by Justice Abella) recognized that the contemporary environment of consumer contracts is distinct from the commercial environment in which the contract rules have developed over the years. The majority recognized that these contracts are now ubiquitous and are based on the inequality of bargaining powers. Justice Abella went further than the majority to encapsulate the reality of these contracts: there is "no bargaining, no choice, no adjustments" (*Douez v. Facebook*, 2017, para. 98), which is at the core of why these contracts challenge the traditional bases of contract law, such as consent, choice, and party autonomy. The majority found Facebook's terms of service to be a valid agreement but did not enforce the forum selection clause, which effectively permitted for the class action against Facebook to proceed in British Columbia. Justice Abella found that the forum selection clause as a contract was not valid since it was unconscionable.

In my view, the Supreme Court's decision in *Douez v. Facebook* (2017) marks a fundamental shift in the court's approach to consumer contracts but is short of revolutionary. The Supreme Court' justices' 4–3 split—as well as the arguments used by the majority (that there is a new social reality in which these contracts are effectively powerful regulators) and the dissent (that the economic reality in which "certainty and predictability of transactions" take precedence)—are indicative of the tension between the old and new paradigms of consumer relationships.

While the Supreme Court recognized in *Douez v. Facebook* (2017) that consumer relationships are different than commercial ones, two years later, in *TELUS Communications v. Wellman* (*TELUS,* 2019), the court failed to recognize that the same dynamic applies to other similarly situated parties, such as small businesses. In the court's view, the case primarily hinged on the statutory interpretation of the Ontario *Arbitration Act* (1991), leaving little room for addressing normative and policy arguments about the role of standard-form contracts and their impact on relationships involving vulnerable parties. Similarly to *Douez v. Facebook*, although with a different split, *TELUS Communications v. Wellman* embodies the tension between maintaining commercial certainty (in the majority decision), and understanding the social and economic reality of "absence of choice" for the weaker parties (in the dissenting decision [*TELUS,* 2019, para. 166]). It is worth noting, however, that Justice Moldaver, writing for the majority, did recognize that there are broader policy implications of these contracts, but that they "are better dealt with directly through the doctrine of unconscionability" (*TELUS,* 2019, para. 85). The doctrine of unconscionability is an equitable doctrine the courts use to deny enforcement of a contract or, more commonly, a clause in a contract. In *Douez v. Facebook*, Justice Abella found Facebook's terms of use unenforceable based on the doctrine of unconscionability. The doctrine is not uniform across Canada, and generally sets a high threshold (Enman-Beech, 2020).

In *Heller v. Uber Technologies* (2019), the Ontario Court of Appeal did what the Supreme Court of Canada in *TELUS* did not, and recognized that in relationships governed by standard-form contracts other similarly situated parties—such as workers in the gig economy—ought to be protected due to the inequality and unfairness of the underlying relationship. In this case, Uber drivers were seeking a declaration that they were employees, not independent contractors; but an arbitration clause in Uber's terms of service required Canadian drivers to arbitrate their claims in the Netherlands, with an upfront filing fee of $14,500. Revolving around the enforceability of this arbitration clause, the case was all about access to justice and access to class proceedings as a meaningful dispute resolution mechanism for class-wide claims. In its decision, the Ontario Court of Appeal recognized that workers in the gig economy are as equally vulnerable as consumers, and found that an arbitration clause in Uber's terms of service was unconscionable. Yet it remained to be seen if, on appeal, the Supreme Court would carry forward the paradigm shift introduced in *Douez v. Facebook*.

On June 26, 2020, the Supreme Court of Canada issued its decision in *Uber v. Heller*, ruling the arbitration clause in Uber's terms of service was unconscionable, and therefore unenforceable. While, like *TELUS*, *Uber v. Heller* is not a consumer case, the underlying issue of the regulatory power of standard-form contracts is equally applicable to consumer relationships.

The Supreme Court's decision in *Uber v. Heller* might be much more groundbreaking than the court's quite revolutionary decision in *Douez v. Facebook*. First, contrary to the 2017 divided bench, the very strong majority of eight justices to one in *Uber v. Heller* would signal that the court now embraces the new reality of how far-reaching the regulatory power of standard-form contracts has become. Written by Justice Abella and Justice Rowe, the majority judgment lays out a modern version of the unconscionability test that is particularly tailored to standard-form contracts in the mass-market environment. Concurring, Justice Brown agreed with the unforceability of the arbitration clause, but on the ground that it "undermine[d] the rule of law by denying access to justice" (*Uber v. Heller*, 2020, para. 101). On the opposite end, the dissenting opinion by Justice Coté is a treatise on freedom of contract and party autonomy, showing the rift between the old and new paradigms. Second, the majority and the concurring judgments distinctly recognize that, while being a procedural mechanism, arbitration clauses have a direct impact on the substantive rights under the contract, and effectively eliminates any rights of the weaker party when it prevents access to an appropriate adjudicatory mechanism. Thirdly, and perhaps most importantly, the Supreme Court recognized that standard-form contracts are a necessary tool in today's mass market, but put on notice the drafters of these agreements: going forward both procedural and substantive clauses will be subject to a closer judicial scrutiny.

Conclusion: Ways Forward

It has taken almost twenty years for the courts to recognize the radically different reality of the contemporary society in which we are consumers first—a necessary rationale to start recalibrating certain aspects of contract law. In today's society, where our lives are largely digital, the line is blurring between a consumer, who acquires digital services, and a citizen, who uses those digital services to be informed or participate in civic discourse. Citizenry in a digital context is often premised on digital consumerism, and both activities are tightly wrapped into standard-form contracts. Boilerplate contracts have thus migrated even further, from a purely commercial environment to a consumer environment, and now to citizenship and participation in a digital context.

Contracts have been a regulatory tool for private economic relationships, yet they are increasingly being used to regulate socio-economic rights (such as the right to work) and a wide range of social relationships that often include significant public interest (such as civic participation). As a result, standard-form contracts have become a powerful tool that extend the boundaries of private ordering into somewhat of an unchartered territory with significant risks for the public. By supercharging contracts with procedural limitations (such as forum selection clauses, arbitration clauses, and class action waivers), businesses are making it difficult, if not impossible, for users to challenge their practices before the courts. This effectively shields businesses from any oversight over their practices and makes them into powerful gatekeepers of numerous social interactions, including access to and provision of information.

A robust and multifaceted research and policy agenda is urgently required in order to strengthen consumer rights, preserve the integrity of civic participation, and prevent further erosion of human and democratic rights by non-negotiated standard-form contracts:

- First, given the diversity of contracts (and the relationships they regulate), a more nuanced, empirically based approach to identifying risks and challenges is required for meaningful evidence-based policy-making. While it is easy to paint all standard-form contracts with the same "unfairness" brush, not all of them are the same or produce the same impact, given the wide range of relationships they regulate and the multitude of provisions they include. Cataloguing the provisions (Marotta-Wurgler, 2007), identifying their negative impact, and correlating the contracts with the market power and market options would be the first step, and would provide a sound empirical basis for identifying appropriate and proportionate regulatory approaches.

- Second, Canada needs to learn from other comparable jurisdictions, such as from the European Union's (EU) New Deal for Consumers (*Directive [EU] 2019/2161*, 2019) and Australia's comprehensive legislative review of consumer law (2018). Canada also needs to overcome federal-provincial jurisdictional issues and create a strong and well-rounded consumer rights framework that would be applicable across industries, across federal and provincial borders, and across a myriad of regulatory schemes and regulatory agencies. Basing this consumer rights framework on the consumers-first paradigm would help resolve the current reluctance to limit the reach of contracts, since contracts are currently seen exclusively as economic regulators.
- Third, a uniform legislation that limits the reach of standard-form contracts, and that applies to not only consumer relationships but other similarly situated relationships, would go far in addressing some of the current tensions. The legislation could use as a model, or expand on, the EU Directive on unfair terms in consumer contracts (*Directive 2005/29/EC*, 2005) or the American Law Institute's draft "Restatement of the law of Consumer Contracts" (McGowan, 2019). In addition, providing a uniform format and simplifying the language of the contracts would go far in fostering digital and legal literacy, and helping people understand their rights and obligations (Shade et al., in Chapter 3).
- Finally, and perhaps more importantly, given that standard-form contracts act as entry points to all aspects of digital life, it is imperative that the narrow view of standard-form contracts as economic regulatory mechanisms gives way to a more expansive view of boilerplate contracts as social regulatory mechanisms. Only by changing this starting viewpoint can we shift the thinking and corresponding regulatory approaches to contracts both in the areas of consumer relationships as well as social or civic relationships. The Supreme Court of Canada may have just done that in *Uber v. Heller*, but it remains to be seen whether the Supreme Court's recognition of the new social reality of these contracts and the corresponding shift in the way they are enforced are carried forward by that Court itself, as well as the lower courts, in both the consumer context and, more importantly, the

broader social context of these contracts—until regulators and legislators finally act.

References

Arbitration Act, 1991, SO 1991, c. 17.

Bakos, Y., Marotta-Wurgler, F., & Trossen, D. R. (2014). Does anyone read the fine print: Consumer attention to standard-form contracts. *Journal of Legal Studies, 43*(1), 1–35.

Ben-Shahar, O. (2007). *Boilerplate: The foundation of market contracts.* Cambridge University Press.

Ben-Shahar, O. & Schenier, C. (2014). *More than you wanted to know: The failure of mandated disclosures.* Princeton University Press.

Best, A. (1981). *When consumers complain.* Columbia University Press.

Cho, J., Keum, H., & Shah, D. (2015). News consumers, opinion leaders, and citizen consumers: Moderators of the consumption—participation. *Journalism & Mass Communication Quarterly, 92*(1), 161–178.

Cohen, J. E. (1988). Copyright and the jurisprudence of self-help. *Berkeley Technology Law Review, 13*(3), 1089–1143.

Defoe, D. (1726). *The complete English tradesman, in familiar letters: Directing him in all the several parts and progressions of trade.* Printed for Charles Rivington. https://babel.hathitrust.org/cgi/pt?id=nnc1.0112322717&view=1up&seq=29

Dell Computer Corp. v. Union des consommateurs, [2007] 2 SCR 801.

Directive 2005/29/EC of the European Parliament and of the Council of 11 May 2005 concerning unfair business-to-consumer commercial practices in the internal market, O.J., L. 149, 11.6.2005, 22–39.

Directive (EU) 2019/2161 of the European Parliament and of the Council of 27 November 2019 amending Council Directive 93/13/EEC and Directives 98/6/EC, 2005/29/EC and 2011/83/EU of the European Parliament and of the Council as regards the better enforcement and modernisation of Union consumer protection rules, O.J., L. 328, 18.12.2019, 7–28.

Douez v. Facebook Inc., 2017 SCC 33.

Dubois, E. and Martin-Bariteau, F. (2020). Citizens and their political institutions in a digital context. In W. H. Dutton (Ed.), *A research agenda for digital politics.* Edward Elgar. https://papers.ssrn.com/sol3/papers.cfm?abstract_id=3499315

Enman-Beech, J. (2020). Unconscionable inaccess to justice. *Supreme Court Law Review.* Advance online publication. https://papers.ssrn.com/sol3/papers.cfm?abstract_id=3467019

Heller v. Uber Technologies Inc., 2019 ONCA 1.

Jacobsen, E. (2017). Political consumption—citizenship and consumerism. In M. Keller, B. Halkier, T. A. Wilska, & M. Truninger. (Eds.), *Routledge Handbook on Consumption* (pp. 181–190). Routledge.

Kanitz v. Rogers Cable Inc., [2002] OJ No 665, [2002] 58 OR (3d) 299.

Kerr, I. R. (2005). If left to their own devices …: How DRM and anti-circumvention laws can be used to hack privacy. In M. Geist (Ed.), *In the public interest: The future of Canadian copyright law* (pp. 167–210). Irwin Law.

Marotta-Wurgler, F. (2007). What's in a standard-form contract? An empirical analysis of software license agreements. *Journal of Empirical Legal Studies, 4*(4), 677–713.

McGowan, D. (2019). Consumer contracts and the restatement project (Paper no. 19–424). *San Diego Legal Studies.* https://papers.ssrn.com/sol3/papers.cfm?abstract_id=3446802

Pavlović, M. (2016). Contracting out of access to justice: Enforcement of forum selection clauses in consumer contracts. *McGill Law Journal, 62*(2), 389–440.

Productivity Commission (2018). *Review of Australia's Consumer Policy Framework.* Productivity Commission Inquiry Report no 45, Australian Government. https://www.pc.gov.au/inquiries/completed/consumer-policy/report

Radin, M. J. (2013). *Boilerplate: The fine print, vanishing rights, and the rule of law.* Princeton University Press.

Rakoff, T. D. (1983). Contracts of adhesion: An essay in reconstruction. *Harvard Law Review, 96*(6), 1173–1284.

Ramsay, I. (1985). Framework for regulation of the consumer marketplace. *Journal of Consumer Policy, 8*(4), 353–372.

Ramsay, I. (1993). Consumer law and structures of thought: A comment. *Journal of Consumer Policy, 16*(1), 79–94.

Rudder v. Microsoft Corp., [1999] OJ No 3778, [1999] 2 CPR (4th) 474.

Scammell, M. (2000). The Internet and civic engagement: The age of the citizen consumer. *Political Communication, 17*(4), 351–355.

TELUS Communications Inc. v Wellman, 2019 SCC 19.

Tilden Rent-A-Car Co. v Clendenning (1978), 83 DLR (3d) 400.

Trebilcock, M. J. (1995). Critiques of the limits of freedom of contract: A rejoinder. *Osgoode Hall Law Journal, 33*(2), 353–377.

Trentmann, F. (2016). *The empire of things: How we became a world of consumers, from the fifteenth century to the twenty-first.* HarperCollins.

Trigg v. MI Movers International Transport Services Ltd. et al., (1991) 4 OR (3d) 562, 50 OAC 321 (CA).

Uber v. Heller, 2020 SCC 16.

Werden, G. J. (2011). Consumer welfare and competition policy. In J. Drexl, W. Kerber, & R. Podszun (Eds.), *Competition policy and the economic approach* (pp. 11–43). Edward Elgar Publishing.

CHAPTER 9

A Human Rights-Based Approach to Data Protection in Canada

Teresa Scassa

Abstract

The rapidly changing digital and data landscape has placed increasing pressure on Canada's existing data protection frameworks. Individual-oriented consent-based mechanisms no longer seem adequate or appropriate to address the challenges posed by the ubiquitous and continuous harvesting of massive amounts of data through the Internet of Things, and its use in big data analytics, artificial intelligence, and machine learning. This paper explores the potential for a shift in paradigm—to a human rights-based approach to data and privacy.

Canadian privacy law is at a crossroads. While data protection law stagnates, data collection continues to increase in volume and variety. New technologies are connecting our bodies, homes, vehicles, and even our cities, to the Internet of Things (IoT). There are ever fewer areas of human life untouched by rampant data collection. Not only is the collection of personal data ubiquitous and continuous, it is often of extraordinary detail and quality. In this sense, as noted in the Introduction to this book, individuals enact their citizenship in a digital context on a daily basis, and privacy is intrinsically intertwined with it.

In addition to dramatic changes in the scope and scale of data collection, the surging digital and data economy find new applications for data at an astounding rate. Big data analytics have developed into artificial intelligence (AI) and machine learning. These technologies rely on massive quantities of data, and many of the new applications are aimed at products or services customized for individuals or for "categories" of individuals. AI applications for government and private sector actors alike will profile, sort, categorize, and make decisions that both define and impact individuals and groups.

The *Personal Information Protection and Electronic Documents Act* (PIPEDA) of 2000, Canada's main private sector data protection law, was not built for the burgeoning data economy. The House of Commons Standing Committee on Access to Information, Privacy and Ethics (ETHI) held a number of hearings over the past two years that touch on privacy concerns, including hearings on the reform of PIPEDA (ETHI, 2018a), the applicability of privacy laws to political parties (Office of the Privacy Commissioner of Canada [OPC], 2018), the Facebook-Cambridge Analytica scandal (ETHI, 2018b, 2018c), and the Sidewalk Toronto's proposed smart city development (Vincent, 2019). Both the federal Smart Cities Challenge and the controversial Sidewalk Toronto proposal have sparked important debates about managing privacy in increasingly networked and technologically enabled public and private contexts (Canadian Press, 2018).

In May 2019, the federal government announced its *Digital Charter*, a political declaration articulating a set of principles for digital policy development. Among these principles, three touch on issues of importance to PIPEDA reform: control and consent; transparency, portability, and interoperability; and strong enforcement and real accountability. In addition, the government has released a discussion paper outlining some of the data protection reform issues it is considering (ISED, 2019).

Although there are signs that law reform is likely to occur at the federal level in Canada, it is not clear how extensive or transformative this reform will be. This chapter argues for a paradigm shift in Canadian data protection law—one that reframes privacy as a human right, rather than as a trade-off in the race to innovate or to carry out business in Canada.

The Need for PIPEDA Reform

There is no constitutional right to privacy in Canada beyond the Section 8 right in the *Canadian Charter of Rights and Freedoms* (1982) to be free from unreasonable search and seizure by government actors. In spite of this, courts have held that both the federal public sector *Privacy Act* (1985) and PIPEDA have quasi-constitutional status. This means that courts must interpret the rights protected by these laws generously (Curran, 2014). PIPEDA is a data protection law built around consent in consumer-business relationships. The law itself is premised upon a need to balance the privacy rights of individuals with the needs of businesses to collect, use, and disclose personal information (PIPEDA, 2000, s. 3). Although informed consent is, in many contexts, a means of preserving individual dignity and autonomy, in the contemporary data protection context it has become increasingly unmanageable as a basis for the collection, use, or disclosure of personal information. Individuals are overwhelmed by requests for consent, by lengthy and incomprehensible privacy policies, and by the reality of practical exclusion from digital services if consent is not granted (OPC, 2017). In addition, the speed and complexity of the data economy means that an organization's purposes for collection are often unclear and may shift over time. The implications or consequences of granting consent are not always evident, and these too may evolve.

The highly individualist orientation of the consent model is also no longer adequate to address all privacy concerns. Privacy rights are increasingly understood as having collective and not just individual dimensions. Titus Stahl notes that traditional conceptions of privacy focus on the collection of "specific information about specific individuals," whereas indiscriminate mass surveillance technologies affect almost everyone (2016, p. 33). Behavioural data collected from individuals can be used to profile individuals, groups, and communities. Alessandro Mantelero (2016) argues for a concept of "collective data protection" (p. 246), noting that "the most important concern in this context is the protection of groups from potential harm due to invasive and discriminatory data processing" (p. 249). He argues that collective privacy interests "have a supra-individual nature and a collective dimension, which are not adequately addressed by the existing data protection legal framework." An example of the collective dimension of privacy rights can also be seen in the Cambridge

Analytica scandal. There, although there was large-scale misuse of personal information, the most important harms were public ones: the manipulation of voters with a view to subverting democracy.

The traditional consent model reflected in PIPEDA creates an illusion of control that is typically exercised once and fleetingly. Yet dramatic increase in the importance of data has led to calls for data protection laws to provide new mechanisms for individuals to assert control over their data—ones that go well beyond the initial point of data collection. From the right of erasure to rights of data portability, new approaches to privacy attempt to address what has been a steady undermining of individual control over identity and autonomy in digital realms. In addition, privacy advocates maintain that without strong oversight and enforcement, data protection is largely meaningless. PIPEDA, built on a soft-touch ombuds model (Scassa, 2019; Stoddart, 2005), has come under fire for its relatively weak enforcement (Martin-Bariteau, 2019; Scassa, 2018).

Concerns over privacy in relation to the use of personal data or data derived from human activity in data analytics, AI, and related data-driven technologies extend to human welfare more generally. The use of data in profiling and targeting activities—whether it is of individuals or groups—can be biased, and can lead to discrimination, exclusion, and marginalization (Barocas & Selbst, 2016). The growing concentration of consumer data in the hands of major corporations and technology giants also raises competition law and consumer protection issues. Further, there are serious concerns that the changing nature of data processing, and in particular the use of AI and machine learning, make it difficult to understand how data is used and how decisions are made. Transparency, which has long been a core value associated with data protection, is significantly challenged in both public and private sectors. Joel Reidenberg states that "typically, democracies shield the privacy of citizens from the state and make the activities of the state transparent" (2015, pp. 449–450). He observes that rather than the traditional concept of a transparent government and a private citizen, governments and corporations are increasingly opaque, and citizens more transparent to them.

Canada's struggles with these issues do not occur in a vacuum. The EU's *General Data Protection Regulation* (GDPR) of 2016, which lays out the rules for data protection in all EU states, has set a new global standard—one which must be matched by those jurisdictions wishing to maintain transborder flows of personal data. The GDPR is an ambitious law that seeks to balance the needs of government and industry to collect, process, and share data with the privacy rights of individuals. While it is not necessary to adopt the GDPR wholesale in Canada, there is no doubt that it will have a significant impact in driving reform of Canada's privacy laws. Yet these changes should not be motivated exclusively by the fear of being excluded from the economic benefits of continued transborder data flows. Given the significant actual and potential impacts of data-driven technologies in contemporary society, Canadians both need and deserve a principled human rights-based framework for privacy protection.

A Rights-Based Approach to Data Protection

Canada is a signatory to a number of international human rights instruments that recognize privacy as a human right. For example, Article 12 of the *Universal Declaration of Human Rights* (UNDHR) provides: "No one shall be subjected to arbitrary interference with his privacy, family, home or correspondence, nor to attacks upon his honour and reputation. Everyone has the right to the protection of the law against such interference or attacks" (UNDHR 1948). This same right is found in Article 17 of the *International Covenant on Civil and Political Rights* (ICCPR 1966). The UN Human Rights Committee (1988) has interpreted Article 17 of the ICCPR as requiring the protection of individuals from interference with their privacy not just by the state but also by other persons, both legal and natural. It also includes a right to the protection of the law against incursions on the right—in other words a right to effective legal recourse for breach of privacy rights. The New Zealand Human Rights Commission has stated that, as expressed in the UNDHR and the ICCPR, the right links "the human rights concepts of personal autonomy and dignity" (2018, p. 8).

> In 2013, the UN General Assembly adopted its resolution on the *Right to Privacy in the Digital Age*. This resolution reaffirmed the rights set out in Article 12 of the UNDHR and Article 17 of the ICCPR, and noted as well that "the exercise of the right to privacy is important for the realization of the right to freedom of expression and to hold opinions without interference, and is one of the foundations of a democratic society" (UN General Assembly, 2013, p. 1). The link to these other rights serves as a reminder that while privacy is an individual right, it has broader

collective dimensions as well. As Mantelero (2016) notes, both privacy and data protection play an important role in safeguarding not only individual interests, but also the quality of society in general. Freedom of association, limits to disproportionate surveillance practises, and prevention of discrimination based on sensitive personal data are just few examples of the social effects of safeguarding the right to privacy and personal information. Values such as democracy and pluralism are strictly related to the protection of these rights. (p. 245)

A human rights-based approach to privacy not only recognizes a fundamental right to privacy, but also acknowledges the interrelationship between privacy and the right of individuals to exercise their other rights and freedoms with autonomy and dignity. Further, the human right to privacy must be supported by legislation that renders the right effective and realizable.

Privacy as a Human Right and PIPEDA

Although Section 3 of PIPEDA acknowledges the existence of a right to privacy, this is undercut by the almost simultaneous recognition of the need of organizations to collect, use, and disclose personal information. This brief mention of a simple privacy right can be compared and contrasted with the recitals of the GDPR—the introductory statement of principles of the regulation—which situate that instrument's regulation of data processing within the context of a much broader range of human rights. Reidenberg (2015, p. 460) suggests that "the GDPR [seeks] to match political rights to new economic issues such as profiling, data security breach, and corporate responsibility. Europe looks at citizen transparency from the perspective of privacy as a fundamental right."

Throughout a total of 173 recitals, the GDPR makes repeated references to fundamental rights of individuals in relation to data processing. These include the right to be protected in data processing, as well as the right to be protected against the multiple harms that can flow from the processing of personal data. The GDPR's second recital reads:

The principles of, and rules on the protection of natural persons with regard to the processing of their personal data should, whatever their nationality or residence, *respect their fundamental rights and freedoms,* in particular their right to the protection of personal data. This Regulation is intended to contribute to the accomplishment of an area of freedom, security and justice and of an economic union, to economic and social progress, to the strengthening and the convergence of the economies within the internal market, and to the well-being of natural persons. (emphasis added)

While the actual provisions of the GDPR establish the rules for data processing, the recitals ground these processes in an articulation of the rights. By contrast, Section 3 of PIPEDA casts the right to privacy narrowly by framing it solely as a privacy right, and by balancing it against the interest of organizations in the collection, use, and disclosure of personal data.

Although it might be easy to dismiss the GDPR's recitals as being a lofty excess of verbiage, the framing of legislation is important to its interpretation. For example, the GDPR introduces the concept of "legitimate interest" for data processing (GDPR, 2018, Recital 47). This is meant as a kind of workaround to consent in a rapidly evolving data economy. An organization may have a legitimate interest in processing data it has already collected, but it might be unduly burdensome to obtain fresh consents for this processing. While the GDPR allows organizations to assert "legitimate interest" as a basis for the use of personal data, it must be weighed against the human rights of affected individuals and will only be justified where the impact on those human rights is not disproportionate to the goals sought to be obtained. The concept of legitimate interest has been mooted in Canada as an aspect of PIPEDA reform, and if it were added it would benefit from being incorporated within a framework that acknowledges and gives priority to human rights.

It is also noteworthy that some of the new rights recognized in the GDPR are much easier to reconcile with a broader view of privacy as a human right than they are with the narrower concept of data protection. For example, the right to be forgotten is complicated when framed in terms of data protection, since it typically involves information that has entered the public domain. Yet the right to be forgotten is not simply a right to privacy in the sense of shielding one's personal information from public view; rather, it is also tied to a right to self-actualize, and to potentially even redefine oneself to the world.

The right to data portability is similarly not strictly a right to privacy. Basic data protection law addresses an organization's need to obtain consent to the collection, use, or disclosure of personal information. But data portability is about an individual's right to control their personal data. The individual is entitled to ask for their data that is in the hands of an organization and to port it, in machine-readable formats, to another organization. It is not privacy in the narrow sense that is enhanced by such a right, but rather autonomy and freedom.

The rights in the GDPR around transparency of automated processing of data and the right to an explanation of automated decision-making are similarly not privacy rights in the strict sense. Rather, they are rights that enable individuals to protect themselves against potential bias and injustice.

Although a human rights-based approach to privacy is an important aspect of basic data protection, it is clear that it is also valuable because it both includes and extends beyond privacy rights. For example, the GDPR, in Recital 4, acknowledges the importance of "the respect for private and family life, home and communications, the protection of personal data, freedom of thought, conscience and religion, freedom of expression and information, freedom to conduct a business, the right to an effective remedy and to a fair trial, and cultural, religious and linguistic diversity." The recognition of other rights and freedoms directly impacted by the protection of privacy shifts the GDPR away from a narrower, consent-based paradigm of classic data protection in which an individual negotiates for the collection, use, or disclosure of their personal information in exchange for products or services.

Models for a Human Rights-Based Approach

In addition to the GDPR, there are several past and current models that offer some insights into how a human rights-based approach might be structured for people's digital lives. In 2001, Senator Sheila Finestone introduced Bill S-21, *An Act to guarantee the human right to privacy (Privacy Charter)*. The bill's preamble declared that privacy was "a basic human right of every individual and a fundamental value reflected in international human rights instruments to which Canada is a signatory." It also linked privacy to the public good because of the role it plays in establishing "relations of mutual trust and confidence that are fundamental to the Canadian social fabric." Finally, the preamble linked privacy to the preservation of democracy and to the "full and meaningful enjoyment and exercise of many of the rights and freedoms guaranteed by the *Canadian Charter of Rights and Freedoms*" (*Privacy Charter*, 2001).

The bill's stated purpose was to give effect to basic principles that highlighted the importance of the right to privacy, the existence of a legal right to privacy, and the limitations on privacy rights. Section 3 defined the right to privacy as including physical privacy, the freedom from surveillance, the freedom for interception and monitoring of communications, and "freedom from the collection, use and disclosure of their personal information" (*Privacy Charter*, 2001). Section 4 gives individuals the right to claim and enforce their privacy rights; in Section 4(3), it also prohibits the unjustifiable infringement of a person's right to privacy (*Privacy Charter*, 2001).

Limitations on the right to privacy were acknowledged in the *Privacy Charter*. Although Section 5 began with the principle that any interference with an individual's privacy is an infringement, infringements can be justified if they are "reasonable and can be demonstrably justified in a free and democratic society" (*Privacy Charter*, 2001). To be justifiable, an infringement would have to be lawful and necessary to achieve a sufficiently important objective linked to the public good or to the need to respect another human right. The objective that motivates the infringement must not be capable of being achieved by a less privacy-infringing means and the importance of the objective and its beneficial effects would have to outweigh the detrimental privacy impacts. The consent of the impacted individual will also negate infringement.

The rights in the bill were to be given substantive effect in a number of ways. The Minister of Justice was tasked with overseeing all government bills and prospective regulations to ensure that they were consistent with the *Privacy Charter* (2001, s. 6). Private sector actors were also bound to comply with it in all of their contracts (s. 6). The *Privacy Charter* was to prevail over any inconsistent federal legislation unless another statute expressly declared that it operated notwithstanding (s. 11). This feature sought to import some of the weight of constitutional rights without the need for a painful and potentially fruitless constitutional amendment process. Past experience with the

Canadian Bill of Rights (1960) suggests that such a framework might not be particularly helpful (Hogg, 2007). However, the *Privacy Charter* may have sought to avoid the weaknesses of the *Canadian Bill of Rights* by incorporating a provision (s. 4) that would give Canadians the ability to claim and enforce their rights.

In 2004, the British Columbia Information and Privacy Commissioner (BC Commissioner) recommended the adoption, in the province, of some form of a "privacy charter" that would more deeply embed privacy considerations into government law and policy-making. The recommendation was to require government bodies to assess the privacy impacts of any "law, policy, program or technology under consideration" (Office of the Information and Privacy Commissioner [OIPC], 2004). The assessment would be guided by a privacy charter that either would become part of the *Freedom of Information and Protection of Privacy Act* (FIPPA) or be found in a freestanding statute. Although privacy impact assessments (PIAs) were required by FIPPA at the time, the BC Commissioner believed that all they did was assess technical compliance. The BC Commissioner was concerned that "a PIA that only assesses technical compliance fails to account for the wider risks that initiatives can raise for the personal privacy of individuals whose lives and personal information are affected" (OIPC, 2004, p. 26). The recommendation was never adopted.

The *Privacy Charter* was controversial, and it failed for a number of reasons (Shade, 2009). Canada's Privacy Commissioner at the time, George Radwanski, refused to endorse the bill because it "comports itself as if there were no privacy legislation in place, as if we did not have a *Privacy Act*, which is a good piece of law, and as if we did not have the new Bill C-6, the private sector act, which is also a good piece of law" (Radwanski, 2001, para. 12). Commissioner Radwanski was concerned that the bill would create two-track recourse, with the *Privacy Charter* creating broad and open-ended rights, and public and private sector data protection laws creating carefully constructed and balanced frameworks that would be marginalized by the new right. The Senate Committee that considered Bill C-6 was concerned about its interface with the *Criminal Code*, and saw a need for the scheme to be more integrated with the Office of the Privacy Commissioner.

The *Privacy Charter* was a product of its particular moment in history. It was introduced in the Senate at a time when PIPEDA was still in bill form, and thus there was no previous experience with the oversight of private sector data collection, use, or disclosure. Governments were preoccupied with security in a post-9/11 environment, and there were new measures being proposed that would dramatically increase the surveillance capacities of the state. Public preoccupations with privacy were therefore primarily turned toward concerns over state surveillance. While state surveillance remains a significant concern today, the widespread and ubiquitous data collection by the private sector results in a convergence with the surveillance state, creating a much greater need to recognize the relationship between human rights and ubiquitous data collection. Further, private sector surveillance—labelled "surveillance capitalism" by Shoshana Zuboff (2015)—is a growing concern. The size and complexity of the GDPR is an indication that addressing data protection requires far more than a simple set of rules; what it may instead require is the situating of the data protection regimes within a human rights-based framework.

The *Privacy Charter* recognized that privacy rights were not absolute, but it provided no specific framework in which competing rights could be identified or weighed. Both PIPEDA and the *Privacy Act*, as data protection statutes, attempt to negotiate competing rights and interests in relation to the collection, use, and disclosure of personal information. In fact, the bulk of both statutes reflects a direct engagement with this balancing. This suggests that a broader human rights-based approach might most effectively be incorporated into each statute through an expanded statement of principles that provides a framework within which the legislation should be interpreted.

The Quebec *Charter of Human Rights and Freedoms* offers an interesting model that combines privacy with other human rights. This provincial law takes precedence over other legislation in the province unless another provincial statute specifically declares that it does not apply (Quebec *Charter*, s. 52). While the Quebec *Charter* is not a privacy charter *per se*, it contains several provisions that have a strong connection to privacy values. Article 1 establishes, "a right to life, and to personal security, inviolability and freedom"; Article 4 provides that "every person has a right to the safeguard of his dignity, honour and reputation"; and Article 3 provides for the "freedom of conscience, freedom of religion, freedom of opinion, freedom of expression, freedom of peaceful assembly and freedom of association." Each of these rights is linked to the values associated with privacy, and all would apply, for example, to the interpretation of privacy rights under the *Civil Code*, or to data protection rights under Quebec's *Act Respecting the Protection of Personal Information in the Private Sector*. The Quebec *Charter* also provides for specific privacy rights in Article 5: "Every person has a right to respect for his private life." The inviolability of the home is protected in Article 7, Article 8 provides a broad right against anyone entering on a person's property or taking anything therefrom without consent, and Article 9 states that "every person has a right to non-disclosure of confidential information." The Quebec *Charter* also includes the right to be free from discrimination, something that is becoming increasingly important in the context of data processing. Article 24.1 of the Quebec *Charter* provides for a right to be free from unreasonable search and seizure at the hands of the state. The document also contains a series of economic and social rights, among which is found, in Article 44, the "right to information to the extent provided by law." The provisions of the Quebec *Charter* apply broadly across public and private sectors alike: There is a right of action and a right to compensation, including punitive damages established by Article 49. While many of the rights and freedoms contain their own limitations in the wording of articles that establish them, the fundamental rights and freedoms found in Articles 1 through 8 of the Quebec *Charter* are made subject, in Article 9, to "a proper regard for democratic values, public order and the general well-being of the citizens of Quebec." The Quebec *Charter* has been relied upon to protect privacy rights on its own and in combination with separate privacy rights found in the Quebec *Civil Code*. The rights in the *Civil Code* are also in part implemented by separate public and private sector data protection laws in Quebec.

Both the *Privacy Charter* and the Quebec *Charter* offer examples of how a broader human rights perspective could inform a legislative approach to data protection law in Canada. Of course, Canadian federalism adds a layer of complexity to data protection, since privacy is neither exclusively a matter of federal or provincial jurisdiction (Kratchanov, 1995). PIPEDA is justified as federal legislation under the "trade and commerce" power, which limits its application to the collection, use, or disclosure of personal information to the context of commercial activity (s. 4.1.a). PIPEDA's odd constitutional status and its relationship to provincial private sector data protection statutes in Quebec, Alberta, and British Columbia make adopting a human rights-based approach through an independent legislative instrument complicated. However, the values that should guide the interpretation of PIPEDA could be grounded in either the preamble of the statute or in a reworked Section 3.

Conclusion

More than ever, big data issues raise crucial privacy concerns as well as complex, interrelated human rights issues. Although acknowledged by the courts as quasi-constitutional in nature, PIPEDA is a data protection statute that makes only a brief nod to privacy rights in the same provision that balances them against the needs of organizations to collect, use, and disclose personal information. Further, it does not acknowledge the complex range of privacy interests in the big data era, nor does it acknowledge the relationship between the protection of privacy and the safeguarding of other human rights values. As we move toward reform of PIPEDA, it is time to recognize the important and interconnected human rights dimensions of privacy. Although a set of recitals in a preamble or a legislative provision setting out the human rights basis for the protection of privacy may seem like cosmetic changes, they would serve important goals. The first of these is to give legislative voice to the principles and human rights values that are meant to underlie data protection law in Canada. The second is to provide concrete direction for the interpretation of provisions that, while also serving to oil the machinery of commerce and innovation, should never do so at the expense of fundamental human rights.

Acknowledgements

This paper draws upon research that was funded by the Office of the Privacy Commissioner of Canada in early 2019. All views expressed are the author's own.

References

Act Respecting the Protection of Personal Information in the Private Sector, CQLR c P-39.1 (1993).

Barocas, S., & Selbst, A. D. (2016). Big data's disparate impact. *California Law Review, 104,* 671–732.

Bill S-21, An Act to guarantee the human right to privacy [Privacy Charter]. (2001). 37th Parliament, 1st Session.

Canada, House of Commons, Standing Committee on Access to Information, Privacy and Ethics [ETHI]. (2018a, February). *Towards privacy by design: Review of the Personal Information Protection and Electronic Documents Act.* Report no. 12. 42nd Parliament, 1st Session. https://www.ourcommons.ca/DocumentViewer/en/42-1/ETHI/report-12/

Canada, House of Commons, Standing Committee on Access to Information, Privacy and Ethics [ETHI]. (2018b, December). *Democracy under threat: Risks and solutions in the era of disinformation and data monopoly.* Report no. 17. 42nd Parliament, 1st Session. https://www.ourcommons.ca/Content/Committee/421/ETHI/Reports/RP10242267/ethirp17/ethirp17-e.pdf

Canada, House of Commons, Standing Committee on Access to Information, Privacy and Ethics [ETHI]. (2018c, June). *Addressing digital privacy vulnerabilities and potential threats to Canada's democratic electoral process.* Report no. 16. 42nd Parliament, 1st Session. https://www.ourcommons.ca/Content/Committee/421/ETHI/Reports/RP9932875/ethirp16/ethirp16-e.pdf

Canadian Bill of Rights, SC 1960, c. 44 (1960).

Canadian Charter of Rights and Freedoms, Part I of the Constitution Act of 1982, Schedule B of the Canada Act (UK), 1982, c. 11 (1982).

Charter of Human Rights and Freedoms, CQLR, c. C-12 (1975).

Civil Code of Quebec, CQLR, c. CCQ-1991 (1991).

Curran, B. (2014). Alberta (Information and Privacy Commissioner) v. United Food and Commercial Workers, Local 401. *Alberta Law Review, 52*(1), 185–197.

Freedom of Information and Protection of Privacy Act [FIPPA], RSBC, c 165 (1996).

Hogg, P.W. (2007). *Constitutional Law of Canada,* 5th ed., Carswell.

Innovation, Science and Economic Development Canada [ISED]. (2019). *Strengthening privacy for the digital age: Proposals to modernize the Personal Information Protection and Electronic Documents Act.* https://www.ic.gc.ca/eic/site/062.nsf/eng/h_00107.html

International Covenant on Civil and Political Rights [ICCPR]. New York, 16 December 1966, United Nations Treaty Series, vol. 999, no. 14668, p. 171.

Kratchanov, D. C. (1995). *Personal information and the protection of privacy 1995.* Uniform Law Conference of Canada. https://www.ulcc.ca/en/annual-meetings/430-1995-quebec-qc/civil-section-documents/246-personal-information-and-the-protection-of-privacy-1995?showall=1&limitstart=

Mantelero, A. (2016). Personal data for decisional purposes in the age of analytics: From an individual to a collective dimension of data protection. *Computer Law and Security Review, 32,* 238–255.

Martin-Bariteau, F. (2019, May 7). Qu'attendons-nous pour protéger la vie privée ? *Policy Options.* https://policyoptions.irpp.org/magazines/may-2019/quattendons-nous-pour-proteger-la-vie-privee/

New Zealand Human Rights Commission. (2018). *Privacy, data and technology: Human rights challenges in the digital age.* https://www.hrc.co.nz/files/5715/2575/3415/Privacy_Data_Technology_-_Human_Rights_Challenges_in_the_Digital_Age_FINAL.pdf

Office of the Information and Privacy Commissioner for British Columbia [OIPC]. (2004). *Submission of the Information and Privacy Commissioner to the Special Committee to Review the Freedom of Information and Protection of Privacy Act.* https://www.oipc.bc.ca/special-reports/1274

Office of the Privacy Commissioner of Canada [OPC]. (2017). *2016-17 Annual report to Parliament on the Personal Information Protection and Electronic Documents Act and the Privacy Act.* https://www.priv.gc.ca/en/opc-actions-and-decisions/ar_index/201617/ar_201617/#heading-0-0-3-1

Office of the Privacy Commissioner of Canada [OPC]. (2018). *Securing trust and privacy in Canada's electoral process: Resolution of the federal, provincial and territorial information and privacy commissioners.* https://www.priv.gc.ca/en/about-the-opc/what-we-do/provincial-and-territorial-collaboration/joint-resolutions-with-provinces-and-territories/res_180913/

Personal Information Protection and Electronic Documents Act [PIPEDA], SC, c. 5 (2000).

Privacy Act, RSC, c. P-21 (1985).

Radwanski, G. (2001, September 20). *Testimony to the Standing Senate Committee on Social Affairs, Science and Technology.* 37th Parliament, 1st Session. https://www.priv.gc.ca/en/opc-actions-and-decisions/advice-to-parliament/archive/02_05_a_010920/

Regulation (EU) 2016/679 of the European Parliament and of the Council of 27 April 2016 on the protection of natural persons with regard to the processing of personal data and on the free movement of such data, and repealing Directive 95/46/EC (General Data Protection Regulation) [GDPR], O.J., L. 119, 4.5.2016, p. 1–88.

Reidenberg, J. R. (2015). The transparent citizen. *Loyola University Chicago Law Journal, 47,* 437–463.

Scassa, T. (2018, June 7). Enforcement powers key to PIPEDA reform. *Policy Options.* https://policyoptions.irpp.org/magazines/june-2018/enforcement-powers-key-pipeda-reform/

Scassa, T. (2019). Moving on from the ombuds model for data protection in Canada. *Canadian Journal of Law and Technology, 1,* 90–98.

Shade, L. R. (2009). Reconsidering the right to privacy in Canada. *Bulletin of Science, Technology & Society, 28*(1), 80–91.

Stahl, T. (2016). Indiscriminate mass surveillance and the public sphere. *Ethics Information Technology, 18*, 33–39.

Stoddart, J. (2005). *Cherry picking among apples and oranges: Refocusing current debate about the merits of the ombuds-model under PIPEDA.* Office of the Privacy Commissioner of Canada. https://www.priv.gc.ca/en/opc-actions-and-decisions/research/explore-privacy-research/2005/omb_051021/

The Canadian Press. (2018, December 7). Sidewalk Labs's vision and your data privacy: A guide to the saga on Toronto's waterfront. *The Globe and Mail.* Retrieved June 24, 2019, from https://www.theglobeandmail.com/canada/toronto/article-sidewalk-labs-quayside-toronto-waterfront-explainer/

United Nations General Assembly. (1948, 10 December). Resolution 217 A (III), *Universal declaration on human rights* [UNHDR]. http://www.un.org/en/universal-declaration-human-rights/

United Nations General Assembly. (2013, December 18). Resolution 68/167, *The right to privacy in the digital age*, A/RES/68/167. https://undocs.org/A/RES/68/167

United Nations Human Rights Committee. (1988, 8 April 1988). *CCPR general comment No. 16: Article 17 (right to privacy), the right to respect of privacy, family, home and correspondence, and protection of honour and reputation.*

Vincent, D. (2019, February 19). Waterfront Toronto officials to face grilling in Ottawa over Sidewalk Labs plans. *The Toronto Star.* https://www.thestar.com/news/gta/2019/02/19/waterfront-toronto-officials-to-face-grilling-in-ottawa-over-sidewalk-labs-plans.html

Zuboff, S. (2015). Big other: Surveillance capitalism and the prospects of an information civilization. *Journal of Information Technology, 30*, 75–89.

CHAPTER 10

Making Sense of the Canadian Digital Tax Debate

Michael Geist

Abstract

Few Canadian digital policy issues have proven as confusing as the ongoing debate over digital taxation. While there is general agreement that a neutral tax policy should apply to the online world, the issue has been muddled by both nomenclature and corporate efforts to use digital tax policy for competitive advantage. With politicians fearing voter backlash over the perception of increased taxes, Canadian digital tax policy has struggled to keep pace, leading to a predominantly hands-off approach. The result is an uneven digital policy playing field that leaves domestic firms disadvantaged and government coffers missing out on hundreds of millions of dollars. This chapter seeks to unpack the digital tax policy debate by examining the various meanings, the core policy choices, and the potential to develop a fair digital policy structure. The chapter begins with a discussion of digital sales taxes, followed by corporate income taxes, and the finally mandated contributions by companies active in the digital economy, including online service providers and Internet access providers.

F ew Canadian digital policy issues have proven as confusing as the ongoing debate over digital taxation. While there is general agreement that a neutral tax policy should apply to the online world, the issue has been muddled by both nomenclature and corporate efforts to use digital tax policy for competitive advantage. With politicians fearing voter backlash over the perception of increased taxes, Canadian digital tax policy has struggled to keep pace, leading to a predominantly hands-off approach. The result is an uneven playing field in digital tax policy that leaves domestic firms disadvantaged and government coffers missing out on hundreds of millions of dollars.

The most obvious example of confused policy-making involves the taxation of digital services such as Netflix. The term "Netflix tax" has been politically toxic for many years, dating back to the 2015 federal election campaign when then prime minister, Stephen Harper, pledged that, if re-elected, his government would not institute a "Netflix tax" (Geist, 2019a). The Liberals responded with a "no Netflix tax" promise of their own (Geist, 2019a), which became government policy when Justin Trudeau was elected and became prime minister a few months later. Yet the words "Netflix tax" mean different things to different people, including digital sales taxes, corporate taxes, or mandated contributions in support of Canadian content production.

The confusion is nicely illustrated by an exchange between NDP MP Peter Julian and Prime Minister Justin Trudeau during question period in the House of Commons in 2018. Julian asked:

> Speaking of letting the wealthy off the hook, the government seems more than happy to let web giants continue to make huge profits without contributing to the Canadian economy. While the rest of the world is trying to make these companies pay, the Liberals are doing the opposite. They are making deals with Netflix and other companies, and offering massive tax breaks. Canadians pay their taxes and expect companies to do the same. When will the Liberals start making web giants pay their fair share? (House of Commons, 2018, p. 16751)

Trudeau responded:

> Mr. Speaker, the NDP is proposing to raise taxes on the middle class, which is something we promised we would not do and have not done. We explicitly promised in the 2015 election campaign that we would not be raising taxes on Netflix. People may

remember Stephen Harper's attack ads on that. They were false. We actually moved forward in demonstrating that we were not going to raise taxes on consumers, who pay enough for their Internet at home. (House of Commons, 2018, p. 16751)

Julian's question seems to refer to corporate income taxes, while Trudeau's response takes aim at either sales taxes or mandated cultural contributions. Beyond the confusion, the conversation mainly considered the Internet from a content consumption perspective while, from education to government, it became an integral part of Canadians' daily lives to enact their citizenship. As such, this chapter seeks to unpack the digital tax policy debate by examining its various meanings, the related core policy choices, and the potential to develop a fair digital policy structure. The chapter begins with a discussion of digital sales taxes, followed by corporate income taxes and, finally, the mandated contributions by companies active in the digital economy, including online service providers and Internet access providers.

Digital Sales Tax

The prospect of extending sales taxes—namely GST/HST in Canada— to digital sales has emerged as a challenging policy issue in countries around the world. The basic principle is relatively straightforward: sales taxes should be applied equally to the sales of all goods (and services for those countries that tax both goods and services) without regard for whether the good or service is tangible or intangible, or sold by a domestic or foreign firm. The need for equal application of sales tax policy is aimed at ensuring that equivalent goods and services are treated equally. Moreover, there is concern that applying sales tax collection obligations solely to domestic firms could place them at a marketplace disadvantage since foreign firms would enjoy a perceived cost advantage for consumers given the "tax free" status of their goods or services.

The need to address the digital sales tax issue was raised in Canada in 2014 when the Conservative government used its budget bill to launch a public consultation on the matter (Geist, 2015). Years later, the Liberal government advised that Canada was awaiting an international agreement on digital sales taxes before implementing any domestic reforms. In 2018, Finance Minister Bill Morneau indicated that the government would support a quick resolution of the issue, but that provincial digital sales tax initiatives would not spark a matching federal tax until the global issues were resolved (Curry, 2018).

The ongoing delays reflect the realization that creating a global sales tax system that requires foreign providers to register and remit sales taxes is fraught with complexity (Dourado, 2018). Registration requirements alone create new costs that some businesses may be unwilling to bear. In order to avoid burdening small businesses, countries may set a revenue threshold before registration and collection requirements kick in. In fact, some businesses may simply decide to avoid or block the taxing market altogether, leading to services that either decline to sell locally or increase their prices to account for the regulatory cost burden.

The complexity of digital sales tax collection was highlighted by government officials at a 2016 hearing of the House of Commons Standing Committee on Canadian Heritage (CHPC):

> E-commerce sales by foreign-based companies can present a challenge for proper sales tax collection. Foreign-based Internet vendors' businesses with no physical presence in Canada are generally not required to collect GST/HST on their sales. Instead, in the case of physical goods that are purchased online and shipped to Canada by post or courier, the applicable customs duties and GST/HST would generally be collected by the Canada Border Services Agency at the time the goods are imported.
>
> In cases other than the importation of physical goods, the GST/HST legislation imposes a general requirement to self-assess the tax. For businesses that would be entitled to recover any tax payable by claiming input tax credits, there is generally no requirement to self-assess tax on such imports. The challenges related to the proper collection of sales tax on digital supplies by foreign-based vendors are not unique to Canada. It's a difficult issue for all jurisdictions with a sales tax. (CHPC, 2016, paras. 11–12)

Indeed, the challenges of imposing a general sales tax requirement on foreign digital firms became readily apparent in 2018 when the Province of Quebec became the first Canadian jurisdiction to establish digital sales tax collection and remission requirements (Quebec Ministry of Finance [QMF, 2018, p. 137]). Yet despite assurances that digital sales taxes are relatively easy to implement, the Quebec plan demonstrates the complexity associated with requiring thousands of online companies around the world to implement dozens or even hundreds of new tax requirements.

The provincial government established a lightweight registration system for foreign companies to ease the administrative burden associated with signing up for provincial sales tax collection. But while the basic framework raises few concerns, enforcement presents an enormous challenge as tax authorities try to persuade online businesses with no presence in the province to register, collect, and remit the applicable sales tax. The government promised to work with businesses to assist with compliance in the first year, but thereafter it warned that "the penalties provided for in the existing tax legislation will be imposed on non-resident suppliers that have not complied with the new obligations" (QMF, 2018, p. 137).

For some businesses, the cost of compliance with the provincial requirements may far exceed the actual tax payments. Without a global standard, the Quebec government has arbitrarily set the threshold for sales tax registration and collection at $30,000 in provincial revenues. That is low compared to many other countries that have adopted digital taxes: the Japanese threshold is over $120,000, the Saudi Arabian threshold is over $340,000, the Swiss threshold is over $135,000, and the New Zealand threshold is over $55,000 (Geist, 2018a).

Many businesses may also have to rework their customer relationships in order to collect increased personal information. For example, some digital services may not currently gather detailed geographic information on their subscribers, but the Quebec tax rules effectively mandate the collection and use of location-based information.

With a 9.75 percent tax rate, the low threshold sets the bar at less than $3,000 in annual sales taxes for some businesses, meaning compliance costs alone could easily exceed the tax revenues and cause some companies to rethink providing service in the province. That points to at least one tax trade-off: the benefits of increased tax revenues set off against decreased consumer choice as some businesses exit the Quebec market.

The enforcement challenges extend to consumers, some of whom may try to avoid paying provincial sales taxes by claiming residency elsewhere. The government has identified measures to target sales tax evaders, with penalties of $100 or 50 percent of the applicable sales tax (Geist, 2018a). In order to identify instances of sales tax evasion, the government plans to collect customer information from out-of-country operators such as Netflix, though it is unclear how it will compel those companies to hand over subscriber lists or other relevant data.

The sales tax issue has been framed by some as a "tax holiday" for companies (NDP, 2018a). Yet the reality is that, when applicable, sales taxes are paid by consumers, not companies. Companies resident in Canada are merely required to collect and remit the applicable sales taxes. The tax does not come out of earnings or represent a gain for the companies who act as intermediaries by collecting the sales tax and remitting it to the government.

In fact, for some digital companies, even the collection and remittance of the sales tax is borne by their users. For example, Uber, the popular ride-sharing service, advises its Canadian drivers that they are required to collect and remit sales tax. Once a driver has obtained a sales tax identification number, Uber will facilitate the collection of the sales tax with each ride and provide a weekly breakdown of the sales tax collected in the prior week to its drivers. The sales tax collected by Uber on behalf of its drivers is paid to the drivers, who are required to file an annual sales tax declaration to the Canada Revenue Agency (CRA) along with any sales tax owing. In other words, sales taxes are paid by riders, but the annual filings fall to the drivers, with Uber facilitating the process by initially collecting the applicable sales tax (Uber, n.d.). A similar system is used by Airbnb, whose lodging providers may also be subject to municipal occupancy taxes (Airbnb, n.d.).

As governments race to catch up to the growth of e-commerce, there has long been a seeming inevitability to the imposition of digital sales tax. However, the experience to date demonstrates that, for the moment, shifting sales tax to a global Internet environment remains easier said than done.

Corporate Income Tax

The debate over "Netflix taxes" has also included discussion over whether the company must pay corporate income tax in Canada. The income tax issue was raised by the NDP in 2018, who called on the government to ensure that Internet companies pay taxes on profits made in Canada (NDP, 2018b). While the income tax issue is an important one, it is not a digital tax issue per se. Rather, it reflects ongoing corporate tax challenges that implicate all multinational companies that strategically structure themselves in the most tax advantageous manner.

Further, the debate on the issue is not limited to Canada. Countries around the world struggle with the same question (Alberici, 2018; Leahy, 2017). Indeed, the issue was raised at the Canadian Senate committee hearing on the issue, with an official from the CRA commenting:

> It is also important to understand the current corporate tax system, which is essentially based on the notion of a permanent establishment, which is a traditional concept. For example, when a company does business in another country and has employees and plants in that country, it clearly has a permanent establishment. The general concept of taxation is based on these notions.
>
> A company that does business in another country and sells digital products does not necessarily have a physical presence. Consequently, some important questions arise with respect to income taxation. The key question is whether these permanent establishment concepts on which tax treaties are based still represent the best way to tax those businesses and to determine whether value is being created in the source country by those electronic transactions. If that is the case, one must determine the approach that should be used to tax properly, but also to ensure that the ultimate result is not double taxation of the business in question.
>
> This therefore requires discussions at the international level, such as those currently being held at the OECD, for example. I think the OECD communiqués attest to the fact that the various OECD members have agreed to take time to analyze this question. The ideal solution is to come up with joint and coordinated options or new standards to prevent double taxation. (Senate Standing Committee on Transport and Communications, 2018, paras. 55–57)

In 2019, the corporate income tax issue emerged as a federal election issue as several political parties committed to establishing a special tax on digital companies. For example, the Liberal Party promised to implement a 3 percent tax on revenues in Canada of large technology companies. The Conservatives introduced a similar plan for a 3 percent tax on large tech companies that provide social media, search, and online marketplace services (in other words, Facebook, Google, and Amazon, but not Netflix). But the Conservative platform also noted that the preference would be for those companies to invest and further establish themselves in Canada. If they do so, the Conservative Party promised to waive the extra tech company corporate tax (Geist 2019b).

While the prospect of implementing a Canadian digital specific corporate tax remains uncertain, a similar proposal in France has drawn the ire of the US government. In December 2019, the United States threatened to implement billions in retaliatory tariffs against France if it proceeded with a 3 percent tax on digital companies. The United States argued that the proposal discriminated against US companies (Palmer, 2019).

In other words, the income tax question is not limited to Canada, nor to digital companies. There is a general consensus on the need to address income tax standards to ensure fair taxation without double payment in multiple jurisdictions.

Mandated Contributions or Taxes in Support of Canadian Culture

While the application of sales taxes to companies such as Netflix may be relatively uncontroversial, the use of the tax system or other regulated payments in furtherance of other government policies has proven far more divisive. For example, in June 2019, then-Canadian Heritage Minister Pablo Rodriguez seemingly embraced a mandated contribution requirement, stating that "everyone has to contribute to our culture. That's why we'll require web giants to create Canadian content [and] promote it on their platforms" (Rodriguez, 2019). The comment marked a significant shift in government policy. Where previously it had emphasized the need for contributions that may vary depending on the type of service, Rodriguez appeared to be making an explicit endorsement of requirements for digital streaming services to provide funding for the creation of Canadian content (Geist, 2018b).

The Canadian cultural sector has relied on three key arguments in support of mandated contribution requirements: (1) the system is necessary to ensure that investment in Canadian film and TV production is not placed at risk, (2) digital streaming services benefit from an unfair advantage, and (3) other jurisdictions, such as the European Union (EU), have already implemented mandated contributions for digital media providers.

This chapter provides an alternate perspective: (1) investment in television and film production in Canada is at an all-time high; (2) the same rules apply to foreign and domestic online video services, and the Canadian broadcasting sector is actually the recipient of significant regulatory advantages; and (3) comparisons to the EU's approach are selective and inapt.

First, regarding investment, the data demonstrates that there is no Canadian content emergency. The most recent industry data confirms that the total value of the Canadian film and television production sector nearly reached $9 billion in 2018, an all-time record, with overall production increasing by 5.9 percent. Notably, the increased funding came primarily from distributors and foreign financing, not from broadcasters (CMPA, 2018).

Second, the same rules apply to foreign and domestic online video services. Proponents argue that services such as Netflix enjoy an unfair advantage because they face no mandatory contribution requirements, while broadcasters and broadcast distributors (BDUs) face regulations that require contributions (30 percent of revenues for broadcasters, 5 percent of revenues for BDUs). The critics of the current system argue that the Netflix investment in Canada is below either percentage and that the absence of required contributions creates an uneven playing field (CMPA, 2019).

However, the most apt comparison to Netflix is not to broadcasters or BDUs, but rather to competitive online video services. These services, whether Canadian or foreign, are all subject to the same requirements—namely, no mandated Canadian content contributions. For example, Bell's Crave, which frequently promotes US programming such as *Seinfeld* and *The Sopranos*, does not face any Canadian content contribution or spending requirements. In fact, the Canadian Radio-television and Telecommunications Commission (CRTC) even created a "hybrid model" in 2015 that allows for video distribution through BDU systems and the Internet without any Canadian-content requirements (Dobby, 2018).

In reality, Canadian broadcasters and BDUs benefit from significant regulatory advantages. Indeed, while some prefer the comparison to broadcasters or BDUs (arguing that the service feels similar to Canadian subscribers), the reality is that both Canadian broadcasters and BDUs are subject to mandated contributions as part of a regulatory quid pro quo in which they receive significant benefits for being part of the regulated system. Both broadcasters and BDUs have benefited from limited competition due to foreign investment restrictions, which caps the percentage that foreign companies may own of Canadian broadcasters or BDUs.

For broadcasters, other advantages include simultaneous substitution, which allows Canadian broadcasters to replace foreign signals with their own. The industry says this policy alone generates hundreds of millions of dollars in revenues for Canadian broadcasters (CRTC, 2016a). Moreover, Canadian broadcasters benefit from must-carry regulations, which require BDUs to include many Canadian channels on basic cable and satellite packages. These rules provide guaranteed access to millions of subscribers, thereby increasing the value of the signals and the fees that can be charged for their distribution (CRTC, 2019). They also enjoy market access protection, which has shielded Canadian broadcasters from foreign competition, such as HBO or ESPN, for decades (Sokic, 2019), as well eligibility for Canadian funding programs, for which companies like Netflix may be ineligible (Buckner, 2019).

BDUs also enjoy their own set of advantages over online service providers. These include bundling benefits, which allow BDUs to bundle less popular Canadian channels with more popular US signals, thereby guaranteeing more revenues (CRTC, 2016b). They are also beneficiaries of copyright retransmission rules, which create an exemption in the *Copyright Act* to allow BDUs to retransmit signals without infringing copyright. This retransmission occurred for many years without any compensation (Canadian Communications Systems Alliance Inc, 2018).

Third, comparisons to the EU are selective and inapt. Proponents point to European regulation as evidence that others have introduced domestic content regulatory requirements on services such as Netflix and say that Canada should follow suit. They argue that Europe envisions requirements that 30 percent of the Netflix catalogue constitute European programming and seek a similar mandate in Canada (Friends, 2020). However, the European rules, which do not take effect until 2020, do not include Europe-wide mandated payments. Indeed, the European Commission (EC) states:

> The new rules clarify the possibility for Member States to impose financial contributions (direct investments or levies payable to a fund) upon media service providers, including those established in a different Member State but that are targeting their national audiences. This would be a voluntary measure for Member States, not an obligation at EU level. (EC, 2018, para. 24)

Moreover, the content requirements are continent-wide, not limited to a single country. The European requirement of 30 percent incorporates all twenty-eight EU Member States (Donders et al., 2018). Once spread across all member states, the requirement is not particularly onerous since it effectively envisions a few percent of the overall catalogue per country. The percentage of Canadian content on Canadian Netflix is already comparable to the per-European country amount (Geist, 2018c). In fact, the EC emphasizes: "We also need to pay attention to new market entrants and small players. The new rules also include a mandatory exemption for companies with a low turnover and low audiences. It could also be inappropriate to impose such requirements in cases where—given the nature or theme of the on-demand audiovisual media services—they would be impracticable or unjustified" (EC, 2018, para. 29).

Supporters of mandated contributions for Canadian content production have also insisted that similar obligations be extended to Internet and wireless providers. They argue that the Internet is rapidly replacing the broadcast system in Canada and therefore should be expected to contribute in much the same manner.

This argument is not a new one. In fact, as far back as 1998, the CRTC conducted hearings on "new media" in which groups argued that the dial-up Internet was little different than conventional broadcasting and should be regulated and taxed as such (CRTC, 1998). In other words, groups have been arguing for new "Netflix taxes" well before Netflix was a global streaming service.

For example, broadcast lawyer Peter Grant, who in 2019 sat on the broadcast and telecom review panel examining Canadian communications laws, told the CRTC more than twenty years ago that if broadcast-quality video ever reached a certain level of market penetration on the Internet, the Commission should "require certain obligations about some funding as a proportion of the revenue from this particular activity to go into a fund or whatever" (CRTC, 1998, pp. 2550–2551). Grant continued by arguing that websites were the equivalent of programming undertakings and that Internet providers were broadcast distribution undertakings (i.e., the Internet was the equivalent of cable distribution).

The argument received a modern endorsement from the CRTC in 2018 with the release of its *Harnessing Change* report. It stated: "There are numerous services in Canada that connect Canadians to content, whether through the Internet or broadcast networks, such as cable or satellite. Demand for these services is almost wholly driven by demand for audio and video content, yet the Canadian market for this content is only supported by BDUs, television programming and radio services" (CRTC, 2018, "Conclusions and Potential Options," para. 36).

The reality, however, is that Internet use is about far more than streaming videos or listening to music. Those are obviously popular activities, but numerous studies point to the fact that they are not nearly as popular as communicating through messaging and social networks; engaging in electronic commerce or Internet banking; or searching for news, weather, and other information (CIRA, 2019; Statistics Canada, 2014). From the integral role of the Internet in our education system to the reliance on the Internet for health information (and increasingly telemedicine) to the massive use of the Internet for business-to-business communications, Internet use is about far more than cultural consumption. Yet proponents of an Internet tax envision the Internet as little more than cable television and want to implement a taxation system akin to that used for cable and satellite providers.

Precisely because the Internet is such an integral part of the daily lives of most Canadians, ensuring universal, affordable access is a competing policy goal that should not be so easily discarded. The CRTC provided little more than an unconvincing assurance that the impact of new Internet taxes would be "cost neutral"—even though Canadians who only rely on Internet access will clearly pay more under such a system.

To date, the government has indicated that it opposes an "approach that increases the cost of services to Canadians" (LeBlanc, 2018). In fact, the government rejected an Internet tax proposal last year on affordability grounds:

> The Committee's [CHPC] recommendation to generate revenue
> by expanding broadcast distribution levies so that they apply

to broadband distribution would conflict with the principle of affordable access. The open Internet has been a powerful enabler of innovation, driving economic growth, entrepreneurship, and social change in Canada and around the world. The future prosperity of Canadians depends on access to an open Internet where Canadians have the power to be freely innovative, communicate, and access the content of their choice in accordance with Canadian laws. Therefore, the Government does not intend to expand the current levy on broadcast distribution undertakings. (Geist, 2017, para. 3)

Notwithstanding the rejection, the Internet tax issue resurfaces again and again.

Conclusion

The past two decades have been marked by near-continuous efforts to use the digital tax issue as a policy lever to benefit one set of stakeholders over another. In the nascent days of e-commerce, a hands-off approach was promoted as an ideal mechanism to help support a relatively small commercial sector. As the digital economy has grown, the debate has gradually shifted, first toward tax fairness and a neutral, level playing field and later to using the digital economy to support sectors that have struggled to adapt to the changing environment. For Canadian digital policy-makers, the challenge is compounded by a confusing public debate with little agreement on what basic terms mean, much less how Canada should proceed.

Despite growing momentum to institute a variety of new taxes, evidence suggests that the case for many new taxes is weak. The implementation of a digital sales tax seems inevitable, though Canada should ensure that its approach is consistent with emerging international standards. Similarly, calls for a new corporate tax on digital companies should be held in abeyance until a global approach to the issue can be developed. Further, using the tax or levy system to fund the creation of Canadian content based on inaccurate claims about a level playing field places the remarkable domestic film and television production success story at risk. Making sense of the digital tax debate ultimately depends upon sensible policies, something that may prove challenging in the absence of an evidence-based analysis of the tax implications of the digital economy.

Acknowledgements

My thanks to Elizabeth Dubois and Florian Martin-Bariteau for their feedback and leadership on Canadian digital policy and this important initiative, to Felice Yeung and Meghan Sali for their exceptional research assistance, and to the anonymous reviewers for their helpful suggestions. Thanks as well to the Canada Research Chair program and Social Sciences and Humanities Research Council of Canada for their financial assistance. Any errors or omissions are the sole responsibility of the author.

References

Airbnb. (n.d.). *Occupancy tax collection and remittance by Airbnb in Canada.* Retrieved April 1, 2020, from https://www.airbnb.ca/help/article/2283/occupancy-tax-collection-and-remittance-by-airbnb-in-canada

Alberici, E. (2018, February 15). *Why many big companies don't pay corporate tax.* ABC News. https://www.abc.net.au/news/2018-02-14/why-many-big-companies-dont-pay-corporate-tax/9443840

Buckner, D. (2019, January 30). *Cultural funding fight with Netflix reignites age-old debate—what is Cancon anyway?* CBC. https://www.cbc.ca/news/business/netflix-cancon-broadcasters-crtc-1.4997568

Canada, House of Commons. (2018, February 5). *Debates, 148*(257). 42nd Parliament, 1st Session. https://www.ourcommons.ca/Content/House/421/Debates/257/HAN257-E.PDF

Canada, House of Commons, Standing Committee on Canadian Heritage [CHPC]. (2016, December 1). [Evidence]. Meeting no. 41. 42nd Parliament, 1st session. http://www.parl.gc.ca/HousePublications/Publication.aspx?Language=e&Mode=1&Parl=42&Ses=1&DocId=8666889

Canada, Senate, Standing Committee on Transport and Communications. (2018, May 29). [Evidence]. Issue no. 36. 42nd Parliament, 1st session. https://sencanada.ca/en/Content/Sen/Committee/421/TRCM/36ev-54106-e

Canadian Communications Systems Alliance Inc. (2018, September 6). *Submission for consideration in the Standing Committee on Industry, Science and Technology statutory review of the Copyright Act.* https://www.ourcommons.ca/Content/Committee/421/INDU/Brief/BR10008889/br-external/CanadianCommunicationSystemsAllianceInc-e.pdf

Canadian Internet Registration Authority [CIRA]. (2019). *2019: Canada's internet factbook.* https://cira.ca/resources/corporate/factbook/canadas-internet-factbook-2019

Canadian Media Producers Association [CMPA]. (2018). *Profile 2018: Economic report on the screen-based media production industry in Canada.* https://telefilm.ca/wp-content/uploads/profile-2018.pdf

Canadian Media Producers Association [CMPA]. (2019). *Broadcasting and Telecommunications Legislative Review Panel responding to the new environment: A call for comments.* https://cmpa.ca/wp-content/uploads/2019/01/CMPA-Yale-Panel-Submission.pdf

Canadian Radio-television and Telecommunications Commission [CRTC]. (1998, December 3). *Public hearing examining new media.* https://crtc.gc.ca/eng/transcripts/1998/tb1203.htm

Canadian Radio-television and Telecommunications Commission [CRTC]. (2016a, August 19). *Broadcasting regulatory policy 2016-334 and broadcasting order CRTC 2016-335.* https://crtc.gc.ca/eng/archive/2016/2016-334.htm

Canadian Radio-television and Telecommunications Commission [CRTC]. (2016b, November 21). *Broadcasting decision CRTC 2016-458.* https://crtc.gc.ca/eng/archive/2016/2016-458.htm

Canadian Radio-Television and Telecommunications Commission [CRTC]. (2018). *Harnessing change: The future of programming and distribution in Canada.* https://crtc.gc.ca/eng/publications/s15/pol1.htm

Canadian Radio-television and Telecommunications Commission [CRTC]. (2019, May 23). *Ensuring a place for Canadian services.* https://crtc.gc.ca/eng/cancon/c_services.htm

Curry, B. (2018, October 12). Canada won't act alone on new tax rules for digital giants: Morneau. *The Globe and Mail.* https://www.theglobeandmail.com/politics/article-canada-wont-act-alone-on-new-tax-rules-for-digital-giants-morneau/

Dobby, C. (2018, March 12). CRTC proposes looser rules if CraveTV, Shomi are offered to all. *The Globe and Mail.* https://www.theglobeandmail.com/report-on-business/crtc-to-force-broadcasters-to-offer-cravetv-shomi-to-all-canadians/article23420361/

Donders, K., Raats, T., Komorowski, M., Kostovska, I., Tintel, S., & Iordache, C. (2018). *Obligations on on-demand audiovisual media services providers to financially contribute to the production of European works: An analysis of European member states' practices.* Vrije Universiteit Brussel. http://smit.vub.ac.be/wp-content/uploads/2018/12/VUB-VOD-report-2018-.pdf

Dourado, A. P. (2018). Debate: Digital taxation opens the Pandora box: The OECD interim report and the European Commission proposals. *Intertax, 46*(6/7), 565–572.

European Commission [EC]. (2018, June 7). *Digital single market: Updated audiovisual rules* [Press release]. http://europa.eu/rapid/press-release_MEMO-18-4093_en.htm

Friends of Canadian Broadcasting (2020). *Submission to the Broadcasting and Telecommunications Legislative Review Panel.* https://www.ic.gc.ca/eic/site/110.nsf/vwapj/884_FriendsofCanadianBroadcasting_11_EN_CA.pdf/$FILE/884_FriendsofCanadianBroadcasting_11_EN_CA.pdf

Geist, M. (2015, January 23). Is the digital taxman headed to Canada? Geist. *The Toronto Star.* https://www.thestar.com/business/2015/01/23/is-the-digital-taxman-headed-to-canada-geist.html

Geist, M. (2017, October 19). *Government rejects call for an internet tax: "Conflicts with principle of affordable access."* Michael Geist. http://www.michaelgeist.ca/2017/10/government-rejects-call-internet-tax-conflicts-principle-affordable-access/

Geist, M. (2018a, April 3). Quebec shows that taxing digital sales is easier said than done. *The Globe and Mail.* https://www.theglobeandmail.com/business/commentary/article-quebec-shows-that-taxing-digital-sales-is-easier-said-than-done/

Geist, M. (2018b, June 6). *Math not magic: If Melanie Joly Mandates internet taxes, consumers will foot the bill.* Michael Geist. http://www.michaelgeist.ca/2018/06/math-not-magic-if-melanie-joly-mandates-internet-taxes-consumers-will-foot-the-bill/

Geist, M. (2018c, October 25). *Making sense of the Canadian digital tax debate, part 2: Mandated Canadian content contributions aka a "Netflix tax."* Michael Geist. http://www.michaelgeist.ca/2018/10/making-sense-of-the-canadian-digital-tax-debate-part-2/

Geist, M. (2019a, August 7). Election 2019: Return of the Netflix tax debate. *The Globe and Mail.* https://www.theglobeandmail.com/business/commentary/article-election-2019-return-of-the-netflix-tax-debate/

Geist, M. (2019b, October 15), Who owns the internet? *The Globe and Mail.* https://www.theglobeandmail.com/business/commentary/article-who-owns-the-internet/

Leahy, P. (2017, December 2). Ireland to fight proposed EU digital tax on internet giants. *The Irish Times.* https://www.irishtimes.com/business/economy/ireland-to-fight-proposed-eu-digital-tax-on-internet-giants-1.3312834

LeBlanc, D. (2018, June 4). Panel to redraft broadcasting laws as Ottawa eyes foreign firms such as Netflix, Facebook. *The Globe and Mail.* https://www.theglobeandmail.com/politics/article-federal-government-wants-new-legal-powers-over-foreign-online/

NDP [@NDP]. (2018a, April 15). *Tax exemptions given to web giants like Netflix, Facebook, and Google cost Canadians nearly $1B every year in lost tax* [Tweet]. Twitter. https://twitter.com/NDP/status/985510633583104000

NDP. (2018b, August 28). *Protect our culture and end special treatment for web giants* [Press release]. https://www.ndp.ca/news/protect-our-culture-and-end-special-treatment-web-giants

Palmer, D. (2019, December 2) U.S. threatens tariffs on $2.4B French cheeses, other goods in tax dispute. *Politico.* https://www.politico.com/news/2019/12/02/us-threatens-tariffs-on-24b-french-cheeses-other-goods-in-tax-dispute-074835

Quebec Ministry of Finance [QMF]. (2018, March). *The Québec economic plan.* http://www.budget.finances.gouv.qc.ca/budget/2018-2019/en/documents/AdditionalInfo_18-19.pdf#page=137

Rodriguez, P. [@pablorodriguez]. (2019, June 26). *Thanks to @JanetYale1 & panel for their work. We will be ready to legislate once we receive their recommendations* [Tweet]. Twitter. https://twitter.com/pablorodriguez/status/1143906301002620928

Sokic, N. (2019, May 23). Protected industries: Why more than a third of the Canadian economy is walled from competition. *The Financial Post.* https://business.financialpost.com/news/economy/protected-industries-why-more-than-a-third-of-the-canadian-economy-is-walled-from-competition

Statistics Canada. (2014, November 19). *Infographic: internet use and e-commerce—Data from the 2012 internet user survey.* https://www.statcan.gc.ca/pub/11-627-m/11-627-m2014003-eng.htm

Uber. (n.d.). *Sales tax in Canada.* Retrieved April 1, 2020, from https://www.uber.com/ca/en/drive/tax-information/

CHAPTER 11

Online Abuse, Chilling Effects, and Human Rights

Jonathon W. Penney

Abstract

Online harassment, cyberbullying, hate, and other forms of online abuse pose a significant threat to human rights in Canada. Now, the country is at a crossroads: it will face American pressure to adopt a broad immunity model similar to Section 230 of the *Communications Decency Act* (CDA) or, at long last, take more robust action to address cyberharassment and other online abuse, beyond the piecemeal approach used today. Central to this regulatory debate are concerns and claims about "chilling effects"—that is, the idea that certain regulatory actions may "chill" or deter people from exercising their rights online and in other digital contexts. Such claims, and in particular claims about speech chill, have long been raised to oppose measures addressing online abuse. In this chapter, I argue that such chilling-effect claims, which are advanced to oppose measures taken to curb online harassment and abuse, neglect other kinds of chilling effects. I argue that such abuse chills the rights of victims. And, drawing on new empirical research on this point, I argue that such legal interventions—like cyberharassment laws—rather than having a chilling effect, can also have a salutary impact on the speech and engagement of victims whose voices have been typically marginalized. I will also discuss the important implications these findings have for Canadian law and policy.

Online harassment, cyberbullying, hate, and other forms of online abuse pose a significant threat to human rights in Canada. A 2016 survey, for example, found almost half of young Canadians have experienced online harassment (Global News, 2016). A poll last year found a third of parents knew a cyberbullying victim (Abedi, 2018). Such harassment has a range of harmful and negative impacts. For example, researchers tracking online hate and disinformation in the 2019 Canadian election suggested such abuse may be harming Canadian democracy (Fionda, 2019). Indeed, with women and minorities disproportionately targeted by such online abuse, it threatens deliberative and participatory democracy, which requires diverse perspectives and voices (Citron & Penney, 2019).[1] Not surprisingly, a 2016 poll found that Canadians wanted more to be done to "curb online abuse" (BBC, 2016). This has led to calls to regulate social media platforms (e.g., Farber & Balgord, 2018; Elghawaby, 2018), including by the House of Commons Standing Committee on Access to Information, Privacy and Ethics (Solomon, 2018).

Yet, other than a few limited exceptions—such as Quebec's *Act to Establish a Legal Framework for Information Technology* (AELFIT)— governments in Canada have been "wary" to regulate social media companies to address these challenges (Elghawaby, 2018). Moreover, Canada faces pressure to adopt a permissive regulatory framework that shields online service providers (OSPs) from doing more to address online abuse. The new *Agreement between Canada, the United States of America, and the United Mexican States* (CUSMA), signed in 2018, includes provisions that may require Canada to adopt an even more permissive regulatory framework for OSPs similar to Section 230 of the CDA, which provides OSPs with broad immunity, shielding them from liability for user-generated content and from lawsuits relating to how they moderate content (Laidlaw, 2020, p. 3).

Though Section 230 is treated as a "sacred cow" with "near constitutional status" in the United States, especially in the technology industry (Citron & Wittes, 2017, pp. 409–410), it has also been controversial. The most powerful OSPs today are popular US-based social media platforms like Facebook, Google, Twitter, among others, which all enjoy sweeping protection from tort liability for most forms of user-generated content, thanks to Section 230. This, critics argue, has given these companies far too much unchecked power over digital rights (Klonick, 2017, pp. 1613–1614). These broad legal protections, for instance, mean these platforms have little incentive to address online abuse (Citron & Wittes, 2017, p. 411, pp. 413–414).

Canada is thus at a crossroads. It will face American pressure to adopt a "broad immunity" model similar to Section 230 or finally take stronger action to address cyberharassment, hate, and other online abuse. Central to this regulatory debate are concerns and claims about "chilling effects"—that is, the idea that certain laws or state or corporate activities may "chill" or deter people from exercising their rights, particularly online and in other digital contexts. Such claims have long been raised to oppose legislative measures addressing online abuse (Franks, 2018, pp. 339–340). In fact, concerns about chilling effects on speech and innovation was a central justification for enacting Section 230, and in early decisions like *Zeran v. AOL* (Ciolli, 2008, pp. 147–148; Klonick, 2017, pp. 1607–1608).

Yet, there has been strikingly little systematic study of such "chilling effect" claims in various areas of law over the years. Part of the problem is that chilling effects are often subtle, difficult to measure, and require interdisciplinary research and methods going beyond traditional legal analysis. After an extensive literature review, Leslie Kendrick found in 2013 that empirical support for such chilling effect claims was "flimsy" and required additional study (p. 1536).

Today there is a growing body of literature investigating, exploring, and documenting "chilling effects" in a range of contexts (see Townend, 2014; Stoycheff, 2016; Stoycheff et al., 2017; Stoycheff et al., 2019; Stoycheff et al., 2020; Penney, 2016, 2017; Marthews & Tucker, 2017; Wahl-Jorgensen et al., 2017; Dencik & Cable, 2017; Citron & Penney, 2019). Drawing on this research, I argue that chilling effect claims advanced to oppose measures taken to curb online harassment and abuse neglect other kinds of chilling effects—how such abuse chills the rights of victims. And, drawing on new empirical research, I argue that contrary to critics, such legal interventions—like cyberharassment laws—rather than having a chilling effect, actually may encourage more online speech and engagement, particularly for women—the usual targets of such abuse. These findings have important implications for Canadian law and policy, which I will also discuss.

Chilling Effects and Platform Responsibilities

Canadian governments have, as noted, been reticent to regulate social media platforms to address cyberharassment and similar online abuse. And the few measures that *have* been taken are quite narrow with limited success. The federal government enacted a "revenge porn" criminal offence in 2015, but it is unclear if this provision might also be applied to platforms or businesses, and so far none have been charged (Slane & Langlois, 2018, p. 50). Nova Scotia, for its part, enacted a *Cyber-Safety Act* in 2013 to tackle cyberbullying, but it was struck down as unconstitutionally broad two years later by the Nova Scotia Supreme Court. The Nova Scotia government has no plans to re-legislate (Slane & Langlois, 2018, p. 61). Quebec enacted the AELFIT in 2001—which provides for liability for intermediaries once made aware of "illicit activities"—but it has not been effectively enforced (Slane & Langlois, 2018, pp. 50–51). The result has been that platforms and other OSPs are "mostly left alone" in Canada, with online abuse, sexual exploitation, and harassment able to persist (Slane & Langlois, 2018, p. 51, p. 46). Not surprisingly, many experts believe far more can be done (Elghawaby, 2018).

Chilling effect claims have been a key challenge in this context. Such claims and concerns have often been raised to criticize, oppose, or challenge laws and other measures taken to address cyberharassment and similar forms of online abuse. The first type of chilling effect claim is the more general form: that, no matter what is being addressed—online harassment, defamation, etc.—any regulatory measures at all that impose liability on OSPs would lead to chilling effects on digital speech.

This was, essentially, the conclusion of the US Fourth Circuit Court of Appeal's famous 1997 decision *Zeran v. America Online* (*Zeran v. AOL*), which first found OSPs had broad immunity from tort liability under Section 230 of the CDA. The facts involved a case of online harassment whereby an unidentified person posted on AOL's message board false and defamatory messages about the plaintiff, Kenneth Zeran, who sued AOL for failing to remove the postings promptly once notified. In dismissing Zeran's lawsuit, the Fourth Circuit found that imposing liability on AOL for how it dealt with user-generated content would have "chilling effects" on online speech. In fact, a primary reason Section 230 was enacted in the first place was to guard against such chilling effects, after the New York

Supreme Court found Prodigy liable in its 1995 decision *Stratton Oakmont v. Prodigy Services* (1995; Ciolli, 2008, pp. 147–148; Klonick, 2017, pp. 1607–1608).

The second type of chilling effects claim is that raised specifically about laws and other measures pursued to address online harassment and abuse. That is, such laws typically target or seek to deter certain kinds of online harassment, hate, and abuse, and would thus have a "chilling effect" on the people's online speech and expression (Citron & Penney, 2019, p. 2327). In the United States, courts have struck down such laws on "numerous occasions" for possible chilling effects on speech protected by the First Amendment (Diaz, 2016). These arguments have also been successfully raised in Canada. Critics of Nova Scotia's *Cyber-Safety Act* argued it could "dramatically chill constitutionally protected speech" (Fraser, 2014). The statute was later struck down as unreasonably limiting freedom of expression under the *Canadian Charter of Rights and Freedoms* (Slane & Langlois, 2018, p. 61). And efforts to expand Canada's "revenge porn" laws have been criticized as having a "chilling effect" on journalism (Pearson, 2016).

The Chilling Effects of Online Abuse

Chilling effect claims have been a key legal, normative, and public policy challenge to bettering measures to tackle online harassment, bullying, and other online abuse, including in Canada. But there are important problems with these claims.

First, they largely neglect other chilling effects; that is, the chill or silencing effect that online harassment and abuse has on the speech and engagement of victims. Scholars such as Danielle Citron and Mary Ann Franks have long documented these corrosive impacts on victims of online abuse (see Citron, 2014, pp. 196–198). Online harassment, bullying, hate, "doxxing," and revenge porn all have a silencing effect on victims (Franks, 2018, p. 307; Citron, 2014, pp. 196–197). Such abuse has a "totalizing and devastating impact" upon victims (Citron, 2014, p. 29). In fact, silencing victims is often the primary motivation for such abuse (Citron, 2014, p. 196). Moreover, these chilling effects have a disproportionate impact on the speech and engagement of certain people, such as minority populations, already marginalized due to systematic and overt barriers (Franks, 2018, p. 307).

Second, while a cyberharassment law—or other measures taken to address online abuse—likely will chill at least some speech, empirical evidence suggests that this chill pales in comparison to the impact on victims. As Franks points out, there is "ample evidence" for "how harassment chills freedom of expression, mobility, and association" (2018, p. 307). However, she goes further, noting that these impacts have "a greater chilling effect than any governmental action," (p. 307) and current research supports this claim. Studies have shown how, for example, street harassment inflicts great costs on women, including a loss of freedom of speech and mobility (Franks, 2018, p. 307). There are, furthermore, countless cases where online hate speech or "cyber mobs" threaten victims into silence, forcing them to change how they live and act (Franks, 2018, p. 307; Citron, 2014, pp. 196–197). Moreover, my own previous research work (Penney, 2017), found in a comparative study of different hypothetical "chilling effect" scenarios (that is, scenarios where state or corporate action might chill people's online activities), the scenario involving personally received and targeted threats had the greatest chilling effect across a range of different activities and contexts, more so than even scenarios involving government or corporate surveillance.

Such silencing effects of online abuse are often ignored by policy-makers, by critics of such anti-abuse laws, and by courts evaluating them (Franks, 2018, p. 340). However, new empirical evidence suggests such laws may not only deter or limit online abuse but also help encourage greater online speech and engagement by victims. This salutary effect is the result of the law's expressive function.

The Expressive Impact of Online Abuse Laws

Most literature on legal compliance holds that people comply with the law either because of its coercive force—to avoid legal punishments or penalties—or because they believe the law is legitimate. That is, they believe the law is worthy of compliance (Geisinger & Stein, 2016, pp. 1061–1062). However, a growing body of work focuses on the "expressive" function of law—that is, on how legal frameworks can shape behavioural norms by changing the social meaning of behaviour (Geisinger & Stein, 2016, p. 1062; McAdams, 2015).

There are different theories as to how the law's expressive function impacts behaviour, but most scholarship focuses on what

Richard McAdams (2015) calls the "informational" and "coordinating" mechanisms of law's expressive effects (p. 6). On the former, a law provides information about how people should act, providing a signal about societal consensus or wider popular attitudes about social behaviour. Through this message to the broader population about what is considered acceptable and unacceptable behaviour, a law has its expressive impact—people internalize that message and alter their behaviour accordingly (Geisinger & Stein, 2016, p. 1062). The coordination mechanism of a law speaks to its function in providing a focal point for people to coordinate and organize their activities, leading to wider societal mobilization or social movements, and ultimately shifts in social behaviour (McAdams, 2015, p. 5). These mechanisms work together in a law's expressive impact. A good example of this is how, over time, anti-smoking laws changed public attitudes about smoking, leading fewer people to smoke (Geisinger & Stein, 2016, p. 1062). These laws provided information to the wider public by signalling that a new anti-smoking consensus was forming, and were also a focal point for citizens to coordinate their action to advocate for additional law reforms or more effective enforcement.

Can cyberharassment laws also have such expressive impacts? And if so, what are they? A new article that I co-authored with Citron, a leading privacy and online abuse expert (Citron & Penney, 2019), discusses new empirical evidence that such laws can have a salutary impact on people's online speech and engagement, particularly for women. The notion that law can empower the speech of victims is not new. For instance, the idea that law reforms could better give victims a voice was a core of the victim's rights movement, starting in the 1970s and continuing today (Eisenberg, 2015, p. 620). Citron (2009) has previously discussed law's expressive function in combating online harassment. As with chilling effects, however, there has been little systematic empirical research done on law's expressive function, including its salutary impact in this context.

Drawing on expressive law theory by McAdams (2015) and others, it is possible see how law's expressive function could have this impact. By enacting a cyberharassment law, a democratic society provides important information to educate the public— that online harassment and abuse are unacceptable behaviours. It also sends a message to online-abuse victims that their speech and engagement in online contexts are important and worthy of protection. These would all be informational mechanisms of the law's expression function. A new cyberharassment law could also provide a focal point for broader reforms or additional enactments addressing other forms of online abuse, such as hate or intimate-privacy violations. These would be consistent with coordinating mechanisms.

Beyond a theoretical case like this, however, our article provides an empirical foundation for these claims. We analyzed findings from an original online survey, administered to 1296 US-based adult Internet users, which described to participants a series of hypothetical scenario involving different government or corporate activities. Questions sought to elicit behavioural responses to these different scenarios, in order to compare and statistically analyze responses, including in relation to a range of demographic variables, such as age, gender, education and income levels, as well as other variables relating to online behaviour and concerns, such as the amount of time spent online, level of online sharing, level of social network engagement, and privacy concerns in response to the law. One scenario involved participants being made aware that the government had "enacted a new law that introduced tough civil and criminal penalties for posting information or other content online, with the intent to harass or intimidate another person" (Citron & Penney, 2019, p. 2329)—in other words, a law that might be described as a cyberharassment law.

Responses offered a range of insights. First, contrary to what many critics argue, responses suggested the cyberharassment law would have few chilling effects. Of the participants, 87 percent indicated that the cyberharassment law would have "no impact" or render them "somewhat more likely" or "much more likely" to "spend time on the Internet" (Citron & Penney, 2019, p. 2330). Similarly, 62 percent indicated such a law would have "no impact" or render them "more likely" to "speak or write about certain topics online" (p. 2330). Additionally, 67 percent responded that the law would have "no impact" or would render them "somewhat more likely" or "much more likely" to share personally created content online, while 56 percent indicated that the law would either have "no impact" or would render them "more likely" to contribute to social networks online (p. 2330). The findings thus did not provide compelling evidence that a cyberharassment law would have substantial or pervasive chilling effects on online speech and engagement.

Second, the findings suggested cyberharassment laws, rather than chilling speech and engagement, may actually *encourage* these activities, particularly for women. Analysis of the findings revealed a gender effect in response to this law—female participants in the survey were statistically more likely to engage online in response to the cyberharassment law on a range of different counts (Citron & Penney, 2019, pp. 2331–2332). Specifically, women reported being more likely to spend time online more likely to share personally created or authored content online, and more likely to contribute to social network sites online, in response to the government enacting the cyberharassment law. The findings reveal a salutary effect on women's online expression, engagement, and participation—a greater likeliness to speak, engage, and express themselves online in light of a cyberharassment law.

These findings are not necessarily surprising; as women are disproportionately targeted by online harassment and abuse, it makes perfect sense that may also report being more positively impacted by a cyberharassment law and its expressive effects. Of course, there are also important limitations. The survey sample could be more representative and was obtained through an online recruitment service; it thus may be biased by self-selecting respondents. And self-reported responses in online surveys do not always accurately reflect people's actual behaviour. Beliefs do not always match actions.

Indeed, far more research needs to be done to document both the silencing effects of online abuse as well as the expressive law effects in different Canadian contexts—such as different types of online-abuse laws. Complexities should also be investigated: How important is the enforcement of a cyberharassment law to ensuring its expressive impacts? Do these expressive impacts hold for different minority groups and cultural communities in Canada? Both nuanced qualitative and quantitative research is required to answer these difficult questions. That said, our study, and the survey therein, does reflect participants' perspectives and beliefs about how the cyberharassment law would impact their behaviour. Given that the focus here is the law's expressive function—the message it sends to people more generally and victims of online harassment more specifically—then these self-reports are direct evidence of that expressive impact.

Implications

These theoretical and empirical insights have important implications for Canadian law and policy. First, Canadian judges and lawyers need to better take into account the chilling effects of online abuse; that is, how such activities often aim to silence victims and drive them from online spaces and social networks. A good example of this is the Nova Scotia Supreme Court's decision in *Crouch v. Snell* (2015), which struck down the *Cyber-Safety Act* for unconstitutionally limiting rights to expression under Sections 2(b) and 7 of the *Charter of Rights*. The court found the act sought to protect people from "undue harm" to their "reputation" and "well being" due to cyberbullying (para. 147). As well, the court found that the act aimed to "balance" an "individual's right to free speech against society's interests in providing greater access to justice to victims of cyberbullying" (para. 172).

However, the court never acknowledges the speech interests of victims of cyberbullying. As already noted, the main aim of such abuse is typically to silence victims (Citron, 2014, p. 196), often with a "totalizing and devastating impact" (p. 29). Had the court also taken into account the speech and expression rights of victims, then the court's analysis under Section 1 of the *Charter of Rights*—as to whether the law's limitations on the free expression of cyberbullies were reasonable—may have come to a different conclusion.

Second, courts and lawyers should also take into account potential salutary impacts of these laws on victims' online speech and engagement. This is important as the silencing effects of online abuse disproportionately impact the speech and engagement of groups and communities, such as women and visible minorities, already marginalized due to discrimination, racism, and other societal barriers (Franks, 2018, p. 307). If the court in *Crouch v. Snell* (2015) had understood how the *Cyber-Safety Act* may have salutary expressive impacts on victims of cyberbullying—encouraging their online speech and engagement—then its analysis and conclusion may have been different. These points were neither raised nor discussed by the court in its decision.

Third, law- and policy-makers, at a very basic level, must acknowledge the corrosive impact that online abuse has both on victims and on democratic societies more broadly. Such abuse silences victims, weakening public discussion and democratic deliberation. Having acknowledged this, law- and policy-makers then must act.

Furthermore, any response to cyberharassment and other forms of online abuse should take into account the law's expressive impact and function. For example, a new cyberharassment law could include an official preamble clearly describing the government's objectives and aims, and other informational dimensions to strengthen the expressive impact of the law for the public in general and victims in particular. The findings in Citron and Penney (2019) also provide empirical support for important government outreach to affected communities to provide information and education about new laws or initiatives concerning online abuse. Again, this can strengthen the new law's expressive function through better informational mechanisms.

Fourth, any general regulatory framework for platforms and other OSPs should include measures to address cyberharassment and other forms of online abuse. As noted earlier, CUSMA may require Canada to adopt a new regulatory framework for OSPs. If so, it should not adopt one comparable to Section 230 of the CDA. Though acclaimed in the United States as essential to the development of the modern Internet (Citron & Wittes, 2017, pp. 409–410), there is also greater recognition that some of the most harmful chilling effects on human rights online do not concern the activities of OSPs or statutes regulating them, but stem from forms of online harassment, abuse, and privacy violations (Citron, 2014). Naturally, those concerned with addressing these challenges have been increasingly critical of Section 230 (Klonick, 2017, p. 1614). Consistent with those criticisms, and with the insights in this chapter, any new Canadian regulatory framework or scheme must take online abuse seriously. A framework, which includes safe harbours and general or specific legal immunities or protections for OSPs, must include express mandates, provisions, exceptions, and incentives to address cyberharassment and other forms of online abuse. What those provisions may be goes beyond the limited scope of this chapter, but mitigating the chilling effects of online abuse and encouraging the speech and engagement of victims online through expressive laws and other measures should be essential objectives for policy-makers going forward.

Conclusion

Concerns about chilling effects have long been central to debates about the responsibilities of platforms and OSPs in dealing with user activities, particularly concerning user-generated and shared content. For example, the famous 1997 decision in *Zeran v. AOL*, which interpreted Section 230 of the CDA broadly to grant online platforms publishers immunity, was premised on a concern about how content liability would chill speech and innovation. Drawing on new empirical research, this chapter argued that such chilling effect concerns, typically raised to criticize and oppose measures to address cyber-harassment and other forms of online abuse, neglect other forms of chilling effects—the silencing impact of online abuse—as well as the expressive impact of such laws to encourage and empower the speech and engagement of victims. In particular, this chapter argues for the following: (1) more qualitative and quantitative research needs to be done to document the silencing effects of online abuse in Canada as well as the expressive effects of laws that seek to address such online abuse; (2) courts and lawyers must better take into account the silencing effects of online abuse when reasoning about laws and legislation tackling online abuse, as well as about the salutary impacts of such laws; and that (3) Canada should reject a broad immunity model for OSPs and platforms in Canada and act now to better address cyber-harassment and other forms of online abuse.

Notes

1. Data repositories for the study discussed in Citron and Penney (2019) can be found at https://github.com/jwpenney/Cyberharassment_Law_Impact_2019_Study.

References

Abedi, M. (2018, June 27). *Even with more awareness, cyberbullying isn't declining in Canada: Ipsos poll.* Global News. https://globalnews.ca/news/4299734/cyberbullying-cases-awareness-canada-poll/

Act to Establish a Legal Framework for Information Technology [AELFIT], CQLR, c. C-1.1 (2001).

BBC. (2016, October 21). *Canadians want more done to curb abuse on social media.* BBC News. https://www.bbc.com/news/world-us-canada-37723551

Agreement between Canada, the United States of America, and the United Mexican States [CUSMA] (2018). Canada-United States-Mexico Agreement. https://www.international.gc.ca/trade-commerce/trade-agreements-accords-commerciaux/agr-acc/cusma-aceum/text-texte/toc-tdm.aspx?lang=eng

Ciolli, A. (2008). Chilling effects: The Communications Decency Act and the online marketplace of ideas. *University of Miami Law Review, 63*(1), 137–268.

Citron, D. K. (2009). Law's expressive value in combating cyber gender harassment, *Michigan Law Review, 108*(2), 373–416.

Citron, D. K. (2014). *Hate crimes in cyberspace.* Harvard University Press.

Citron, D. K., & Wittes, B. (2017). The Internet will not break: Denying bad Samaritans sec. 230 immunity. *Fordham Law Review, 86*(2), 401–423.

Citron, D. K., & Penney, J. W. (2019). When law frees us to speak. *Fordham Law Review, 87*(6), 2317–2335.

Communications Decency Act [CDA]. 147 USC § 230 (1998).

Crouch v. Snell, 2015 NSSC 340.

Dencik, L., & Cable, J. (2017). The advent of surveillance realism: Public opinion and activist responses to the Snowden leaks. *International Journal of Communication, 11,* 763–781.

Diaz, F. L. (2016). Trolling & the first amendment: Protecting Internet speech in the era of cyberbullies and Internet defamation. *Journal of Law, Technology, and Policy, 2016*(1), 135–159, http://illinoisjltp.com/journal/wp-content/uploads/2016/06/Diaz.pdf

Eisenberg, A. K. (2015). Criminal inflictions of emotional distress. *Michigan Law Review, 113*(5), 607–662.

Elghawaby, A. (2018, August 2). *Social media's self-regulation isn't enough.* Centre for International Governance Innovation. https://www.cigionline.org/articles/social-medias-self-regulation-isnt-enough

Farber, B. M., & Balgord, E. (2018, December 18). New public safety report downplays right-wing extremism. *Toronto Star.* https://www.thestar.com/opinion/contributors/2018/12/18/new-public-safety-report-downplays-right-wing-extremism.html

Fionda, F. (2019, October 15). *How online abuse and hate could be hurting our democracy.* CTV News. https://election.ctvnews.ca/how-online-abuse-and-hate-could-be-hurting-our-democracy-1.4637623

Franks, M. (2018). Fearless speech. *First Amendment Law Review, 17*(Symposium), 294–342.

Fraser, D. T. S. (2014, February 12). *Nova Scotia court issues first cyberbullying prevention order.* Canadian Privacy Law Blog. https://blog.privacylawyer.ca/2014/02/nova-scotia-court-issues-first.html

Geisinger, A. C., & Stein, M. A. (2015). Expressive law and the Americans with Disabilities Act. *Michigan Law Review, 114*(6), 1061–1079.

Global News. (2016, October 21). *Almost half of young Canadians have been harassed on social media, reports poll.* https://globalnews.ca/news/3019354/almost-half-of-young-canadians-have-been-harassed-on-social-media-reports-poll/

Kendrick, L. (2013). Speech, intent, and the chilling effect. *William & Mary Law Review, 54*(5), 1633–1691.

Klonick, K. (2017). The new governors: The people, rules, and processes governing online speech. *Harvard Law Review, 131*(6), 1598–1670.

Laidlaw, E. (2020). Notice-and-notice-plus: A Canadian perspective beyond the liability and immunity divide. In G. Frosio (Ed.), *The Oxford handbook of intermediary liability online.* Oxford University Press.

Marthews, A., & Tucker, C. (2017). The impact of online surveillance on behavior. In D. Gray & S. Henderson (Eds.), *The Cambridge Handbook of Surveillance Law* (pp. 437–454). Cambridge University Press. https://doi.org/10.1017/9781316481127.019

McAdams, R. H. (2015). *The expressive powers of law: Theories and limits.* Harvard University Press.

Pearson, J. (2016, May 12). *Canada's expanding revenge porn laws could threaten journalistic freedom.* Motherboard Tech by VICE. https://www.vice.com/en_us/article/4xaaep/canadas-expanding-revenge-porn-laws-could-threaten-journalistic-freedom

Penney, J. (2016). Chilling effects: Online surveillance and Wikipedia use. *Berkeley Technology Law Journal, 31*(1), 117–182.

Penney, J. (2017). Internet surveillance, regulation, and chilling effects online: a comparative case study. *Internet Policy Review, 6*(2). https://doi.org/10.14763/2017.2.692

Slane, A., & Langlois, G. (2018). Debunking the myth of "not my bad": Sexual images, consent, and online host responsibilities in Canada. *Canadian Journal of Women and the Law, 30*(1), 42–81.

Solomon, H. (2018, December 13). *Regulate social media, says Canadian parliamentary committee.* IT World Canada. https://www.itworldcanada.com/article/regulate-social-media-says-canadian-parliamentary-committee/412940

Stoycheff, E. (2016). Under surveillance: Examining Facebook's spiral of silence effects in the wake of NSA Internet monitoring. *Journalism & Mass Communication Quarterly, 93*(2), 296–311. https://doi.org/10.1177/1077699016630255

Stoycheff, E., Burgess, G. S., & Martucci, M. C. (2020). Online censorship and digital surveillance: The relationship between suppression technologies and democratization across countries. *Information, Communication & Society, 23*(4), 464–490. https://doi.org/10.1080/1369118X.2018.1518472

Stoycheff, E., Liu, J., Xu, K., & Wibowo, K. (2019). Privacy and the panopticon: Online mass surveillance's deterrence and chilling effects. *New Media & Society, 21*(3), 602–619.

Stoycheff, E., Wibowo, K. A., Liu, J., & Xu, K. (2017). Online surveillance's effect on support for other extraordinary measures to prevent

terrorism. *Mass Communication and Society, 20*(6), 784–799. https://doi.
org/10.1080/15205436.2017.1350278

Stratton Oakmont, Inc. v. Prodigy Services Co., 1995 WL 323710.

Townend, J. (2014). Online chilling effects in England and Wales. *Internet
Policy Review, 3*(2). https://doi.org/10.14763/2014.2.252

Wahl-Jorgensen, K., Bennett, L. K., & Cable, J. (2017). Surveillance normalization and critique: News coverage and journalists' discourses around
the Snowden revelations. *Digital Journalism, 5*(3), 386–403.

Zeran v. America Online, Inc. [Zeran v. AOL], 129 F.3d 327 (4th Cir. 1997).

Next Steps for a Connected Canada

Elizabeth Dubois and Florian Martin-Bariteau

C itizenship is digital, and Canada needs to understand the new digital context.

The aim of this collection is to help establish and expand a research and policy agenda for understanding citizenship in a digital context in Canada. We have created this collection with the hope that it can be a useful resource for policy-makers, civil society groups, and researchers, among others, as they advance their work in this area. The goal is to highlight gaps in what we know about how Canadians make use of and interact with digital tools, as well as how Canadians feel about various actors in society making use of digital tools and digital data. Building on the Connected Canada inaugural conference in 2017, which highlighted the value in bringing people together from various sectors, including government, law, journalism, civil society, and academia, this collection extends and broadens the conversations we started at the conference.

In the previous chapters, leading and emerging voices discussed some key and urgent research and policy issues which arise from enacting citizenship in a digital context. Contributors discussed the missing voices in typical conversations about citizenship in digital contexts; government service delivery and multi-stakeholder engagement in policy-making; and a selection of legal challenges for citizens and governments in the digital context. In this final chapter, we present and review their main arguments and identify

15 key recommendations for policy-makers to build a more inclusive, diverse, and safe connected Canada. We then discuss some of the limitations and research needs in order to propose ways to advance research and policy in the Canadian digital context.

Policy Recommendations for a Connected Canada

In this section, we review some of the key recommendations presented in each chapter, and draw links across the various arguments the authors put forward. Notably, we have firmly grounded this work in what is happening in Canada. Yet, there are opportunities for cross-national comparisons and to learn from other countries. For example, Canada and many other countries must grapple with the reality that major technology companies are typically multinational companies based outside their borders (Centre for International Governance Innovation, 2018; Dubois et al., 2019). Canadians can learn from others outside of the country, and we believe that some of the recommendations presented in this book can also be useful to those outside of Canada.

In Part I, "Building an Inclusive Society in a Digital Context," contributors mapped the landscape of civic participation in the current digital context. We sought to incorporate diverse voices and perspectives in order to shed light on some of the types of participation in and experiences of digital society which are less visible in popular discourse, academic research, and policy-making discussions. Our contributors each focused on the notion of equity as a central consideration in research and policy. To date there are voices missing in discussions about how to prioritize, what to spend limited resources on, and which policy issues are most pressing. The chapters focus specifically on a lack of visibility and power among many marginalized communities such as racialized individuals, LGBTQ2S+, Indigenous Peoples, women, and youth. This is because the Internet and related technologies are experienced differently, in part based on an individual's social standing, identity, and relationships to those who currently hold positions of power.

Key recommendations derived from the chapters in Part I include:

1. Make explicit and intentional efforts to include missing voices, notably by incorporating a greater diversity of

individuals from the technology industry, the public policy sector, academia, as well as civil society groups and youth. In tandem, invest in initiatives led by people within diverse communities. In particular, invest in Indigenous-led initiatives, which can contribute to crucial decolonization of the digital sphere and economic reconciliation.

2. Increase access to the Internet and digital tools. Broadband access is still limited and often very expensive in rural and northern communities in Canada.

3. Increase digital literacy and skills through both education and regulation of technology companies. Digital literacy refers to a broad range of skills and might be accomplished in a number of ways, including: develop and implement a digital literacy strategy for K–12 students; require online platforms to be transparent and accountable for their data collection and privacy protection; focus on helping young people understand their digital identity and options for controlling it, including knowledge about datafication as well as privacy protections; fund digital literacy initiatives, particularly ones which are led by those within communities that are not already reached by current initiatives.

4. Make democratic institutions more accessible, representative, and responsive. Consider the ways in which technology can be harnessed to incorporate voices that are not typically included in decision-making processes. This must be balanced with increasing distrust for social media platforms and information found within these platforms.

5. Update existing regulations and implement new policy approaches in order to minimize harms and to respect digital rights. Canada's *Digital Charter* (Innovation, Science and Economic Development [ISED], 2019), for example, outlines broad ideas but implementation is unclear. Crucially, in doing so, policy-makers must consider day-to-day experiences of individuals as priority issues. For example, discrimination and corporate monitoring are routine but require serious consideration by public policy-makers.

In Part II, "Building Democratic Institutions in a Digital Context," contributors reflected on the relationship between citizens and their political and democratic institutions. These chapters show that as digital technology is embedded into the daily lives of individuals, their relationships to their government and journalistic institutions shifts. At the same time, the companies which develop and own these technologies have an increasingly important role to play in influencing these relationships. However, technology companies do not have the good of the Canadian public as their primary concern; governments must. While platforms should, and to some extent do, consider the good of the public in their choices, ultimately they must respond to their shareholders, and they must act in many different national contexts. In order to respond to the needs of citizens in a connected Canada, governments—who hold the public interest paramount—the technology industry, and other actors must work together. The chapters included in Part II consider this from the perspective of digital government and government service delivery, journalism innovation, and policy development around digital rights, but the lessons can extend to other areas. Ultimately, digital technologies are so deeply integrated into people's everyday lives, business, and government that we cannot adequately understand research or policy needs without collaborative approaches.

Key recommendations derived from the chapters in Part II include:

1. Develop partnerships between government and researchers in order to better understand knowledge gaps and opportunities for development of better government services, governance structures, and approaches to other digital government activities. Governments should be proactive in establishing these collaborations.
2. Examine where digital expertise currently lies and where more is needed across teams in various government departments and agencies. In order to address the cross-cutting impacts of digital technology, governmental teams need to have trusted members who are digitally literate and informed about related policy issues.
3. Increase research and education about the trade-off between embedding values such as procedural fairness, privacy, and transparency on the one hand, and fast and innovative approaches to government service delivery and policy-making on the other. Include research into how Canadians currently view this trade-off and what they would ideally like.

4. Embrace experimentation in order to develop innovative responses to new challenges in the journalism industry. This industry faces unprecedented challenges, and it, as well as the government, should experiment with new approaches, which will require research into what works and what does not.

5. Support research into which actors have power in policy-making related to the technology industry and to digital rights. Make efforts to include the voices and perspectives of those who do not have power in the current system.

In Part III, "Rethinking Legal Frameworks for the Digital Context," contributors discussed the effectiveness and fairness of legal frameworks for the digital context. Each contributor focused on a specific issue, discussing challenges of the current framework and recommending key shifts. The chapters consistently noted an erosion of human and democratic rights online. Most current frameworks were initially designed in a commercial-only context, sometimes because of constitutional limitations. However, as noted across the chapters, policy-makers need to acknowledge the new reality: the digital context goes beyond commerce. This change calls for a series of paradigm shifts in policy-making approaches. All the chapters in Part III highlight the need to rethink our frameworks to ensure they adequately protect citizens and to set a level playing field for all actors.

Key recommendations derived from the chapters in Part III include:

1. Adopt a more nuanced, empirically based approach to identifying risks and challenges for meaningful evidence-based policy-making, rather than relying solely on corporate lobbying.

2. Design a comprehensive legal framework for platforms that would neither chill speech nor prevent innovation or access to justice. Platforms should not be immune from liability. Citizens need to be protected online in their everyday life activities without being policed or denied access to justice and privacy rights by non-negotiated contracts.

3. Redesign legal frameworks through a technologically neutral approach—not in favour or against the digital context, nor

to support or constrain a specific sector, industry, or actor. Against the backdrop of an unbalanced relationship between citizens and digital platforms, policy needs to support commerce and innovation; however, it should never do so at the expense of human rights.

4. Overcome federal-provincial/territorial jurisdictional issues to create strong and well-rounded pan-Canadian frameworks for the digital context surrounding consumer rights, privacy, taxation, and freedom of expression. If citizens and corporations, as well as Canada as a whole, are to thrive in the digital and global economy, legal certainty and consistency must be offered across provinces and sectors.

5. Learn from other comparative jurisdictions to build stronger frameworks in line with international standards, rather than trying to reinvent the wheel with complex regulatory schemes.

This collection calls on policy-makers—at all levels of governments—to act to implement these changes, but many of the issues that these recommendations aim to respond to are cross-jurisdictional, highly political, and resource-heavy. This may require trade-offs, negotiation, and coordination among different actors. While policy-makers often need to lead, the implementation of these policy recommendations relies on input from experts and from the people the policies will impact. In the Introduction to this collection, we argued building a resilient and inclusive society in a digital context requires a multi-stakeholder approach. A recommendation implied across all chapters is a need to increase cross-sector collaboration in response to challenges and opportunities afforded by digital technologies. Indeed, the policy shifts recommended throughout this collection require political will—which academia, civil society, journalism, and political parties all play a major role in developing.

Multiple chapters in this collection discuss Canada's *Digital Charter* (ISED, 2019) which is one important political and policy initiative. The *Digital Charter* was released in May 2019 after a series of Government of Canada consultations about the potential need to reform Canadian legal and policy frameworks to respond to the challenges presented by a digital context. The *Digital Charter*, which offers a set of 10 foundational principles for Canadian society to thrive in a digital context, formed a part of the 2019 Liberal Party of Canada's federal election platform. The principles in the *Digital Charter* are: Universal Access; Safety and Security; Control and Consent; Transparency, Portability, and Interoperability; Open and Modern Digital Government; A Level Playing Field; Data and Digital for Good; Strong Democracy; Free from Hate and Violent Extremism; and Strong Enforcement and Real Accountability.

As many chapters in this collection outline, these principles are indeed essential for a connected Canada. Though seen largely as a step in the right direction, the *Digital Charter* is quite broad, lacks commitment, and is non-binding. Many authors in this collection strongly recommend the government push forward and create more specific and actionable changes. As noted in Chapter 8, the *Digital Charter* lacks a proper implementation agenda and, more than a year later, seems to have dropped from the Liberal government's priority list. Consider, for example, privacy and data rights: actual enforcement powers for the regulatory agencies, and updates to the *Privacy Act* (1985) and *Personal Information Protection and Electronic Documents Act* (2000), are crucial, as noted in Chapters 2, 4, and 10. This is especially important because calls regarding privacy rights from academia, civil society, and even Parliament have long been ignored by governments (Martin-Bariteau, 2019).

Ultimately, we believe the policy recommendations highlighted in this collection can act as a compass for the implementation process and as a spark for the government to reignite important conversations about implementation of the *Digital Charter*.

Crucially, while the Government of Canada is an essential player, it cannot act alone. All levels of government must find ways to respond to Canada's digital context and implement the recommendations proposed in this collection. Provincial and municipal governments need to be part of the conversation as some key digital developments are within their jurisdictions and because they are developing digital infrastructures that will directly impact citizen's everyday lives, from digital government service delivery to smart cities.

Finally, as the Canadian Internet Registration Authority (2020) highlights, a foundational building block of a truly connected Canada requires governments to address the current digital divide in Canada and the lack of proper data about connectivity. This will rely on governments at various levels collaborating with the individuals and other actors who are impacted by policy changes, including researchers, the technology industry, the journalism industry, and members of civil society. Canada also needs to build the legal framework for people to be safe online and to offer digital literacy programs to ensure that all people can be part of a connected Canada. It also must be recognized that full participation within a digital context is still a privilege. While everyday life is increasingly impacted by digital tools, a lack of connectivity, of digital skills, and of frameworks protecting vulnerable people within society means that Canada runs the risk of fostering a two-tier society, comprised of the *connected* and the *unconnected*.

What Is Missing: Research Needs for a Connected Canada

A focus on equity in both research and policy work related to citizenship in a digital context is crucial. A diversity of voices and perspectives are required from the very beginning in order to meaningfully incorporate and address equity and to avoid perpetuating existing inequalities. We must recognize that individuals experience the digital world differently, and that those experiences impact how they make use of digital tools, their trust in companies and government, and how data about them should be interpreted by researchers.

As noted in the Introduction, this collection should not be considered an exhaustive list of issues or challenges, and research needs to understand citizenship in a digital context through a particularly Canadian lens. We aimed to start a Canadian conversation and pointed to some of the most pressing concerns, highlighted in the *Canadians in a Digital Context* report (Dubois & Martin-Bariteau, 2018).

Inequity in our social, political, and economic systems continue to impact our experiences of the digital world and limit the participation of some groups of people (Wijesiriwardena, 2017). We take this inequity seriously and have aimed to include research by and about a diverse array of citizens. For example, in Chapter 1, Alexander Dirksen offers a compelling reframing of issues related to digital inclusion in order to underscore the continued role of colonization in digital spaces and to empower Indigenous populations as digital technologies are increasingly integrated into daily life. Other work focuses specifically on the experiences of young people (Chapter 3) and on online harassment which disproportionately impacts marginalized communities (Chapter 11). Over half of our authors identify as women, many currently or have previously lived outside of central

Canada, and they come from a range of academic and professional backgrounds. For each chapter, we also sought out reviewers who reflect Canada's diversity.

That said, work remains to be done. There are a limited number of experts on the Canadian digital context, all of whom are in high demand. This made it difficult to recruit contributors in some cases, and we want to highlight some of the ways this may lead to gaps in the research and policy agenda we have put forward. For example, none of our pieces focused primarily on LGBTQ2S+ communities or the issues faced by individuals in those communities, nor are there LGBTQ2S+ community leaders as authors of our chapters. Similarly, none of our chapters focused specifically on racialized communities or the experience of racialized individuals. Considering specific concerns around personal data, privacy, and identification practices online (Gutierrez, 2018; Manning, 2016; Sanders & Hannem, 2012; Simonite, 2019), and given that we expect some communities to be differently impacted in these cases, this gap needs to be addressed in future work.

We also have limited regional representation among our authors and have not attempted to include local case studies. Often those who focus on regional issues are siloed away from those who focus primarily on national-level issues or from those with regional focuses. This presents a limitation for policy-makers aiming to develop responses which can work cross-nationally and for researchers aiming to learn from the best practices of each other. Connectivity, access, and skill levels with digital technology vary greatly across Canada. In particular, we are missing perspectives on the experiences and impacts of digital technology in the North. We are also missing work that focuses on the experiences of linguistic minority communities that are found across Canada.

Further, we intentionally left aside some discussions that were previously highlighted as essential (Dubois & Martin-Bariteau, 2020). For example, we do not focus on electoral politics and participation, as Elizabeth Dubois co-led another project that addresses key issues related to political uses of digital media during the 2019 Canadian federal election, such as mis- and disinformation, political advertising, and online harassment (Dubois & Owen, 2020). We also leave out a discussion of ethical hacking, whistleblowers, and freedom of the press, as Florian Martin-Bariteau is researching the appropriate framework that will ensure an open, fair, and safe society, and safeguards citizens' digital rights and security.

Important work remains to be done; nonetheless, with this work we have attempted to bridge gaps and include diverse perspectives. We believe that further collaborative efforts such as this book, conferences, and other opportunities for those working in different areas to share their knowledge and experience would go a long way to alleviating the tension between the work done and work that still needs to be done.

The Way Forward for a Connected Canada

The agenda put forward is ambitious. It cannot be tackled by a handful of actors alone and requires a multi-stakeholder approach. More and better data about Canadians' uses and preferences in this digital context are needed. To develop better policies, tools, and research, we need to understand how individuals enact their citizenship.

The Connected Canada conference confirmed that academia, civil society, and government are ready to work together, and this edited collection, as well as related research, demonstrates that a transdisciplinary and multi-stakeholder approach is possible, as well as needed. Collaboration is key to tackling the many challenges and opportunities of an increasingly digital context and to providing access to more and better data about citizenship in a digital context.

Unlike citizens of other countries, Canadians are missing a forum for such a conversation. Certainly, some existing think tanks or university-based research institutes can support this kind of work and could be used to connect communities, promote opportunities, and facilitate the sharing of datasets. However, these kinds of initiatives would be best supported by a non-partisan, pan-Canadian consortium wherein multiple stakeholders, from academia, civil society, governance, and the corporate world contribute their knowledge, experience, and data sets.

We need a multi-stakeholder, pan-Canadian research and policy network for a truly connected Canada.

References

Centre for International Governance Innovation. (2018, February). *A national data strategy for Canada: Key elements and policy considerations* (CIGI Papers No. 160). Centre for International Governance Innovation. https://www.cigionline.org/sites/default/files/documents/Paper%20 no.160_3.pdf

Canadian Internet Registration Authority. (2020, May 7). Submission of the Canadian Internet Registration Authority [to Telecom Notice of Consultation CRTC 2019-406: Call for comments regarding potential barriers to the deployment of broadband-capable networks in underserved areas in Canada]. https://www.cira.ca/sites/default/files/2020-05/CRTC%202019-406%20CIRA%20Submission.pdf

Dubois, E., McKelvey, F. & Owen, T. (2019). What have we learned from Google's political ad pullout? *Policy Options*. http://policyoptions.irpp.org/magazines/april-2019/learned-googles-political-ad-pullout/

Dubois, E., & Martin-Bariteau, F. (2018). Canadians in a digital context: A research agenda for a connected Canada. https://ssrn.com/abstract=3301352

Dubois, E., & Martin-Bariteau, F. (2020). Citizens and their political institutions in a digital context. In W. H. Dutton (Ed.), *A research agenda for a digital politics* (p. 102). Edward Elgar Publishing. https://ssrn.com/abstract=3499315

Dubois, E., & Owen, T. (2020). *Understanding the digital ecosystem: Findings from the 2019 federal election.* Digital Ecosystem Research Challenge. https://www.digitalecosystem.ca/report

Gutierrez, C. (2018, February 20). Data privacy is crucial for the LGBT community. *National Cybersecurity Alliance*. https://staysafeonline.org/blog/data-privacy-crucial-lgbt-community/

Innovation, Science and Economic Development [ISED]. (2019). *Canada's digital charter: Trust in a digital world.* https://www.ic.gc.ca/eic/site/062.nsf/eng/h_00108.html

Liberal Party of Canada. (2019). *Forward: A real plan for the middle class.* https://www2.liberal.ca/wp-content/uploads/sites/292/2019/09/Forward-A-real-plan-for-the-middle-class.pdf

Manning, C. E. (2016, February 22). Privacy is a right, not a luxury—and it's increasingly at risk for LGBT people. *The Guardian*. https://www.theguardian.com/commentisfree/2016/feb/22/privacy-is-a-right-not-a-luxury-and-its-increasingly-at-risk-for-lgbt-people

Martin-Bariteau, F. (2019, May 7). Qu'attendons-nous pour protéger la vie privée ? *Policy Options*. https://policyoptions.irpp.org/magazines/may-2019/quattendons-nous-pour-proteger-la-vie-privee/

Personal Information Protection and Electronic Documents Act, SC 2000, c. 5.

Privacy Act, RSC 1985, c. P-21.

Sanders, C. B., & Hannem, S. (2012). Policy "the risky": Technology and surveillance in everyday patrol work. *Canadian Review of Sociology/Revue canadienne de sociologie, 49*, 389–410. https://doi.org/10.1111/j.1755-618X.2012.01300.x

Simonite, Tom. (2019, July 22). The best algorithms struggle to identify black faces equally. *Wired*. https://www.wired.com/story/best-algorithms-struggle-recognize-black-faces-equally/

Wijesiriwardena, S. (2017, April 19). Is the internet really democratic? How the "wired world" excludes women and other marginalised persons. *World Wide Web Foundation.* https://webfoundation.org/2017/04/is-the-internet-really-democratic-how-the-wired-world-excludes-women-and-other-marginalised-persons/

Contributors

Editors

Elizabeth Dubois and Florian Martin-Bariteau

Dr. Elizabeth Dubois (Ph.D., University of Oxford) is Associate Professor in the Department of Communication at the Faculty of Arts, and Faculty member of the Centre for Law, Technology and Society at the University of Ottawa. Recipient of the 2020 Faculty of Arts Early Researcher of the Year Award, her work examines political uses of digital media, including media manipulation, citizen engagement, and artificial intelligence. She leads a multidisciplinary team that includes political scientists, computer scientists, and communication scholars. She is also a Fellow at the Public Policy Forum of Canada.

Dr. Florian Martin-Bariteau (LL.D., Université de Montréal) is the University Research Chair in Technology and Society at the University of Ottawa, where he is Associate Professor in the Faculty of Law, Common Law Section, and the Director of the Centre for Law, Technology and Society. His research focuses on technology law, ethics, and policy, with a special interest in blockchain, artificial intelligence, cybersecurity, privacy, secrets, and whistleblowers. He is the recipient of the 2019 Common Law Section Emergent Researcher Award.

1. Decolonizing Digital Spaces

Alexander Dirksen

A proud member of Métis Nation British Columbia, Alexander Dirksen has diverse experience as a researcher, public speaker, and strategist. He currently serves as Director of Programs and Community Accountability for Community Knowledge Exchange (CKX) and sits on the City of Vancouver's Urban Indigenous Peoples' Advisory Committee. Previous roles include Manager of Strategy and Engagement with the First Nations Technology Council and Government Relations and Strategic Engagement with Reconciliation Canada. Alexander Dirksen holds an M. A. in Global Affairs from the Munk School of Global Affairs and Public Policy at the University of Toronto and a B.A. (with honours) in International Studies from Simon Fraser University.

2. Telling a Different Story: Canadian Citizens and Their Democracy in the Digital Age

Adelina Petit-Vouriot and Mike Morden

Adelina Petit-Vouriot is Research Analyst at the Samara Centre for Democracy, a non-partisan charity dedicated to strengthening Canada's democracy. She holds an M. A. in Political Science from the University of Toronto. She previously worked at CIVIX, a national civic education charity, developing civic engagement programming and resources for youth.

Dr. Michael Morden is Research Director at the Samara Centre for Democracy. He holds a Ph.D. in Political Science from the University of Toronto. Prior to joining the Samara Centre, Dr. Morden was an SSHRC postdoctoral research fellow in Canadian politics at Western and Wilfrid Laurier Universities, worked at several think tanks (including the Mowat Centre and Mosaic Institute), and was a senior policy advisor for the Government of Ontario.

3. Framing the Challenges of Digital Inclusion for Young Canadians

Leslie Regan Shade, Jane Bailey, Jacquelyn Burkell, Priscilla Regan, and Valerie Steeves

Dr. Leslie Regan Shade is Full Professor at the Faculty of Information, University of Toronto. Her research and teaching focus on the social and policy aspects of information and communication technologies, with particular concerns toward issues of gender, youth, and political economy. Dr. Shade's various publications have explored gender and technological design, social media and social justice, privacy issues in Facebook, the commodification of young people's online spaces, gender and unpaid internships in the creative sector, and digital surveillance in education and at schools. She is a co-investigator on The eQuality Project.

Jane Bailey is Full Professor in Faculty of Law, Common Law Section, at the University of Ottawa, and Faculty member of the Centre for Law, Technology and Society. She teaches courses on cyberfeminism, technoprudence, and contracts. She and Valerie Steeves co-lead The eQuality Project, with Bailey leading the project stream on tech-facilitated violence. She has co-edited five books and over 40 book chapters and articles, and was named Member of the New College of the Royal Society of Canada in 2016. In 2018, she was lead counsel for Samuelson-Glushko Canadian Internet Policy and Public Interest Clinic (CIPPIC) in its intervention before the Supreme Court of Canada in *R v. Jarvis*, a voyeurism case in which a teacher surreptitiously recorded young women while at school.

Dr. Jacquelyn Burkell is Associate Professor in the Faculty of Information and Media Studies and Associate Vice-President, Research, at the University of Western Ontario. Her research focuses on the social impact of technology, examining how technological mediation changes social interaction and information behaviour. One major research focus is privacy in the online context including an examination of online behavioural tracking on consumer health information websites, and research on privacy expectations and practices in online social networks. She is a co-investigator on The eQuality Project, where her work focuses on empirical examinations of attitudes toward and experiences of behavioural tracking, and Associate Member of the Centre for Law, Technology and Society at the University of Ottawa.

Dr. Priscilla Regan is Professor in the Schar School of Policy and Government at George Mason University. Prior to that, she was a senior analyst in the Congressional Office of Technology Assessment (1984–1989). Her primary research focus is the analysis of the social policy and legal implications of organizational use of new information and communications technologies, especially as it relates to privacy and other human rights. She has published over 70 articles or book chapters, as well as *Legislating Privacy: Technology, Social Values, and Public Policy* (UNC Press, 2009), and has co-edited two books. She is a co-investigator on The eQuality Project.

Dr. Valerie Steeves is Full Professor in the Department of Criminology at the University of Ottawa, and Faculty member of the Centre for Law, Technology and Society. Her main area of research is human rights and technology issues. She and Jane Bailey co-lead The eQuality Project, with Dr. Steeves leading the streams on privacy, surveillance, and big data analytics. From 2004 to 2020, Dr. Steeves was the lead researcher on MediaSmart's Young Canadians in a Wired World research project, which has been tracking young people's experiences with networked technologies since 2000. She has written and spoken extensively on privacy from a human rights perspective and is an active participant in the privacy policy-making process in Canada.

4. Government in the Connected Era

Kent Aitken

Kent Aitken is a participant observer of the changing governance environment. He has worked with academic institutions, conferences, and think tanks including the Public Policy Forum and the Mowat Centre to research and communicate about digitally driven trends and challenges. As a public servant, he is a specialist in digital government, community engagement, and transformation projects. From 2016 to 2017, he was the Prime Ministers of Canada Fellow, researching and advising on governance in the digital era. In 2018, he helped launch the Government of Canada's Digital Academy, and he is currently part of the Open and Innovative Government team at the Organisation for Economic Co-operation and Development.

5. Data Governance: The Next Frontier of Digital-Government Research and Practice

Amanda Clarke

Dr. Amanda Clarke is Assistant Professor at the School of Public Policy and Administration, Carleton University. Her research examines public sector reform, policy-making and civic engagement, focusing in particular on the impact of digital technologies on these domains. Her work is published in governance, Canadian public administration, and Internet policy. Dr. Clarke is co-editor of *Issues in Canadian Governance* (Emond, 2018) and author of *Opening the Government of Canada: The Federal Bureaucracy in the Digital* Age (UBC Press, 2019). In 2017, Dr. Clarke was appointed Carleton University's Public Affairs Research Excellence Chair, and, in 2019, the Canada School of Public Service named her Digital Government Research Fellow.

6. The Conversation Canada: Not-for-Profit Journalism Organization in a Time of Commercial Media Decline

Mary Lynn Young and Alfred Hermida

Dr. Mary Lynn Young is Associate Professor within the School of Journalism, Writing, and Media at the University of British Columbia, and a co-founder and board member of The Conversation Canada. She does not own shares in or receive funding from The Conversation Canada. She has held a number of academic administrative positions at the University of British Columbia, including Associate Dean of the Faculty of Arts and Director of the UBC School of Journalism, Writing, and Media (2008–2011). She has recently co-authored two books: *Reckoning: Journalism's Limits and Possibilities* (Oxford, 2020), with Dr. Candis Callison; and *Data Journalism and the Regeneration of News* (Routledge, 2019), with Dr. Alfred Hermida. She has worked as a journalist in Canada and the United States.

Dr. Alfred Hermida is an Associate Professor and Director of the School of Journalism, Writing, and Media at the University of British

Columbia, and a co-founder and board member of The Conversation Canada. He does not own shares in or receive funding from The Conversation Canada. With more than two decades of experience in digital journalism, his research explores the transformation of media, emerging news practises, innovation, and social media. His most recent book is *Data Journalism and the Regeneration of News* (Routledge, 2019), co-authored with Dr. Mary Lynn Young. He was a BBC TV, radio, and online journalist for 16 years.

7. Influencing the Internet: Lobbyists and Interest Groups' Impact on Digital Rights in Canada

Megan Beretta

Megan Beretta is Policy Advisor with the Canadian Digital Service, in the Government of Canada. She graduated from the Oxford Internet Institute, University of Oxford, in 2018, with a Master of Science in the Social Sciences of the Internet. She holds a Bachelor of Social Sciences in Political Science and Communication from the University of Ottawa.

8. Consumers First, Digital Citizenry Second: Through the Gateway of Standard-Form Contracts

Marina Pavlović

Marina Pavlović is Associate Professor in the Faculty of Law, Common Law Section, at the University of Ottawa, and Faculty member of the Centre for Law, Technology and Society. Her expertise is in consumer rights in the digital society, and technology policy and regulation.

9. A Human Rights-Based Approach to Data Protection in Canada

Teresa Scassa

Dr. Teresa Scassa is the Canada Research Chair in Information Law and Policy at the University of Ottawa, where she is Full Professor in the Faculty of Law, Common Law Section, and Faculty member of the Centre for Law, Technology and Society. She is Chair of the Canadian

Statistics Advisory Council, Member of the Digital Strategy Advisory Panel for Waterfront Toronto, and Member of the Canadian Advisory Council on Artificial Intelligence. She is Member of the GEOTHINK research partnership and Senior fellow with Centre for International Governance Innovation's International Law Research Program. She has written widely in the areas of intellectual property law, law and technology, and privacy.

10. Making Sense of the Canadian Digital-Tax Debate

Michael Geist

Dr. Michael Geist is the Canada Research Chair in Internet and E-commerce Law at the University of Ottawa, where he is Full Professor in the Faculty of Law, Common Law Section, and Faculty member of the Centre for Law, Technology and Society. He was appointed to the Order of Ontario in 2018 and has received numerous awards for his work, including the Kroeger Award for Policy Leadership and the Public Knowledge IP3 Award in 2010, the Les Fowlie Intellectual Freedom Award from the Ontario Library Association in 2009, the EFF's Pioneer Award in 2008, and Canarie's IWAY Public Leadership Award for his contribution to the development of the Internet in Canada.

11. Online Abuse, "Chilling Effects," and Human Rights

Jonathon W. Penney

Dr. Jonathon W. Penney is Associate Professor at Osgoode Hall Law School at York University. He is also Research Fellow at the Citizen Lab, based at the University of Toronto's Munk School of Global Affairs and Public Policy, and Research Affiliate of the Berkman Klein Center for Internet and Society at Harvard University.

Index

Law, Technology, and Media

Edited by Michael Geist

The *Law, Technology, and Media* series explores emerging technology law issues with an emphasis on a Canadian perspective. It is the first University of Ottawa Press series to be fully published under an open access licence.

Previous titles in *Law, Technology, and Media* Series

Alana Maurushat, *Ethical Hacking*, 2019

Derek McKee, Finn Makela, and Teresa Scassa, eds., *Law and the "Sharing Economy": Regulating Online Market Platforms*, 2018.

Karim Benyekhlef, Jane Bailey, Jacquelyn Burkell, and Fabie Gélinas, eds., *eAccess to Justice*, 2016.

Michael Geist, *Law, Privacy and Surveillance in Canada in the Post-Snowden Era*, 2015.

Jane Bailey and Valerie Steeves, *eGirls, eCitizens*, 2015.

Lucie Thibault and Jean Harvey, *Sport Policy in Canada*, 2013.

For a complete list of the University of Ottawa Press titles, see:
www.press.uOttawa.ca

www.ingramcontent.com/pod-product-compliance
Lightning Source LLC
Chambersburg PA
CBHW051958270326
41929CB00015B/2699